EDUGORILLA
PUBLICATION

ICSE 10

PHYSICS

12 + 1 SAMPLE PAPERS

SHIVAM TIWARI

EDUCATOR

M.Sc. (Physics), B.Ed. (Science)

BOARD SAMPLE PAPER WITH SOLUTION & ANALYSIS BASED ON LATEST CIRCULAR ISSUED IN JULY FOR 2022-23 EXAM

Title : ICSE Class 10 Physics

Author Name : Mr. Shivam Tiwari

Published By : EduGorilla Community Pvt. Ltd.

Publishers Address : Sector-12/651, First Floor Opp. Arvindo Park, Near Jama Masjid, Indira Nagar, Lucknow, Uttar Pradesh-226016, India

Copyright

ISBN: 9789355564931

+91-63932 16806, +91-78000 04200
book@edugorilla.com
www.edugorilla.com

Disclaimer

Created & Compiled by EduGorilla Publication

Printed by EduGorilla Community Pvt. Ltd.

INDEX

ICSE X PHYSICS

SCIENCE (52)

PHYSICS

SCIENCE PAPER - 1

CLASS X

There will be **one** written paper of **two hours** duration carrying **80 marks** and Internal Assessment of practical work carrying **20 marks**.

Note: Unless otherwise specified, only SI Units are to be used while teaching and learning, as well as for answering questions.

1. Force, Work, Power, and Energy

(i) Turning forces concept; moment of a force; forces in equilibrium; centre of gravity; [discussions using simple examples and simple numerical problems].

Elementary introduction of translational and rotational motions; moment (turning effect) of a force, also called torque and its cgs and SI units; common examples - door, steering wheel, bicycle pedal, etc.; clockwise and anticlockwise moments; conditions for a body to be in equilibrium (translational and rotational); principle of moment and its verification using a metre rule suspended by two spring balances with slotted weights hanging from it; simple numerical problems; Centre of gravity (qualitative only) with examples of some regular bodies and irregular lamina.

(ii) Work, energy, power and their relation with force.

Definition of work. W FS= cosθ; special cases of $\theta = 0^0, 90^0$. W= mgh. Definition of energy, energy as work done. Various units of work and energy and their relation with SI units. [erg, calorie, kW h and eV]. Definition of Power, P=W/t; SI and cgs units; other units, kilowatt (kW), megawatt (MW) and gigawatt (GW); and horsepower (1hp=746W) [Simple numerical problems on work, power and energy].

(iii) Different types of energy (e.g., chemical energy, Mechanical energy, heat energy, electrical energy, nuclear energy, sound energy, light energy).

Mechanical energy: potential energy U = mgh (derivation included) gravitational PE, examples; kinetic energy K= $\frac{1}{2} mv^2$

(derivation included); forms of kinetic energy: translational, rotational and vibrational - only simple examples. [Numerical problems on K and U only in case of translational motion]; qualitative discussions of electrical, chemical, heat, nuclear, light and sound energy, conversion from one form to another; common examples.

(iv) Machines as force multipliers; load, effort, mechanical advantage, velocity ratio and efficiency; pulley systems showing the utility of each type of machine.

Functions and uses of simple machines: Terms- effort E, load L, mechanical advantage MA = L/E, velocity ratio $VR = V_E/V_L = d_E / d_L$, input (W_i), output (W_o), efficiency (η), relation between η and MA, VR (derivation included); for all practical machines η <1; MA < VR.

Pulley system: single fixed, single movable, block and tackle; MA, VR and η in each case. [Pulleys using single tackle]

(v) Principle of Conservation of energy.
Statement of the principle of conservation of energy; theoretical verification that U + K = constant for a freely falling body. Application of this law to simple pendulum (qualitative only); [simple numerical problems].

2. Light

(i) Refraction of light through a glass block and a triangular prism - qualitative treatment of simple applications such as real and apparent depth of objects in water and apparent bending of sticks in water. Applications of refraction of light.
Partial reflection and refraction due to change in medium. Laws of refraction; the effect on speed (V), wavelength (λ) and frequency (f) due to refraction of light; conditions for a light ray to pass undeviated. Values of speed of light (c) in vacuum, air, water and glass; refractive index $\mu = c/V$, $V = f\lambda$. Values of μ for common substances such as water, glass and diamond; experimental verification; refraction through glass block; lateral displacement; multiple images in thick glass plate / mirror; **[Diagrammatic representation not to be tested]**; refraction through a glass prism, simple applications: real and apparent depth of objects in water; apparent bending of a stick under water. (Simple numerical problems and approximate ray diagrams required).

(ii) Total internal reflection: Critical angle; examples in triangular glass prisms; comparison with reflection from a plane mirror (qualitative only). Applications of total internal reflection.
Transmission of light from a denser medium (glass/water) to a rarer medium (air) at different angles of incidence; critical angle (C) $\mu = 1/\sin C$. Essential conditions for total internal reflection. Total internal reflection in a triangular glass prism; ray diagram, different cases - angles of prism (60°,60°,60°), (60°,30°,90°), (45°,45°,90°); use of right-angle prism to obtain $\delta = 90°$ and 180° (ray diagram); comparison of total internal reflection from a prism and reflection from a plane mirror.

(iii) Lenses (converging and diverging) including characteristics of the images formed (using ray diagrams only); magnifying glass; location of images using ray diagrams and thereby determining magnification.
Types of lenses (converging and diverging), convex and concave, action of a lens as a set of prisms; technical terms; centre of curvature, radii of curvature, principal axis, foci, focal plane and focal length; detailed study of refraction of light in spherical lenses through ray diagrams; formation of images - principal rays or construction rays; location of images from ray diagram for various positions of a small linear object on the principal axis; characteristics of images. Sign convention and direct numerical problems using the lens formula are included
(derivation of formula not required).
Scale drawing or graphical representation of ray diagrams not required.

Power of a lens (concave and convex) – [simple direct numerical problems]: magnifying glass or simple microscope: location of image and magnification from ray diagram only [formula and numerical problems **not** included]. Applications of lenses.

(iv) Using a triangular prism to produce a visible spectrum from white light; Electromagnetic spectrum.

Deviation produced by a triangular prism; dependence on colour (wavelength) of light; dispersion and spectrum; electromagnetic spectrum: broad classification (names only arranged in order of increasing wavelength); properties common to all electromagnetic radiations; properties and uses of infrared and ultraviolet radiation.

3. Sound

(i) Reflection of Sound Waves; echoes: their use; simple numerical problems on echoes.

Production of echoes, condition for formation of echoes; simple numerical problems; use of echoes by bats, dolphins, fishermen, medical field. SONAR.

(ii) Natural vibrations, Damped vibrations, Forced vibrations and Resonance - a special case of forced vibrations.

Meaning and simple applications of natural, damped, forced vibrations and resonance.

(iii) Loudness, pitch and quality of sound: Definitions of the characteristics of sound and factors affecting them only.

4. Electricity and Magnetism

(i) Ohm's Law; concepts of emf, potential difference, resistance; resistances in series and parallel, internal resistance.

Concepts of pd (V), current (I), resistance (R) and charge (Q). Ohm's law: statement, V=IR; SI units; experimental verification; graph of V vs I and resistance from slope; ohmic and non-ohmic resistors, factors affecting resistance (including specific resistance) and internal resistance; super conductors, electromotive force (emf); combination of resistances in series and parallel. Simple numerical problems using the above relations. [Simple network of resistors including not more than four external resistors. Internal resistance may be included].

(ii) Electrical power and energy. Electrical energy; examples of heater, motor, amp, loudspeaker, etc. Electrical power; measurement of electrical energy, $W = QV = VIt$ from the definition of pd. Combining with ohm's law $W = VIt = I^2 Rt = (V^2/R)t$ and electrical power $P = (W/t) = VI = I^2R = V^2/R$. Units: SI and commercial; Power rating of common appliances, household consumption of electric energy; calculation of total energy consumed by electrical appliances; $W = Pt$ (kilowatt × hour = kW h), [simple numerical problems].

(iii) Household circuits – main circuit; switches; fuses; earthing; safety precautions; three-pin plugs; colour coding of wires.

House wiring (ring system – no diagrammatic representation), power distribution; main circuit (3 wires-live, neutral, earth) with fuse / MCB, main switch and its advantages - circuit diagram, need for earthing, fuse, 3-pin plug and socket; Conventional location of live, neutral and earth points in 3 pin plugs and sockets.

Safety precautions, colour coding of wires.

(iv) Magnetic effect of a current (principles only, statement of laws not required); electromagnetic induction (elementary).

Oersted's experiment on the magnetic effect of electric current; magnetic field (B) and field lines due to current in a straight wire (qualitative only); Right Hand Thumb Rule – magnetic field due to a current in a loop; Electromagnets: their uses; comparisons with a permanent magnet; conductor carrying current in a magnetic field experiences a force, Fleming's Left Hand Rule, and its understanding, Simple introduction to electromagnetic induction; a magnet moved along the axis of a solenoid induces current,

Fleming's Right Hand Rule and its application in understanding the direction of current in a coil and Lenz's law. Comparison of AC and DC.

5. Heat

(i) Calorimetry: meaning, specific heat capacity; principle of method of mixtures; Numerical Problems on specific heat capacity using heat loss and gain and the method of mixtures.

Heat and its units (calorie, joule), temperature and its units (°C, K); thermal (heat) capacity C' = Q/◎T... (SI unit of C'): Specific heat Capacity C = Q/m◎T (SI unit of C) Mutual relation between Heat Capacity and Specific Heat capacity, values of C for some common substances (ice, water and copper). Principle of method of mixtures including mathematical statement. Natural phenomenon involving specific heat. Consequences of high specific heat of water. [Simple numerical problems].

(ii) Latent heat; loss and gain of heat involving change of state for fusion only. Change of phase (state); heating curve for water; latent heat; specific latent heat of fusion (SI unit). Simple numerical problems. Common physical phenomena involving latent heat of fusion.

6. Modern Physics

Radioactivity and changes in the nucleus; background radiation and safety precautions.

Brief introduction (qualitative only) of the nucleus, nuclear structure, atomic number (Z), mass number (A). Radioactivity as spontaneous disintegration. α, β and γ - their nature and properties; changes within the nucleus. One example each of α and β decay with equations showing changes in Z and A.

Uses of radioactivity - radio isotopes. Harmful effects. Safety precautions. Background radiation.

Radiation: X-rays; radioactive fallout from nuclear plants and other sources.

Nuclear Energy: working on safe disposal of waste. Safety measures to be strictly reinforced.

A NOTE ON SI UNITS

SI units (Systeme International d'Unites) were adopted internationally in 1968.

Fundamental units

The system has seven fundamental (or basic) units, one for each of the fundamental quantities.

Fundamental quantity	**Unit**	
	Name	**Symbol**
Mass	kilogram	kg
Length	metre	m
Time	second	s

Electric current	ampere	A
Temperature	kelvin	K
Luminous intensity	candela	cd
Amount of substance	mole	mol

Derived units

These are obtained from the fundamental units by multiplication or division; no numerical factors are involved. Some derived units with complex names are:

Derived quantity	Unit	
	Name	Symbol
Volume	cubic meter	m^3
Density	kilogram per cubic meter	kg m^{-3}
Velocity	meter per second	m s^{-1}
Acceleration	meter per second square	m s^{-2}
Momentum	kilogram meter per second	kg m s^{-1}

Some derived units are given special names due to their complexity when expressed in terms of the fundamental units, as below:

Derived quantity	Unit	
	Name	Symbol
Force	newton	N
Pressure	pascal	Pa
Energy, Work	joule	J
Power	watt	W
Frequency	hertz	Hz
Electric charge	coulomb	C
Electric resistance	ohm	Ω
Electromotive force	volt	V

When the unit is named after a person, the symbol has a capital letter.

Standard prefixes

Decimal multiples and submultiples are attached to units when appropriate, as below:

Multiple	Prefix	Symbol
10^9	giga	G
10^6	mega	M
10^3	kilo	k
10-1	deci	d
10-2	centi	c
10-3	milli	m
10-6	micro	μ
10-9	nano	n
10-12	pico	p
10-15	femto	f

INTERNAL ASSESSMENT OF

PRACTICAL WORK

Candidates will be asked to carry out experiments for which instructions will be given. The experiments may be based on topics that are not included in the syllabus but theoretical knowledge will not be required. A candidate will be expected to be able to follow simple instructions, to take suitable readings and to present these readings in a systematic form. He/she may be required to exhibit his/her data graphically. Candidates will be expected to appreciate and use the concepts of least count, significant figures and elementary error handling.

Note: Teachers may design their own set of experiments, preferably related to the theory syllabus. A comprehensive list is suggested below:

1. Lever - There are many possibilities with a meter rule as a lever with a load (known or unknown) suspended from a point near one end (say left), the lever itself pivoted on a knife edge, use slotted weights suspended from the other (right) side for effort.

Determine the mass of a metre rule using a spring balance or by balancing it on a knife edge at some point away from the middle and a 50g weight on the other side. Next pivot (F) the metre rule at the
40cm, 50cm and 60cm mark, each time suspending a load L or the left end and effort E near the right end. Adjust E and or its position so that the rule is balanced. Tabulate the position of L, F and E and the magnitudes of L and E and the distances of load arm and effort arm. Calculate MA=L/E and VR = effort arm/load arm. It will be found that MA <VR in one case, MA=VR in another and MA>VR in the third case. Try to explain why this is so. Also try to calculate the real load and real effort in these cases.

2. Determine the VR and MA of a given pulley system.
3. Trace the course of different rays of light refracting through a rectangular glass slab at different angles of incidence, measure the angles of incidence, refraction and emergence. Also measure the lateral displacement.
4. Determine the focal length of a convex lens by (a) the distant object method and (b) using a needle and a plane mirror.
5. Determine the focal length of a convex lens by using two pins and formula $f = uv/(u+v)$.
6. For a triangular prism, trace the course of rays passing through it, measure angles i_1, i_2, A and δ.Repeat for four different angles of incidence
   (say $i_1=40^0$, 50^0, 60^0 and 70^0). Verify $i_1+i_2=A+\delta$ and $A = r_1 + r_2$.

7. For a ray of light incident normally ($i_1=0$) on one face of a prism, trace course of the ray. Measure the angle δ. Explain briefly. Do this for prisms with $A=60^0$, 45^0 and 90^0.
8. Calculate the specific heat capacity of the material of the given calorimeter, from the temperature readings and masses of cold water, warm water and its mixture taken in the calorimeter.
9. Determination of specific heat capacity of a metal by method of mixtures.
10. Determination of specific latent heat of ice.
11. Using as simple electric circuit, verify Ohm's law. Draw a graph and obtain the slope.
12. Set up model of household wiring including ring main circuit. Study the function of switches and fuses.

Teachers may feel free to alter or add to the above list. The students may perform about ten experiments.

Some experiments may be demonstrated.

EVALUATION

The practical work/project work are to be evaluated by the subject teacher and by an External Examiner. (The External Examiner may be a teacher nominated by the Head of the school, who could be from the faculty, **but not teaching the subject in the relevant SECTION/class.** For example, a teacher of Physics of Class VIII may be deputed to be an External Examiner for Class X, Physics projects.)

The Internal Examiner and the External Examiner will assess the practical work/project work independently.

Award of Marks **(20 Marks)** Subject Teacher (Internal Examiner)
10 marks External Examiner
10 marks

The total marks obtained out of 20 are to be sent to the Council by the Head of the school.

The Head of the school will be responsible for the online entry of marks on the Council's C AREERS portal by the due date.

Mind Map : Force

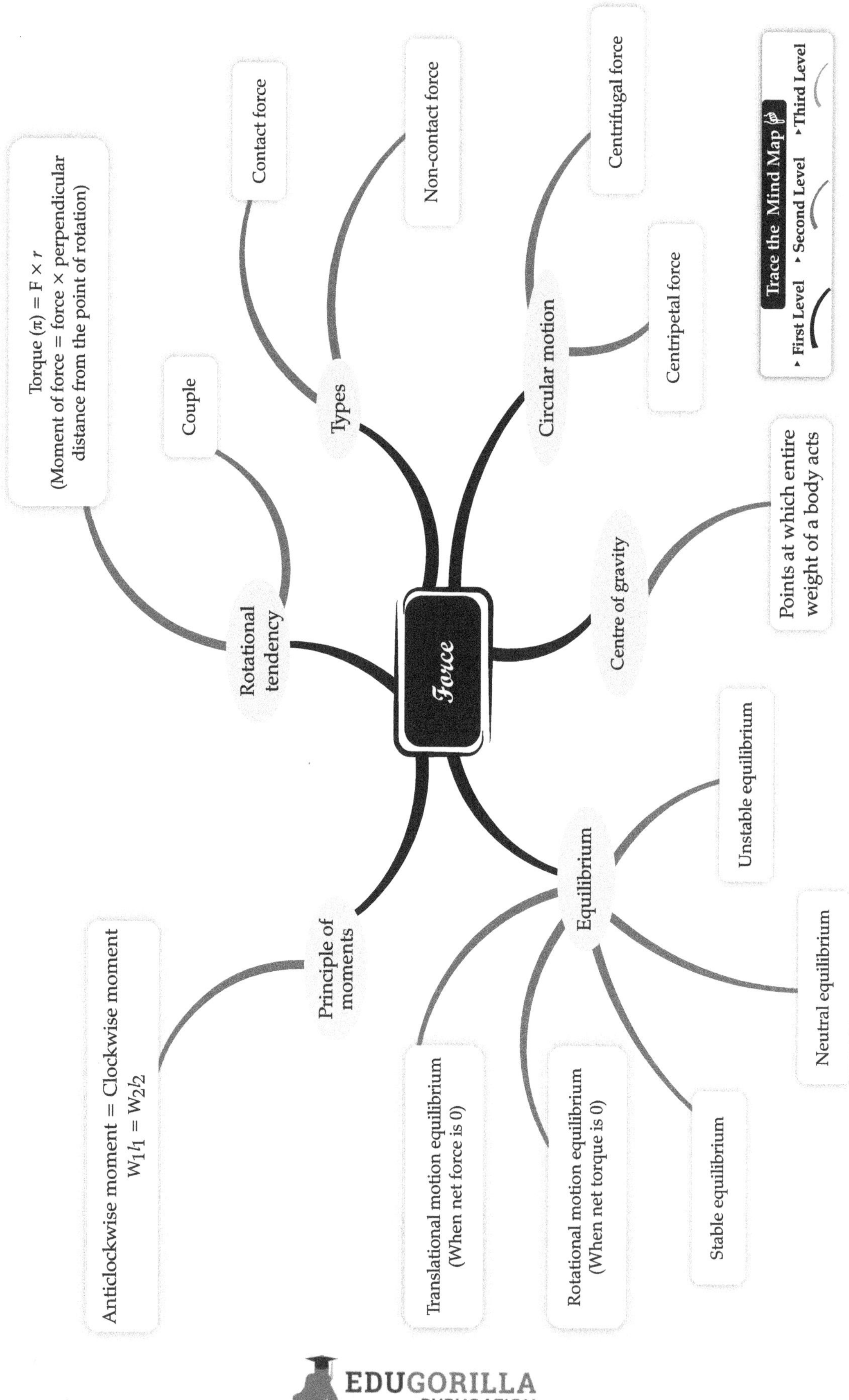

EDUGORILLA PUBLICATION

Mind Map : Work, Power & Energy

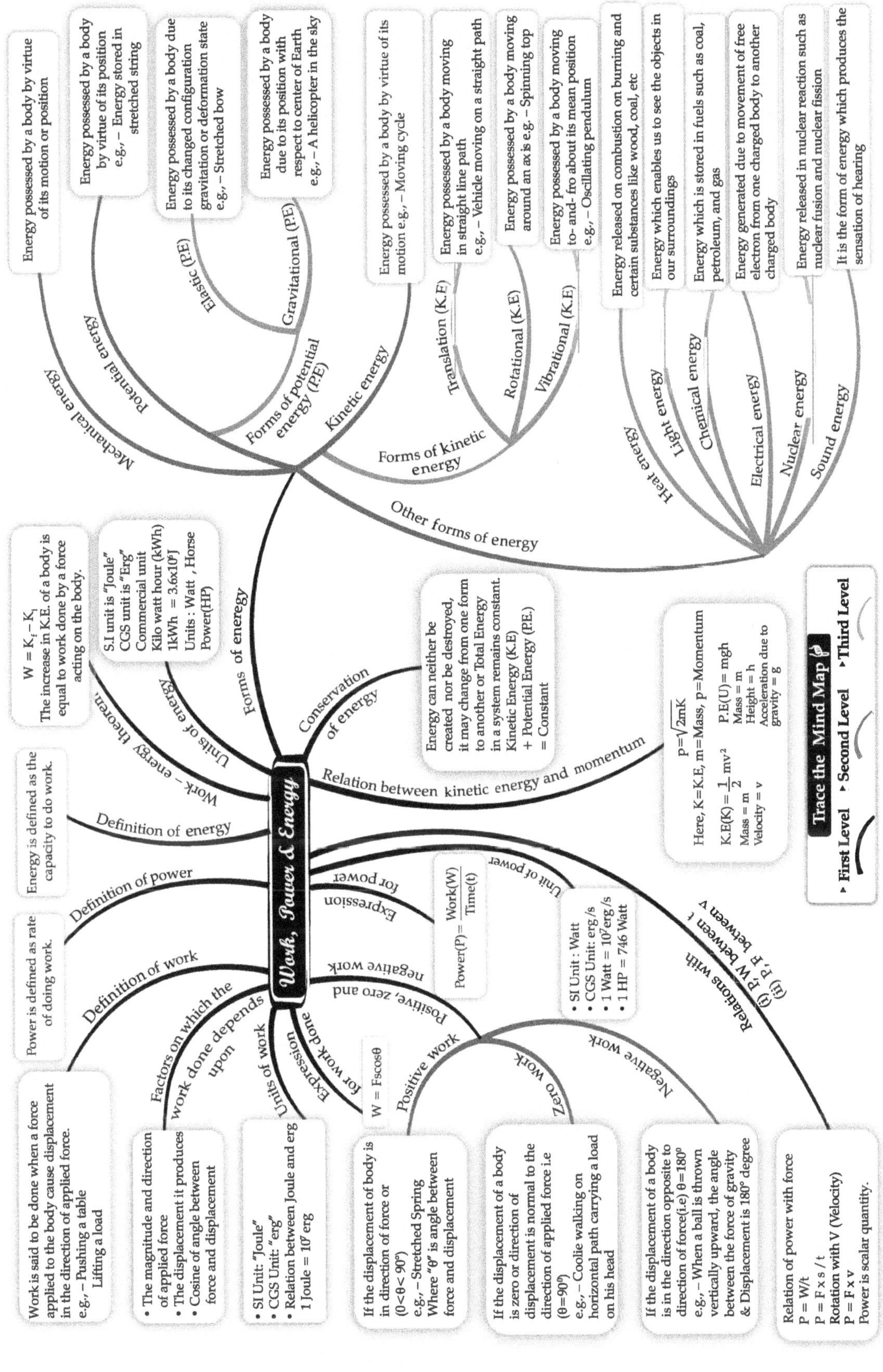

Mind Map : Machines

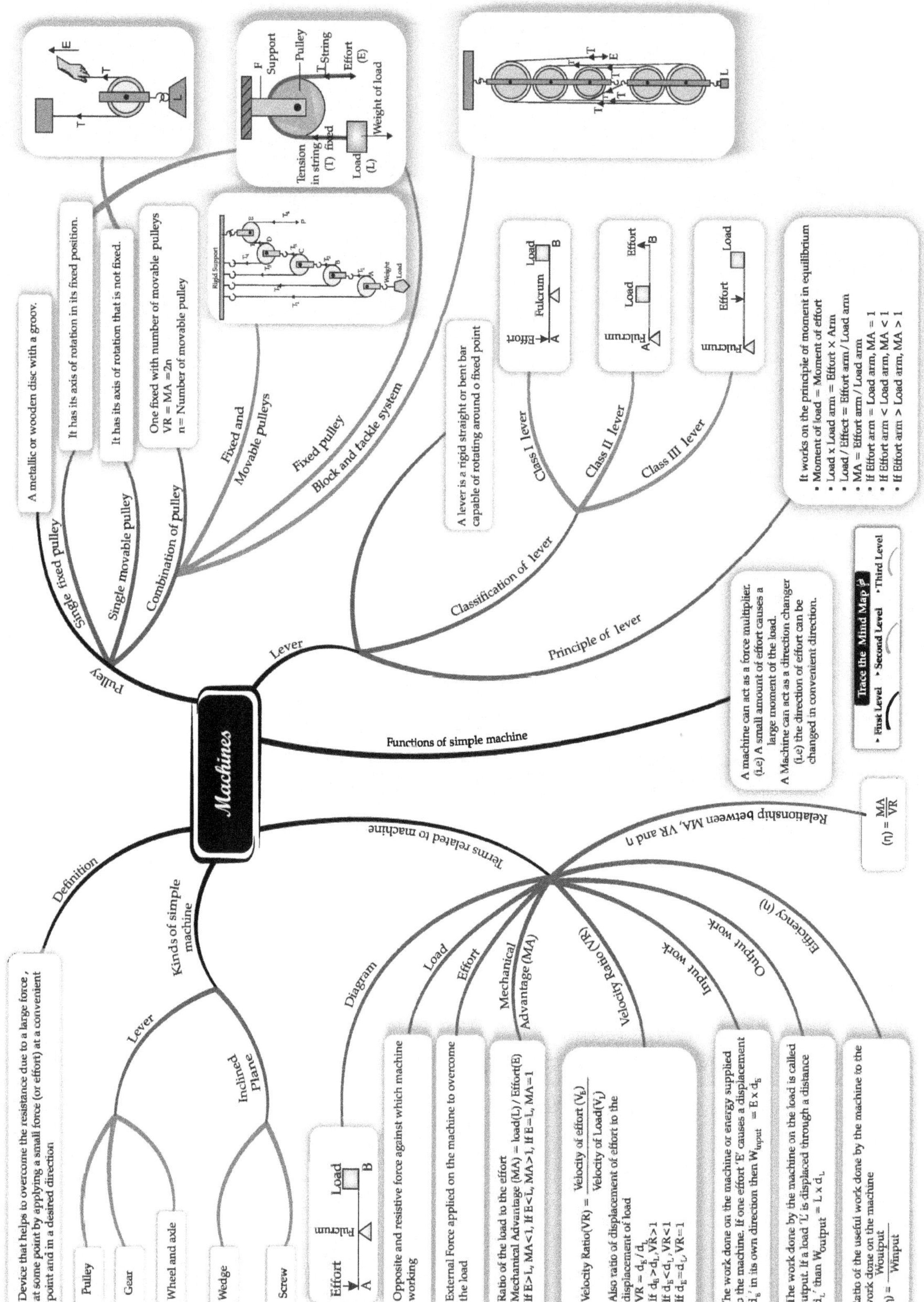

EDUGORILLA PUBLICATION

Mind Map : Refraction of light at plane surfaces

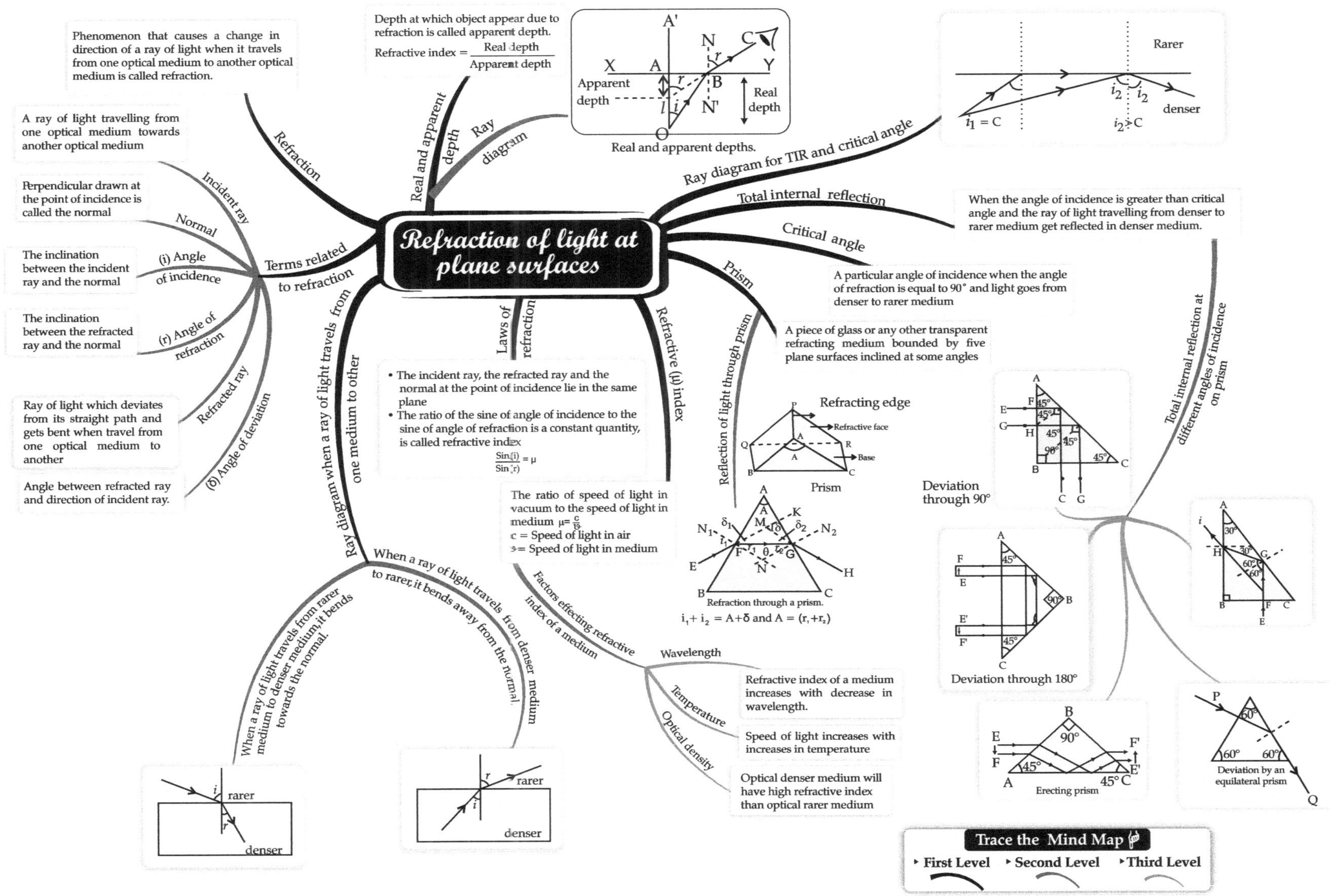

Mind Map : Refraction of light through lens

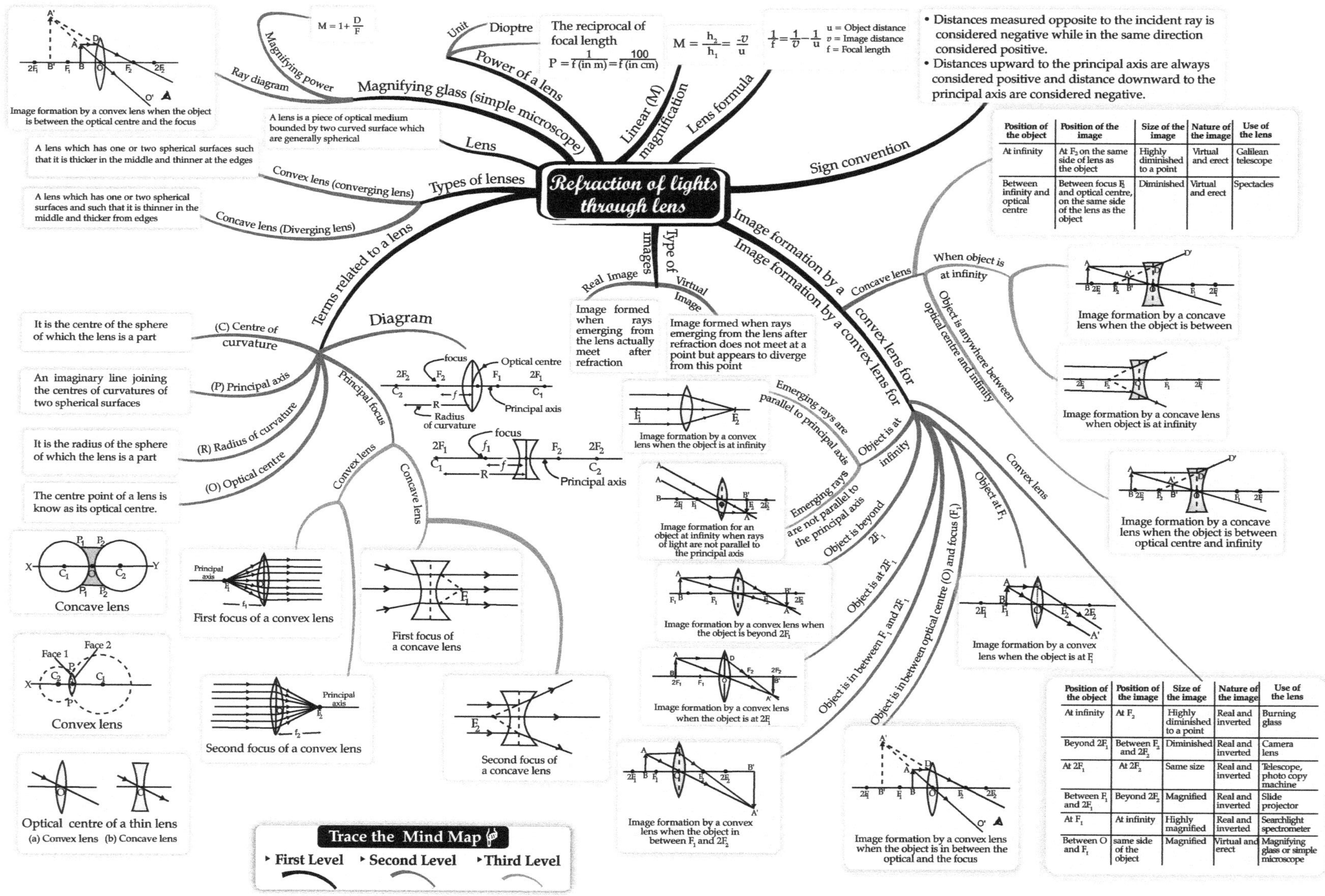

Position of the object	Position of the image	Size of the image	Nature of the image	Use of the lens
At infinity	At F_2 on the same side of lens as the object	Highly diminished to a point	Virtual and erect	Galilean telescope
Between infinity and optical centre	Between focus F_1 and optical centre, on the same side of the lens as the object	Diminished	Virtual and erect	Spectacles

Position of the object	Position of the image	Size of the image	Nature of the image	Use of the lens
At infinity	At F_2	Highly diminished to a point	Real and inverted	Burning glass
Beyond $2F_1$	Between F_2 and $2F_2$	Diminished	Real and inverted	Camera lens
At $2F_1$	At $2F_2$	Same size	Real and inverted	Telescope, photo copy machine
Between F_1 and $2F_1$	Beyond $2F_2$	Magnified	Real and inverted	Slide projector
At F_1	At infinity	Highly magnified	Real and inverted	Searchlight spectrometer
Between O and F_1	same side of the object	Magnified	Virtual and erect	Magnifying glass or simple microscope

EDUGORILLA PUBLICATION

Mind Map : Electromagnetic Spectrum

The Electromagnetic Spectrum

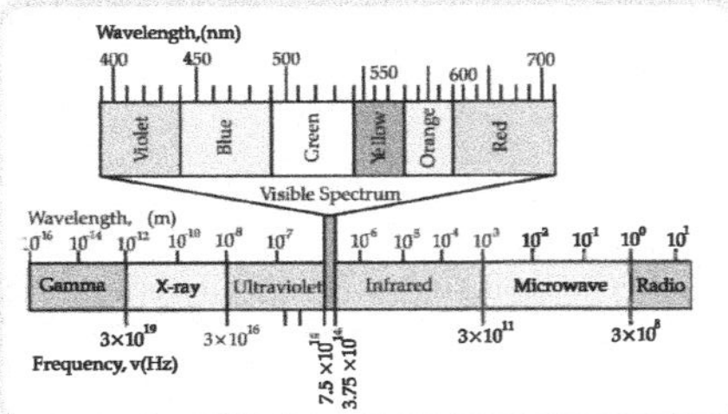

- **Relation between speed (c) (v) frequency and (λ) wavelength:** $C = \upsilon\lambda$
- **Electromagnetic spectrum:** Electromagnetic waves exist in an enormous range of frequencies and this continuous range of frequencies is known as the electromagnetic spectrum.
- **Electromagnetic wave:** Wave that is capable of transmitting its energy through vacuum.
- **Effects of scattering of light:**
  - Red colour during sunrise and sunset
  - Blue colour of the sky
  - White colour of sky at noontime
  - White colour of clouds.
  - Red light used as a danger signal
- **Relationship between intensity of scattered light and wavelength:** $I \propto \frac{1}{\lambda^4}$ Violet light scatters the most while the red light scatters the least.
- **Scattering of light:** Absorption and re-emission of light by the dust and air particles in atmosphere
- **Recombination of colours**

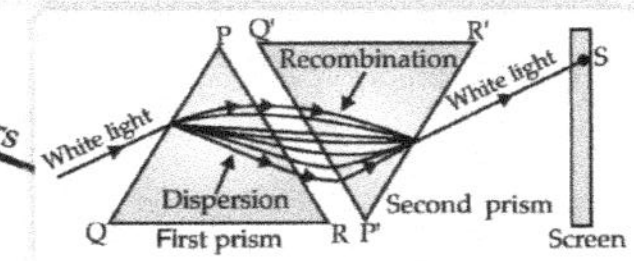

- **Filter the colour by prism**

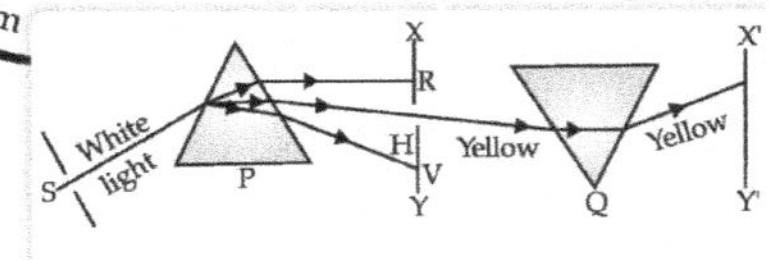

- **Dispersion of white light through prism**

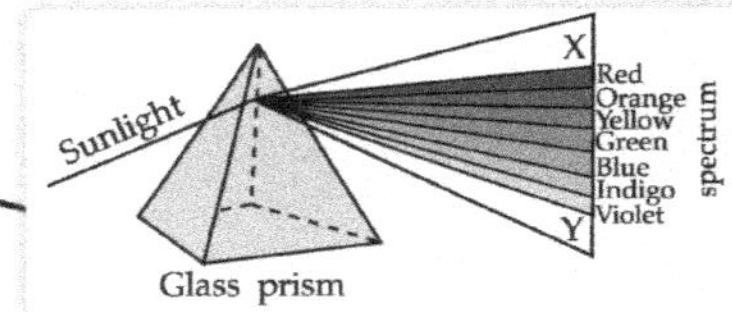

- **Dependence of deviation on colour or wavelength of incident light:**
  - Speed of light decreases with decrease in wavelength of light.
  - As the refractive index of a material increases, angle of deviation also increases.
  - Deviation produced by prism increases with the decreases in wavelength of light.
  - Violet colour with the shortest wavelength has minimum speed and undergoes maximum deviation where as red colour with longest wavelength has maximum speed and undergoes minimum deviation.
- **Properties of electromagnetic waves:**
  - Electromagnetic waves are transverse waves or non-mechanical waves.
  - These wave can propagate through vacuum and thus do not require material medium.
  - Speed of waves of electromagnetic wave is same as the speed of light.
  - These waves exhibit the phenomena of reflection refraction, diffraction, interference and polarisation.
- **Deviation produced by a prism:** Angle of deviation (δ) $= i + e - A$

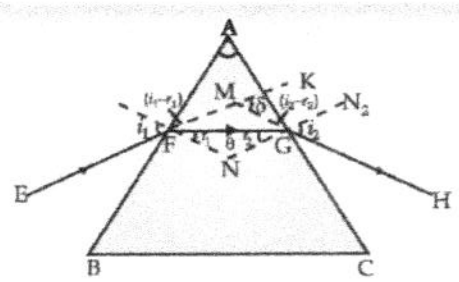

- **Factors affecting the angle of deviation:**
  - Angle of incidence :
  - Refractive index of prism material (μ)
  - Angle of Prism (A)
  - Colour of wavelength of incident light (λ)
- **Characteristics of electromagnetic spectrum:**

Electromagnetic region	Wavelength	Frequency (in hertz)	Source	Detector	Application
Gamma rays	<0.01 nm	$>3 \times 10^{19}$	Cosmic rays, decay of radioactive substances, nuclear fusion and fission reactions	Spectrometer	For killing cancerous cells, for checking welds in industries
X-rays	0.01-10 nm	3×10^{19}- 3×10^{16}	When high velocity electrons collide with a heavy metal target	Photographic plate, fluorescent screen	Medical radiography crystallography, for scanning object
Ultraviolet radiation	10-400 nm	3×10^{16}- 7.5×10^{14}	Sun, mercury vapour lamp, arc spark lamp	Photographic plate, fluorescence, chemical effect on dyes	Sterilisation of surgical instruments, vitamin D production detection of fake gems, forgery
Visible lights	400-800 nm	7.5×10^{14}- 3.75×10^{14}	Sun, electric bulb, flame, hot bodies	Eyes, photographic film	Observing objects, fibre optics
Infrared radiation	800 nm to 1 mm	3.75×10^{14}- 3×10^{11}	Sun, hot bodies such as fire burning gases	Blackened bulb thermometer, thermopile	Night-vision devices, developing photographs, sensor in missiles
Microwaves	1mm-10 m	3×10^{11}- 3×10^{7}	Electronic device special vacuum tubes	Electronic circuits	Radar, television, microwave ovens, cell phones
Radio waves	>10m	below 3.0×10^{7}	Electronic circuits and radio transmitters	Aerials of radio and television receiver	TV and radio broadcasting, navigation

Trace the Mind Map

- First Level
- Second Level
- Third Level

Mind Map : Sound

Sound

Definition
Sound is the form of energy which causes the sensation of hearing. Sound is produced by a vibrating body and it reaches us through the vibrations of a particle.

Characteristics of sound
- **Pitch or shrillness**: It is that characteristic of sound by virtue of which a sharp note can be differentiated from a flat note.
- **Quality or timbre**: When two sounds of same pitch and same loudness originating from two different sources can be distinguished.
- **Loudness and intensity**: **Loudness** is the property of sound that enables to distinguish loud sound from a faint sound when both have same pitch and quality. **Intensity** of sound at a point of medium is the amount of energy flowing per second across a unit area at that point
- **Factors affecting loudness/intensity of sound**
  - Amplitude: $L \propto A^2$
  - Distance: $L \propto \frac{1}{d}$
  - Surface area of vibrating body: Loudness ∝ Surface Area
  - Density of medium: Loudness ∝ Density of medium
  - Resonant body: Loudness ∝ Resonance
- **Difference between forced and resonant vibration**

Difference between forced and resonant vibrations

Forced vibrations	Resonant vibrations
These vibrations of a body are produced by an external periodic force that has a frequency different from the natural frequency of the body.	These vibrations of a body are produced by an external periodic force that has a frequency equal to the natural frequency of the body.
The amplitude of vibration is usual small.	The amplitude of vibration is very large.
The vibrations produced in the body are out of phase with the external periodic force.	The vibrations produced in the body are in phase with the external periodic force.
Once the external periodic force ceases to act these vibrations last for a very small time.	These vibrations last for a long time even after the external periodic force has eased in act.

Resonance
It is the phenomenon in which the frequency of an external force is equal to the natural frequency of the body on which the force acts thereby leading to vibrations with an increased amplitude.

Vibrations
It is a mechanical phenomenon in which oscillation occur about an equilibrium point if a disturbance is caused in the body

- **Types of vibrations**
  - Forced vibration: Vibration that takes place in a body under the influence of an external periodic force eg. swing, tuning fork
  - Damped vibrations: Periodic vibrations of continuously decreasing amplitude due to presence of resistive force are called damped vibrations eg. vibration of simple pendulum in air
  - Free vibrations: Vibration produced in a body on being slightly disturbed and remain sustained in absence of any external force eg. simple pendulum, musical instruments (piano, flute)

Echo
The sound heard after reflection from a distant object after the original sound from the given source dies off.

- Minimum time: The sensation of any sound persists for 0.1 sec. If a sound after reflection reaches the ear in less than 0.1 s, it cannot be distinguished from the original sound.
- Relation (ϑ, d, t): $\vartheta = \frac{2d}{t}$
- Minimum distance: The minimum distance required between the source of sound and reflecting surface to hear an echo is 17m in air.
- wavelength: Wavelength of sound should be less than the size of the reflecting body.

Difference between light waves and sound waves

Light waves	Sound waves
These are electromagnetic waves, *i.e.* non-mechanical in nature.	These are mechanical or elastic waves.
These can travel in vacuum.	These cannot travel in vacuum : required a material medium for propagation
These are transverse waves.	These can be transverse as well as longitudinal waves.
The speed of light waves in air is $3.0 \times 10^8 m s^{-1}$	The speed of sound waves in air is $330 m s^{-1}$
The frequency of visible light waves is in the range of 3.75×10^{14}- 7.5×10^{14}Hz	The frequency of audible sound waves is in the range of 20-20,000 Hz.

Terms related to the wave motion
- Amplitude: It is the maximum displacement of the particle of a medium on the either side of its mean position.
- Time period: It is the time taken by the particle of the medium to complete one oscillation or vibration
- Frequency: It is the number of oscillations completed by a particle in one second.
- wavelength: Distance between two successive waves.
- wave velocity: Distance travelled by a wave in one second
- Relation
  - T & v: Tv = 1
  - ϑ, v, λ: ϑ = vλ

Types of waves
- **Mechanical waves (elastic waves)**: Waves that require material medium for their propagation eg. sound waves, water waves
  - Types of mechanical waves
    - Longitudinal wave: Waves in which particle of medium vibrates about their mean position along the line of direction of propagation of wave.
    - Transverse waves: Waves in which particle of medium vibrates about their mean position at right angle to the direction of propagation of wave.
- **Non-mechanical waves**: Waves that do not require material medium for their propagation eg. all electromagnetic waves
- **Graphical representation**
  - Longitudinal

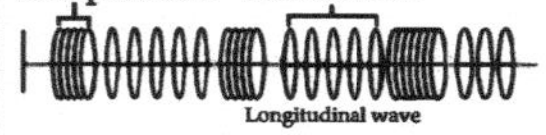

  - Transverse

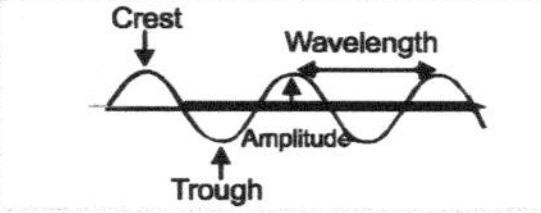

Trace the Mind Map
- First Level
- Second Level
- Third Level

Mind Map : Electricity

Electricity

- **Factors affecting the internal resistance of a cell**
  - Surface area of the electrodes — Surface area is inversely proportional to internal resistance of the cell.
  - Distance between the electrodes — Internal resistance is directly proportional to separation of the electrods.
  - Concentration of the electrolyte — Internal resistance increases the concentration of the electrolyte increases.
  - Temperature of electrolyte — Internal resistance decreases as the temperature of electrolyte increases.
- **Relation between Emf, terminal voltage and resistance of a cell**
  - Internal resistance of a cell (r): $r = [(\frac{E}{V} - 1)R]$
- **Internal resistance of a cell** — The resistance offered by the electrolyte inside the cell to the flow of current.
- **Terminal voltage of a cell (V)**
  - Terminal voltage of a cell is defined as the work done per unit charge carrying around the external circuit of the cell.
  - $V = \frac{W}{q_o}$
  - V=Terminal voltage
  - W=Work done in carrying the unit charge around the external circuit of cell
- **Electromotive force of a cell (E) (EMF)**
  - The Emf of a cell can be defined as the energy spent by the cell per unit charge carrying through its complete circuit.
  - $\varepsilon = \frac{W}{q_o}$
  - Factors affecting Emf of a cell
    - Material of the electrode of a cell
    - Nature and concentration of electrolyte used in the cell
    - Temperature
- **Conductivity / Specific conductance**
  - Conductivity is the reciprocal of resistivity(σ),
  - $\sigma = \frac{1}{\rho} = \frac{1}{R}\left(\frac{L}{A}\right)$
- **Specific resistance or resistivity**
  - The specific resistance of a material may be defined as the resistance of a wire of that material of unit length and unit area of cross section.
  - Unit of Resistivity = ohm. metre (Ω m)
  - Resistivity (ρ)= $R\frac{A}{L}$
  - Factors affecting resistivity
    - Material of the conductor — Resistivity is less for good conductor of electricity.
    - Temperature of the conductor — Resistivity of a metallic conductor increases with the temperature
- **Ohmic and nonohmic Devices**
  - Non-ohmic — Devices that do not obey ohm's law are called non-ohmic devices e.g. : Semiconductor
  - Ohmic — Devices that obey ohm's law are called ohmic devices. e.g. : Metallic conductors
- **Ohm's Law**
  - Current flowing through a conductor is directly proportional to the potential difference applied at its ends
  - $I \propto V$ or $I = GV$, here $G = \frac{1}{R}$
  - or, $V = IR$
  - Unit = Ohm(Ω)
  - $1\ \text{ohm} = \frac{1\ \text{volt}}{1\ \text{ampere}}$
- **Factors affecting the resistance of a conductor**
  - Length of the conductor — The resistance of a conductor is directly proportional to its length, i.e. $R \propto L$
  - Area of the cross section — The resistance of a conductor is inversely proportional to area of the cross section. $R \propto \frac{1}{A}$
  - Formula — $R = \rho\frac{L}{A}$
  - Material of the conductor — Silver, copper and aluminum are the good conductors of electricity and rubber, wood and glass are bad conductors of electricity.
  - Temperature — It increases with the increase in temperature
- **Electric potential and potential difference**
  - The amount of work done in moving a unit positive charge from infinity to a given point in an electric field is called electrical potential at that point.
  - Electric potential = $\frac{\text{Workdone}}{\text{Charge}}$
  - $1\ V = \frac{1\ J}{1\ C}$
  - Unit=Volt (V)
  - The amount of work done in moving a unit positive charge from one point to another point in an electric field
  - $\Delta V = V_2 - V_1$
- **Definition**
  - Current is defined as the rate of flow of charge through conductor.
  - q=Charge, t=Time
  - $I = \frac{ne}{t}$, Here (q=n e) n=Number of electrons e=Charge on each electron
  - Unit — Ampere (A) $1\ A = 1\ Cs^{-1}$
- **Combination of resistors**
  - Series combination
    - Equivalent resistance in series $R_S = R_1 + R_2 + \cdots + R_n$

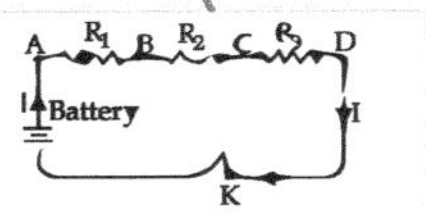

Resistors in series combination

  - Parallel combination
    - Equivalent Resistance in parallel $\frac{1}{R_p} = \frac{1}{R_1} + \frac{1}{R_2} + \cdots \frac{1}{R_n}$

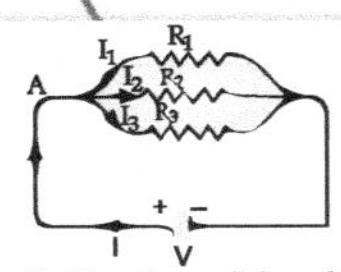

Resistors in parallel combination

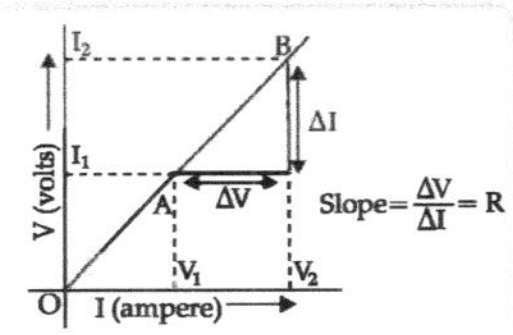

V- I graph for a metallic conductor

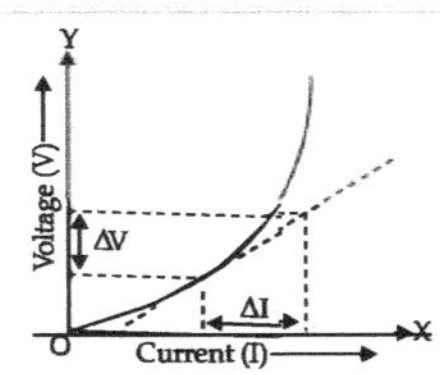

V-I graph for non-ohmic resistors

Trace the Mind Map
- First Level
- Second Level
- Third Level

Mind Map : Electrical Energy and Household Circuits

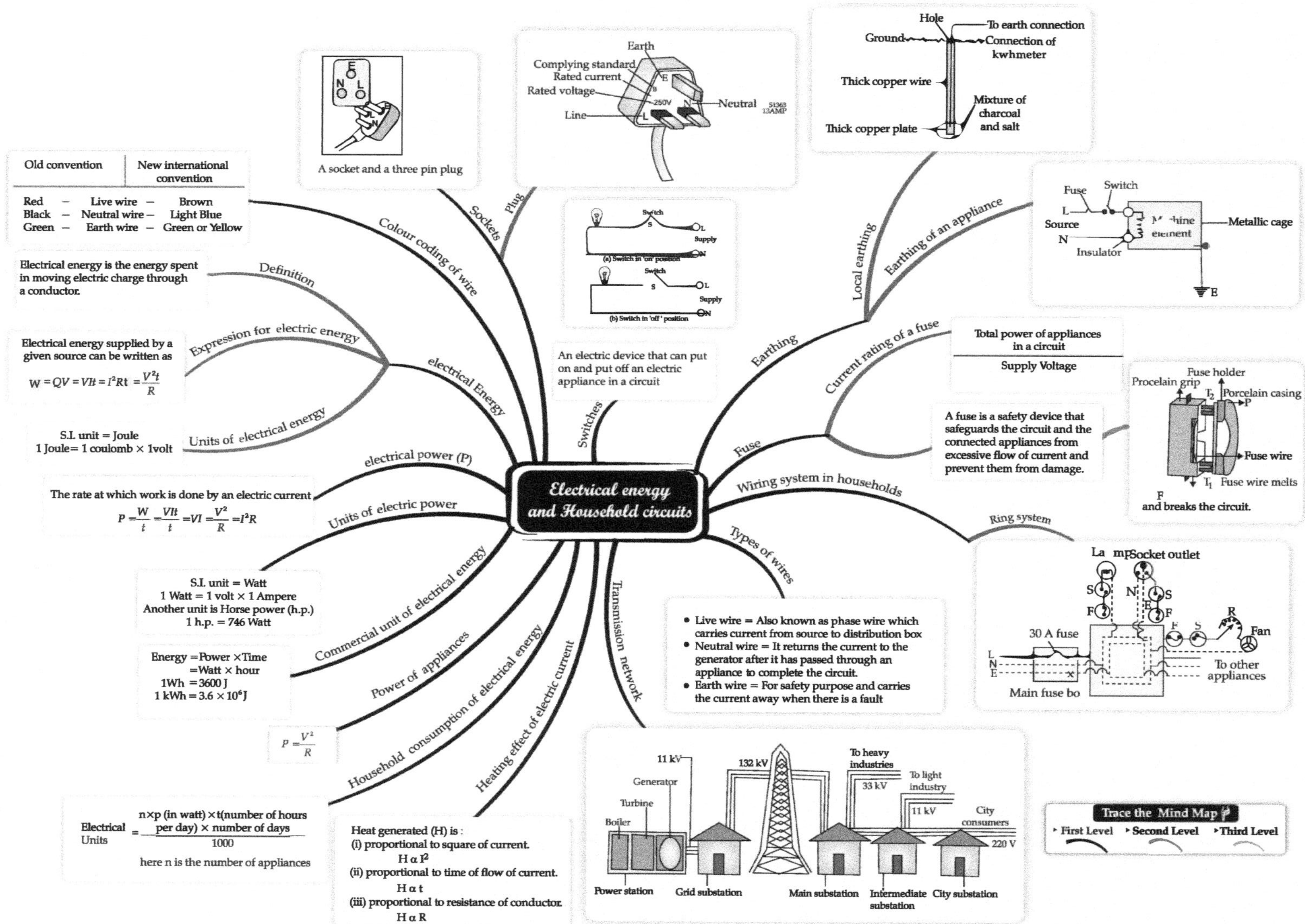

Mind Map : Magnetism

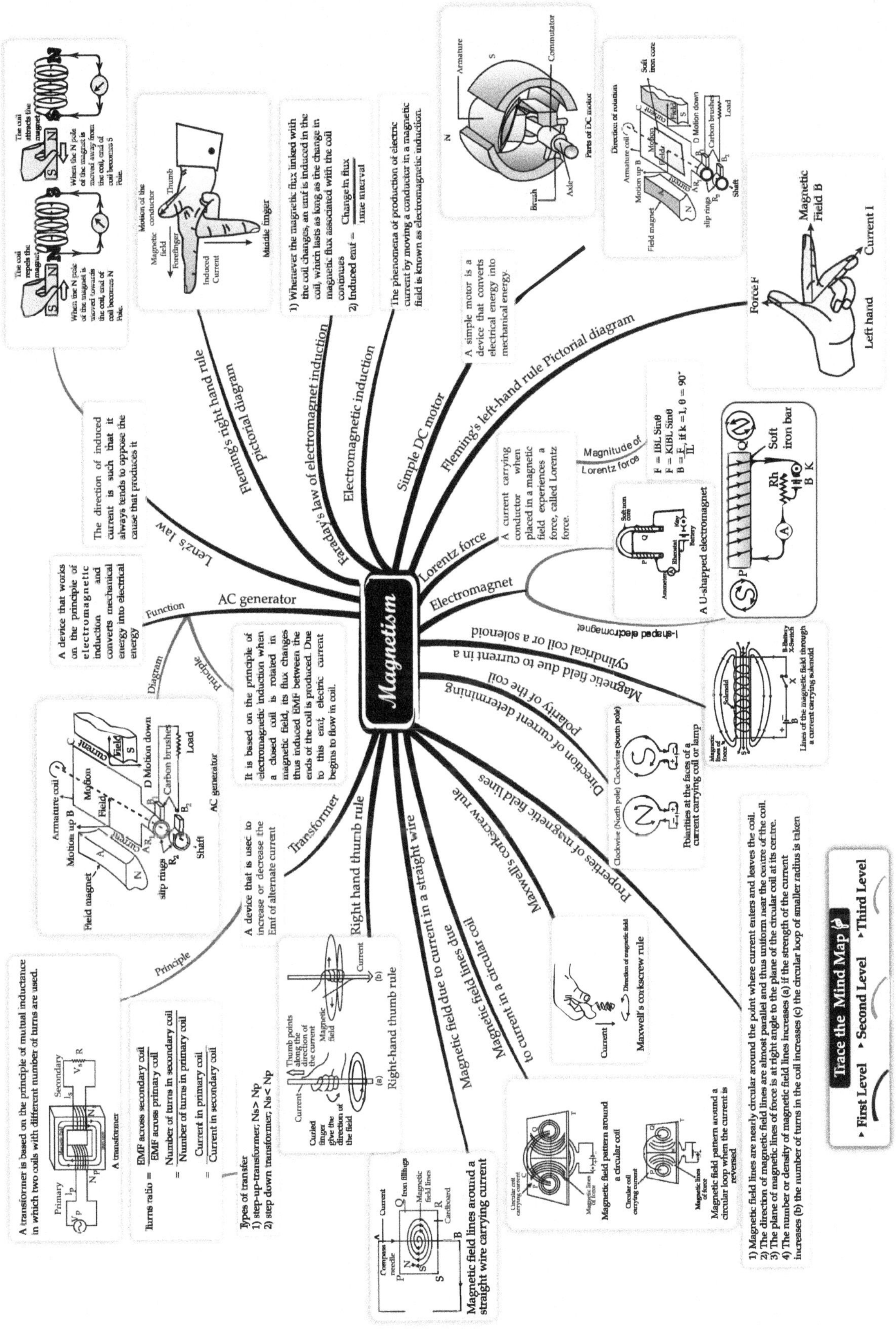

EDUGORILLA
PUBLICATION

Mind Map : Heat

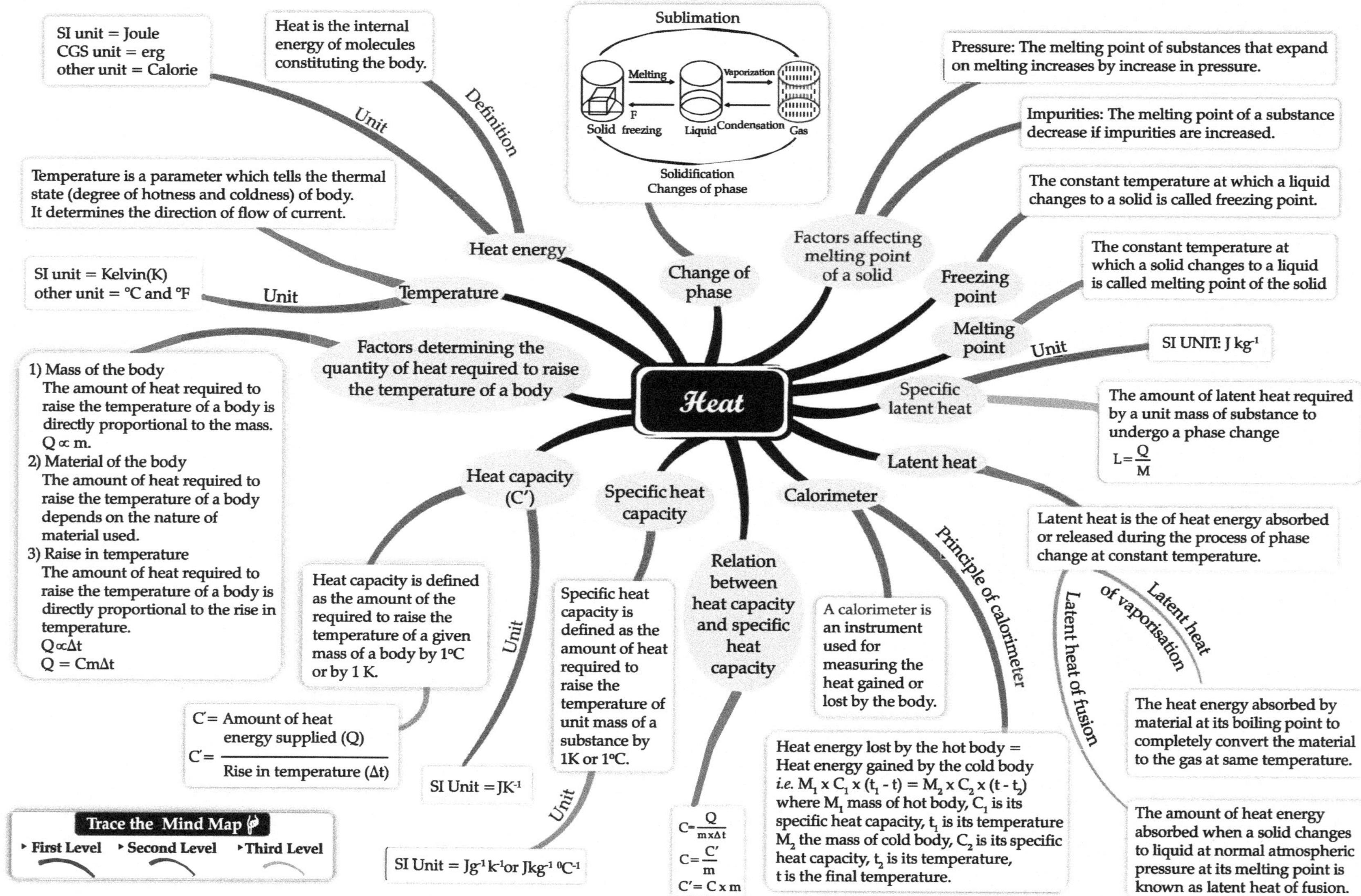

Mind Map : Modern Physics

Modern Physics

Difference between nuclear fission and fusion

DIFFERENCE BETWEEN THE NUCLEAR FISSION AND NUCLEAR FUSION

Nuclear Fission	Nuclear Fusion
It is the process in which a heavy nucleus splits into two light nuclei by bombarding it with slow neutrons.	It is the process in which two light nuclei combine to from a heavy nucleus.
It is a chain reaction.	It is not a chain reaction.
It takes place at normal temperature.	It requires extremely high temperature ($\approx 10^7$K).
Large amount of energy is released.	Energy released is much more than that of fission reaction.
It can be controlled	It can not be controlled.
It leaves behind radioactive wastes.	It does not leave behind any radioactive wastes.
Nuclear bomb is based on the uncontrolled fission reaction.	Hydrogen bomb is based on the uncontrolled fusion reaction.

Nuclear fusion

When two or more light nuclei combine to form a heavy stable nucleus, a part of the mass disappears and is converted into energy. This phenomenon is called nuclear fusion.

$^2_1H + ^3_1H \rightarrow ^4_2He + ^1_0n + 3.3 Mev$

Nuclear fission

Nuclear fission is a process in which a heavier nucleus gets splits into two or more lighter nuclei with the release of large amout

$^{235}_{92}U + ^1_0n \longrightarrow ^{236}_{92}U \longrightarrow ^{144}_{56}Ba + ^{89}_{36}Kr + 3^1_0n + 200 MeV$

Radiations emitted by radioactive nucleus

- Gamma emission: $^A_ZX \rightarrow ^A_Zy + \gamma$ — Parent nucleus, Daughter nucleus, (Gamma radiation)
- Beta emission: $^A_ZP \rightarrow ^A_{Z+1}Q + ^0_{-1}e$ — Parent nucleus, Daughter nucleus, (Beta particle)
- Alpha emission: $^A_ZX \rightarrow ^{A-4}_{Z-2}Y + ^4_2He$ — Parent nucleus, Daughter nucleus, (α-particle)

Structure of atom

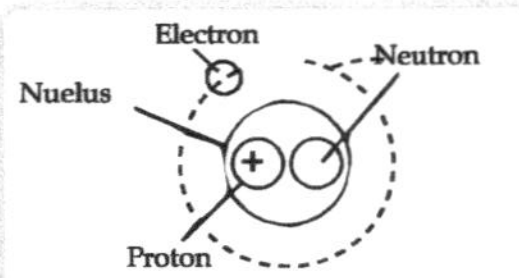

Structure of an atom

Atomic number (z)

The number of protons in the nucleus of an atom is called the atomic number

Mass number

The total number of nucleons (protons + neutrons) in the nucleas of an atom is called the mass number

Relation among A,Z and n

Number of electrons = number of protons = atomic number (z)
Number of protons + number of neutrons = mass number (A)
Atomic number + number of neutrons = mass number
Number of neutrons = mass number - atomic number

Isotopes

Isotopes are the atoms of the same element with the same atomic number (z) but different mass number (A)

Isotopes of hydrogen: ^1_1H Protinum, ^2_1H Deuterium, ^3_1H Tritium

Isobars

Isobar are the atoms of diffrent element with the same mass number but different atomic number

$^{13}_6C$ and $^{13}_7N$

$^{23}_{11}Na$ and $^{23}_{12}Mg$

Isotones

Isotones are the atoms of different mass number (A) and different atomic number (z). different number of electrons and protons but same number of neutrons (A-Z) e.q- $^{23}_{11}Na$, $^{24}_{12}Mg$

Radioactivity

Radioactivity is the phenomenon in which the nucleus of an unstable atom disintegrates and losses energy by emitting invisible radiations e.q- Uranium, Radium, Thorium, etc

Rutherford's experiment

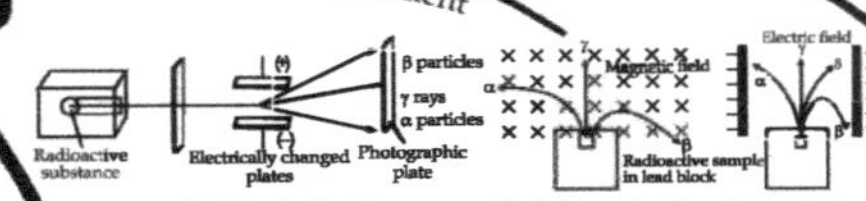

Emission of α, β, γ rays

Deflection of radioactive radiations in magnetic and electric field.

Difference between α, β and γ radiations

Difference between α, β, and γ radiations

Characteristic	α-particle	β-particle	γ-particle
Compositions	A helium nuclei consisting of two protons and two neutrons.	High - energy electron particle.	High - energy electromagnetic radiation.
Charge	Positive and twice to that of a proton (+2e)= $+3.2 \times 10^{-19}$C.	Negative, equal to that of an electron (-e) = -1.6×10^{-19}C.	Neutral, no charge.
Mass	Four times the mass of a proton = 6.68×10^{-27} kg.	Same as the mass of an electron = 9.1×10^{-31}kg.	No mass.
Speed	About 3.33% the speed of light = 10^7 m s^{-1}	About 90% the speed of light = 2.7×10^7 ms^{-1}	Same as the speed of light = 3×10^8 m s^1.
Magnetic and electric field effect	Deflected towards negative plate or terminal.	Deflection towards positive plate or terminal.	No deflection.
Relative angle of deflection	Less	More	Zero
Penetration power	Small, 2.7-8.0 cm in air	Large, 5 m in air.	Very large, 500 m in air.
Absorbed or stopped	Thin cardboard human skin	5 mm thick aluminium sheet, 1 mm thick lead.	30 cm thick iron sheet, 10 cm lead.
Ionising power	Highest 10^4 times that of γ radiations and 10^2 times that of β-particles,	Moderate, 100 times less than α-particles but 100 time more than γ-radiation.	Low 10^4 times of β - particles and 10^2times that of β-particles.
Biological damage	Less damage	More damage	Immense damage.

Trace the Mind Map

▸ First Level ▸ Second Level ▸ Third Level

SOLVED SAMPLE PAPER

ICSE 2023 EXAMINATION

SPECIMEN QUESTION PAPER

PHYSICS

(SCIENCE PAPER - 1)

Maximum Marks: 80

Time allowed: Two hours

Answers to this Paper must be written on the paper provided separately.

You will not be allowed to write during first 15 minutes.

This time is to be spent in reading the question paper.

The time given at the head of this Paper is the time allowed for writing the answers.

SECTION *A* is compulsory. Attempt any four questions from SECTION *B*.
The intended marks for questions or parts of questions are given in brackets [].

SECTION – A (40 Marks)

Answer all the questions from this SECTION

Question 1.

Choose the correct answers to the questions from the given options: **[15]**

(i) S.1. unit of the moment is:

(a) kgf.m
(b) Nm
(c) gf.m
(d) Ncm
Answer. (b)

(ii) Which of the following is the correct expression for gain in kinetic energy, if the initial velocity is not zero?

(a) $k = \frac{1}{2}mv^2$
(b) $k = \frac{mv^2}{4}$
(c) $k = \frac{mv^2}{2t}$
(d) $k = \frac{1}{2}m(v^2 - u^2)$
Answer. (d)

(iii) The energy conversion, when an oscillating pendulum moves from mean to an extreme position is:

(a) Kinetic to potential
(b) Potential to kinetic
(c) Potential to kinetic to potential
(d) Kinetic to potential to kinetic
Answer. (a)

(iv) Which of the following nuclear radiations can be stopped by a sheet of paper?

(a) Alpha

(b) Beta

(c) Gamma

(d) None of these

Answer. (a)

(v) When seven spectral colors pass through a glass block from the air, then which one of the following statements is correct?

(a) In the glass block, speed of blue light > speed of yellow light.

(b) In the glass block, speed of green light > speed of orange light.

(c) In the glass block, speed of violet light > speed of red light.

(d) In the glass block, speed of orange light > speed of indigo light.

Answer. (d)

(vi) In which of the following diagrams is the refraction does not correct:

(a)

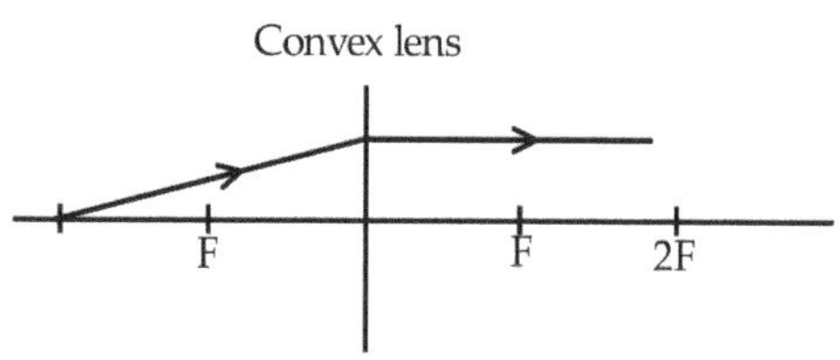

(b)

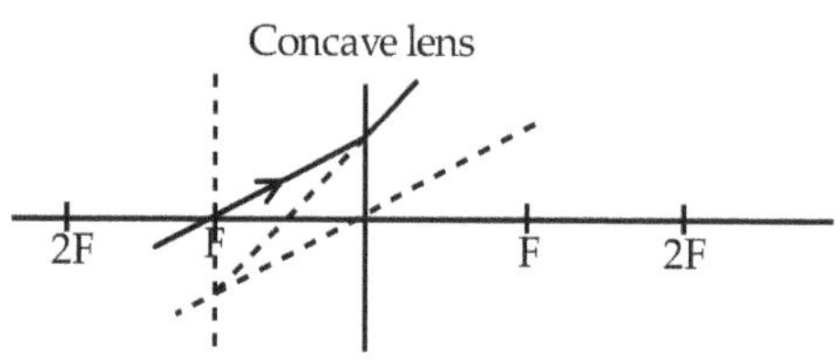

(c)

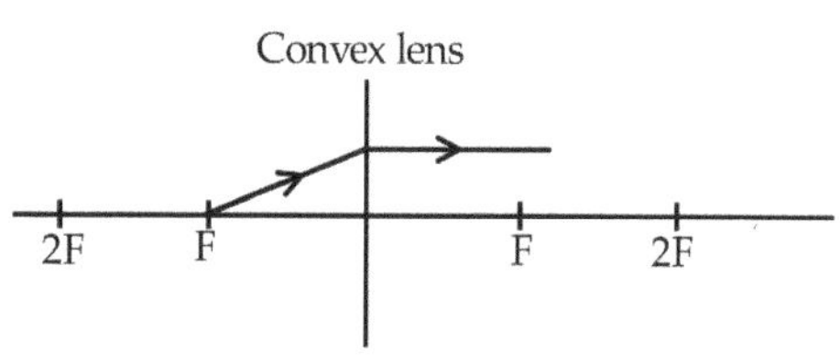

(d)

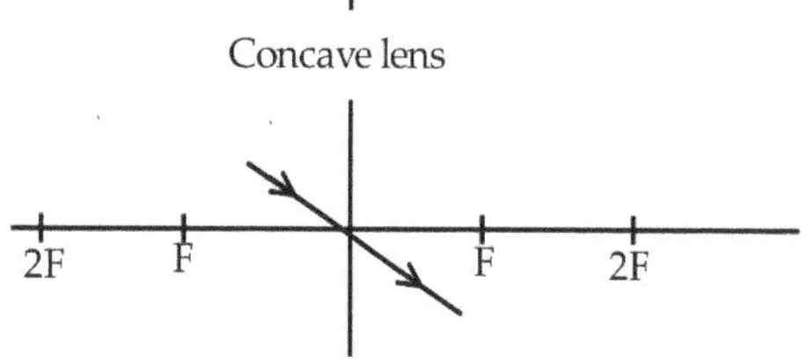

Answer. (a)

(a) Quality

(b) Amplitude

(c) Pitch

(d) Loudness

Answer. (d)

(viii) The ratio of the wavelength of A: to the wavelength of B is:

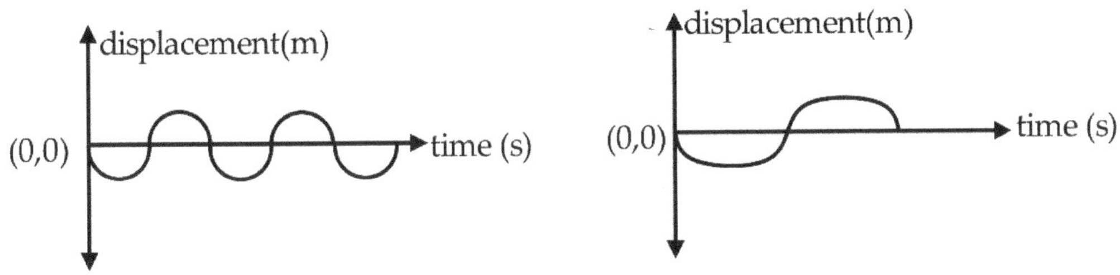

(a) 5: 2

(b) 1:2

(c) 2: 1

Answer. (d)

(ix) The graph shows the I against V relation for three conductors A, B, and C. Choose the correct relation for the resistors of A, B, and C.

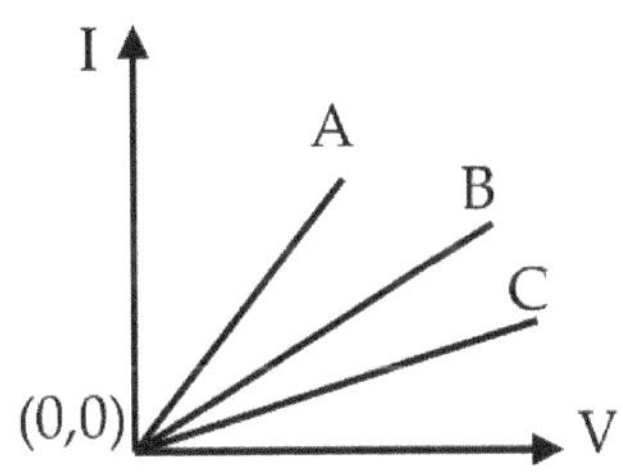

(a) $R_A > R_B > R_C$

(b) $R_B > R_C < R_A$

(c) $R_C > R_B < R_A$

Answer. (c)

(x) Which of the following is the correct color code for the three wires live, neutral, and earth?

(a) Live: Green Neutral: Red Earth: Yellow

(b) Live: Brown Neutral: Red Earth: blue

(c) Live: Brown Neutral: blue Earth: Yellow

(d) Live: Blue Neutral: Brown Earth: Green

Answer. (a)

(xi) When a conductor carrying current is placed in a magnetic field, perpendicular to it then the direction of the force experienced can be found using:

(a) Lenz's law

(b) Fleming's left-hand rule

(c) Flemings right-hand rule
(d) Right-hand thumb rule
Answer. (b)

(xii) Choose the correct statement.
Latent heat absorbed:
(a) Is independent of the mass of the substance.
(b) Is directly proportional to the increase in the temperature of the substance.
(c) Is directly proportional to the specific heat capacity of the substance.
(d) Is directly proportional to the specific latent heat of the substance.
Answer. (d)

(xiii) Which of the following liquids is most suitable for radiators in cars?
(a) Liquid *P* with a specific heat capacity of $4000 Jkg^{-1} K^{-1}$.
(b) Liquid Q with specific heat capacity $2000 Jkg^{-1} K^{-1}$.
(c) Liquid R with a specific heat capacity of $1500 Jkg^{-1} K^{-1}$.
(d) Liquid S with specific heat capacity $2100 Jkg^{-1} K^{-1}$.
Answer. (a)

(xiv) While entering from medium *A* to medium *B* if light slows down then:
(a) $\angle i < \angle r$
(b) $\angle \mathrm{i} = \angle \mathrm{r}$
(c) $\angle \mathrm{i} > \angle \mathrm{r}$
(d) $\angle i \leq \angle r$
Answer. (c)

(xv) The phenomenon of light that causes the diamond to glitter is:
(a) Refraction
(b) Total internal reflection.
(c) Reflection.
(d) Absorption.
Answer. (b)

Question 2.

(i) **(a)** How many pulleys are there in a movable block of a block and tackle system with a velocity ratio of 5? **[3]**
(b) A radioactive nucleus emits a beta particle. Does the position of the daughter nucleus change in a periodic table as compared to the parent nucleus?
(c) To which electrically charged plate the beta radiations will deflect while passing through an electric field?

Answer.
(a) 5 pulleys.
(b) $\mathrm{Z}^{\mathrm{X}^{\mathrm{A}}} \rightarrow \mathrm{z} + 1^{Y^A} + \beta^{-1}$ yes, its gains are in place.

(c) Positive electrically charged plate the beta radiations will deflect while passing through an electric field.

(ii) **(a)** Name the force which produces the maximum moment about. **[2]**

(b) Calculate this moment in the SI unit.

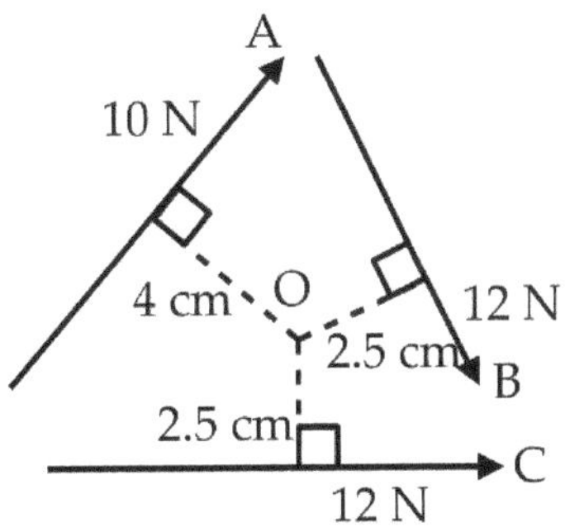

Answer.

(a) Moment of force in maximum when the angle between the r and F is 90^0.

(b) $\tau_A = F \times r$

$$= 10 \times 0.04 \quad \left\{ \begin{matrix} r = 4 \text{ cm} \\ r = \frac{4}{100} = 0.04 \text{ m} \end{matrix} \right\} \text{(Clockwise moment)}$$

$$\tau_A = 0.4 \text{ N} \cdot \text{m}$$

$$\tau_B = F \times r \quad \left\{ \begin{matrix} r = 2.5 \text{ cm} \\ r = \frac{2.5}{1000} = 0.025 \text{ m} \end{matrix} \right.$$

$$= 12 \times 0.025$$

$$\tau_B = 0.3 \text{ N. m (Clockwise moment)}$$

$$\tau_C = F \times r \text{ (Clockwise moment)}$$

$$\{r = 2\text{cm}, \ r = \frac{2}{100}, = 0.02\text{m}\}$$

$$= 12 \times 0.02 \text{ N. m (Anti Clockwise moment)}$$

$$\tau_C = 0.24\text{N. m}$$

$$\tau_{net} = \tau_A + \tau_B + \tau_C$$

$$= (-0.4) + (-0.3) + 0.24$$

$$= -0.4 - 0.3 + 0.24$$

$$\tau_{net} = 0.46\text{N. M[C.W.M.]}$$

(iii) State two factors that affect the center of gravity of the body. **[2]**

Answer.

(a) Mass of a rigid body

(b) Position of mass from the axis.

(iv) If the moment of F about the center of a wheel 0 is 6Nm then calculate the moment of F about A. **[2]**

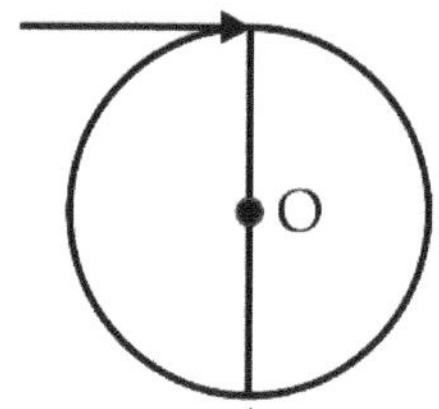

Answer. Moment of a force about the center of wheel 0

$\tau = 6\text{Nm}$

$F = 20 \text{ N}$

$\tau = F \times r_1$

$6 = 20 \times r_1$

$r_1 = \dfrac{6}{20}$

$r_1 = 0.3 \text{ m}, r_1 = r_2$

$r = r_1 + r_2, \; r = 0.3 + 0.3$

$\text{r} = 0.6\text{m}$

Moment of a force about ' A '

$\tau_A = F \times \gamma$

$= 20 \times 0.6$

$\tau_A = 12 \text{ Nm}$

(v) If the kinetic energy of a moving body is, 40 J then what will be its kinetic energy when its velocity is doubled. **[2]**

Answer. $k \cdot \varepsilon_1 = 40 \text{ J}$ $\quad k \cdot \varepsilon_{\text{II}} = ?$

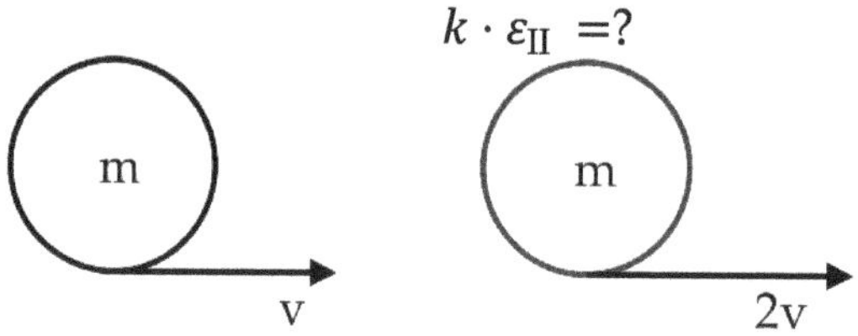

$\dfrac{k \cdot \varepsilon_I}{k \cdot \varepsilon_{II}} = \dfrac{2mv^2}{2\text{m}v^2}$

$\dfrac{40}{k \cdot \varepsilon_{II}} = \dfrac{v^2}{(2v)^2}$

$\dfrac{40}{k \cdot \varepsilon_{II}} = \dfrac{v^2}{4v^2}$

$k \;\; \varepsilon_{II} = 160 \text{ J}$

(vi) A freely suspended pendulum in the air is disturbed once and left to oscillate on its own: **[2]**

(a) Name the type of vibrations.

(b) State one way to decrease the frequency of this vibration.

Answer.

(a) Damped vibration

(b) Increasing the length of a pendulum

$$f = \frac{1}{2\pi}\sqrt{\frac{g}{l}}$$

$$f \propto \frac{1}{\sqrt{l}}$$

(vii) Two copper wires A and B are of the same length present at a temperature 30°C. Radius of A is twice the radius of B. **[2]**

(a) Which wire has greater resistance?

(b) Which wire will have greater resistivity?

Answer.

(a) $r_A = 2r_B$

$R_A > R_B \qquad \left\{R \propto \frac{1}{r^2}\right\}$

(b) Resistivity will be the same.

Question 3.

(i) A lens X can form an image on the screen. **[2]**

(a) Name the lens X.

(b) Is it possible for this lens to form a magnified image?

Answer.

(a) Convex lens

(b) Yes

(ii) **(a)** Is it possible to switch off an appliance by placing the switch in a neutral wire? **[2]**

(b) Is it possible for current to flow between a neutral and an earth wire?

Answer.

(a) Yes

(b) No

(iii) State two factors that affect the strength of an electromagnet. **[2]**

Answer.

(a) No. of turns

(b) Current

(iv) Calculate the heat absorbed by 200 g ice at 0°C to change to water at 60°C. [Specific heat capacity of ice = 2100 J kg^{-1} K^{-1}, Specific heat capacity of water = 4200 J kg^{-1} K^{-1}, Specific latent heat of ice = 336000J kg^{-1}]. **[2]**

Answer. $Q = mL + mc\Delta t$

$= 200 \times 336 + 200 \times 4.2(60 - 0)$

$= 67200 + 200 \times 42 \times 60$

$Q = 117600$ J

(v) What are background radiations? **[2]**

Answer.

Radiation already presents in the atmosphere which is not harmful to human beings is known as background radiation

SECTION – B (40 Marks)

(Attempt any four questions.)

Question 4.

(i) The diagram (not drawn to the scale) below shows the graphical relation between the angle of deviation and angle of incidence when light passes through a triangular prism of angle 62° of a certain glass material. **[3]**

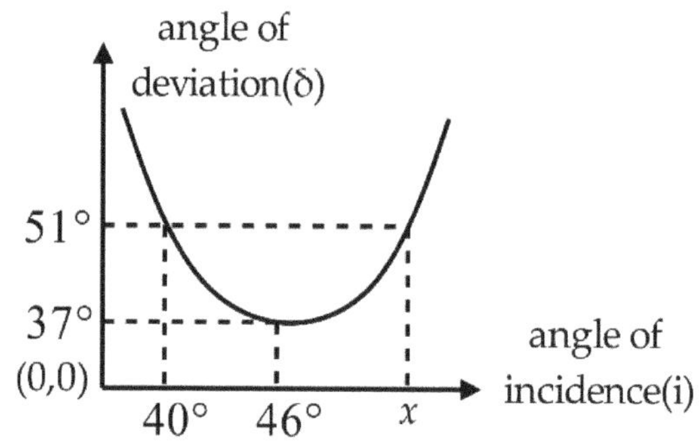

(a) State the angle of minimum deviation of this prism and the corresponding angle of incidence.

(b) Calculate the value of X.

Answer.

(a) The angle of minimum deviation = 37°

the corresponding angle of incidence = 46°

(b) $i + e = \lambda + \delta$

$$x = (46° - 40) + 46°$$
$$x = 52°$$

(ii) Redraw and complete the path of the ray AB till it emerges out of the prism of a critical angle 42°. **[3]**

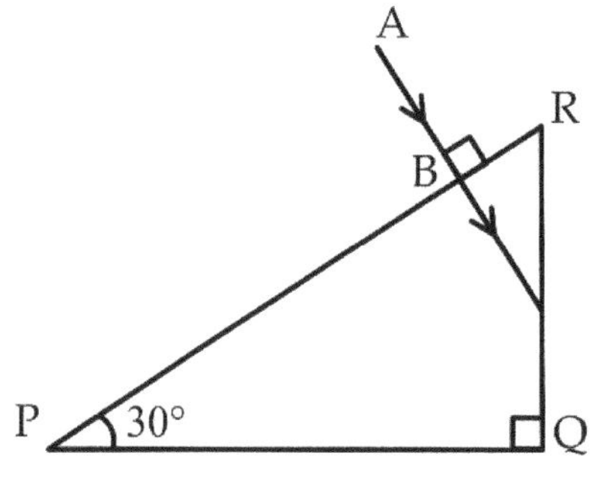

Answer.

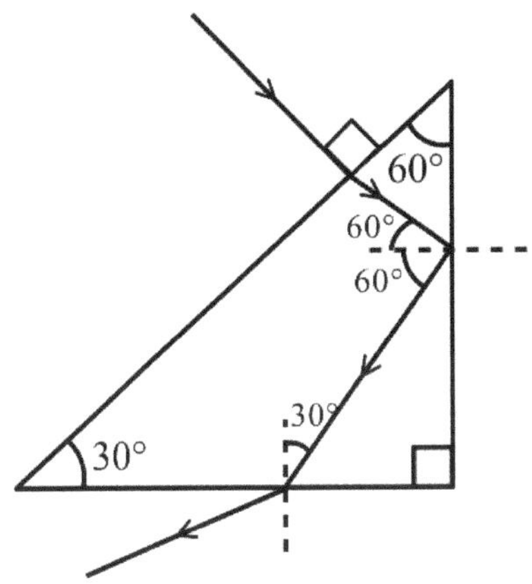

$60 > 40^0$

(iii) The above diagram shows that an observer sees the image of object O at I. **[4]**

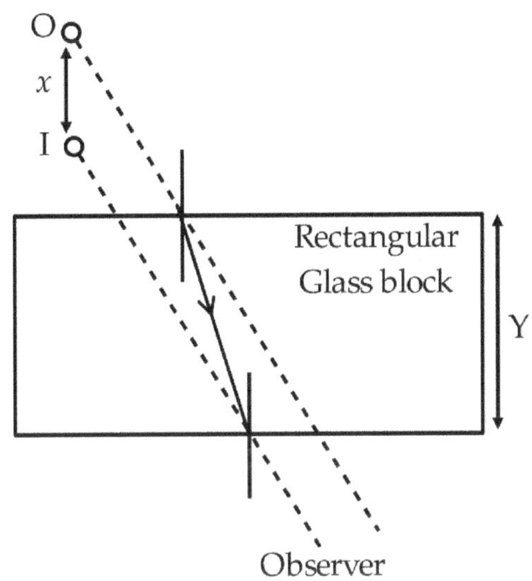

(a) Name and define the phenomenon responsible for seeing the image at a different position.

(b) State the effect on X when:

(i) Y increases

(ii) *Y* decreases

Answer.

(a) Lateral displacement

(b) Increase, decrease.

Question 5.

(i) An object of a height of 20 cm is placed in front of a lens at a distance of 50 cm. Its virtual, diminished image is formed at a distance of 15 cm. **[3]**

(a) Identify the type of lens.

(b) Calculate the focal length of the lens.

Answer.

(a) Concave lens

$u = -50$ cm
$v = -15$ cm

$$\frac{1}{f} = \frac{1}{v} - \frac{1}{u}$$

$$\frac{1}{f} = \frac{1}{-15} - \frac{1}{(-50)}$$

$$\frac{1}{f} = -\frac{1}{15} + \frac{1}{50}$$

$$\frac{1}{f} = -\frac{150}{7}$$

$$f = -21\frac{3}{7} \text{ cm.}$$

(ii) The diagram below shows the extreme colors of a visible spectrum (X and Y). **[3]**

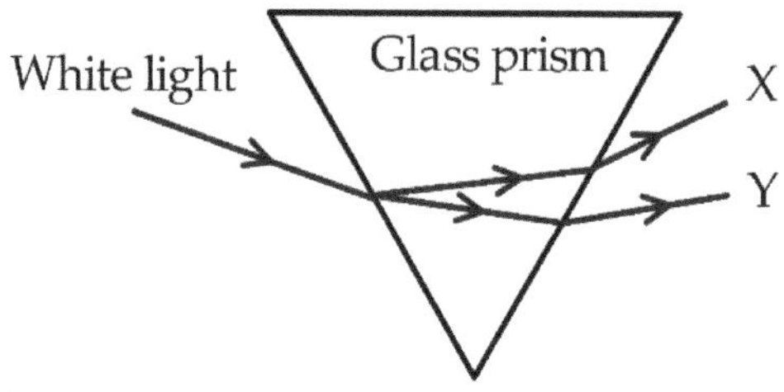

(a) Identify the colors X and Y.
(b) Which color has greater speed in a vacuum?

Answer.
(a) $Y \rightarrow$ Red
(b) $X \rightarrow$ Red

(iii) The diagram below shows an object AB kept in front of the lens. The path of one ray coming from the object is shown. **[4]**

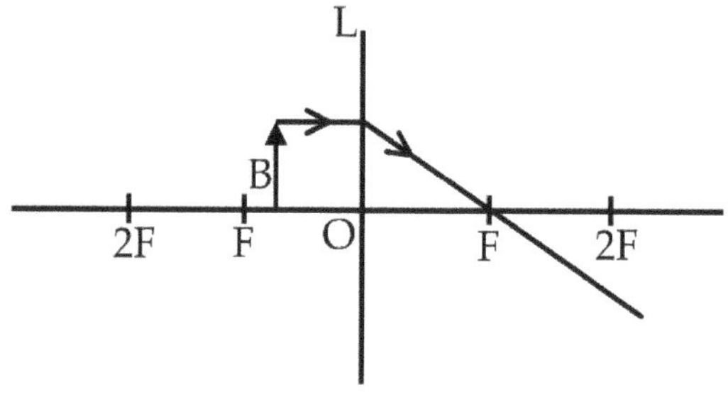

(a) Name the lens L.
(b) Redraw and complete the ray diagram showing the formation of the image.
(c) In which optical instrument is this kind of image formed?

Answer.
(a) Convex lens

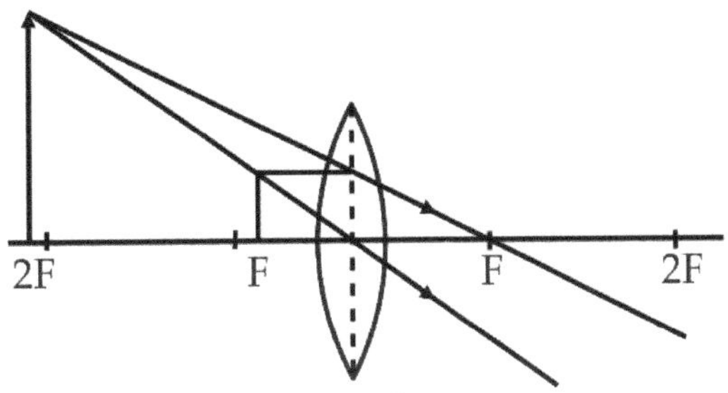

Concex Lens

(c) Simple microscope

Question 6.

(i) The diagram below shows a block and tackle system: **[3]**

(a) Copy and redraw the labeled diagram showing the correct connection of tackle, and the direction of the forces involved to obtain the maximum V.R. and convenient direction.

(b) Calculate the M.A. of this pulley system if its efficiency is 80%.

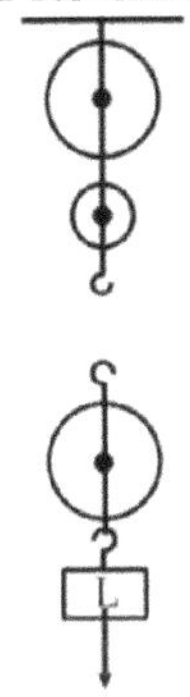

Answer.

(a)

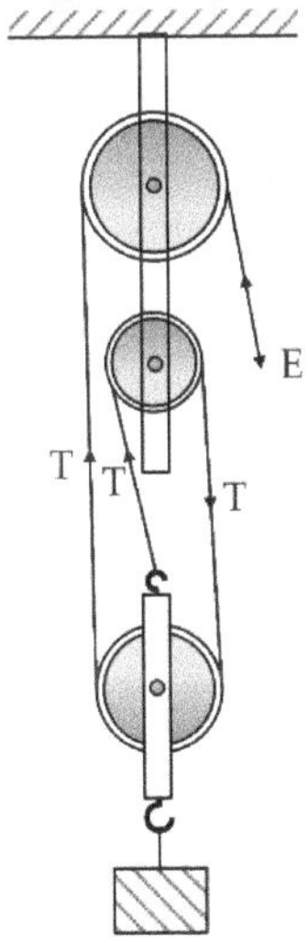

(b) $\eta = 80\%$

$$\text{efficiency} = \frac{M \cdot A}{V \cdot R} \times 100$$

$$\frac{80}{100} = \frac{M \cdot A}{3}$$

$$M \cdot A = \frac{240}{100}$$

$$M \cdot A = 2.4$$

A system of ' n ' pulleys $V \cdot R$ is ' n '

(ii) The adjacent diagram shows a wheel of diameter 40 cm fixed on a wall capable of rotating around its center 0. If the wheel rotates in an anticlockwise direction, then: **[3]**

(a) Calculate the clockwise moment.

(b) State whether X = 100gf or X < 100gf or X > 100gf.

(c) Give a reason for your answer.

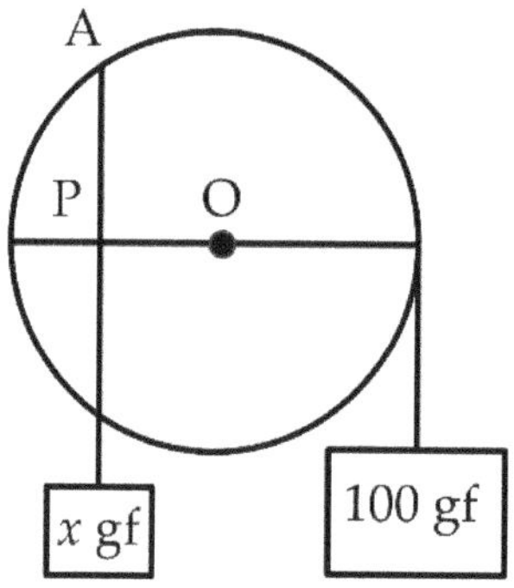

Answer.

(a) clockwise moment

$$= 100 \times \frac{40}{2}$$

$$= 2000 \text{ gf cm}$$

(b) If wheel rotates in anti-clockwise

$$X \propto OP > 100 \times 10$$

$$OP < 20 \text{ cm}$$

$$x \quad > 100\text{gf}$$

(c) Because. $OP < 20cm$.

(iii) A coconut of mass 450 g falls from the top of an 80 m high tree. **[4]**

(a) Calculate the potential energy possessed by the coconut when it is at the top of the tree,

(b) Without calculation, state the kinetic energy with which it strikes the ground and state the principle involved to arrive at the answer in (a). $g = 10 \text{ ms}^{-2}$

Answer.

(a) $m = 450 \text{ g} = \frac{450}{1000} \text{ Kg}$

$$h = 80 \text{ m}$$

$$g = 10 \text{ m/s}^2$$

$$D \cdot \acute{\dot{\varepsilon}} = \text{mgh}$$

$$= \frac{450}{1000} \times 10 \times 8 \Rightarrow 36\text{Joule}$$

(b) By law of conservation of Energy kinetic energy of the coconut at the time of striking

Ground is $36J$

Question 7.

(i) A person standing in front of a cliff fires a gun and hears its echo after 3 s. If the speed of sound in air is 336 ms^{-1}. **[3]**

(a) Calculate the distance of the person from the cliff.

(b) After moving a certain distance from the cliff, he fires the gun again and this time the echo is heard 1.5 s later than the first. Calculate the distance moved by the person.

Answer.

(a)

$$\begin{aligned} v &= 336 \text{ m/s} \\ t &= 3\text{sec.} \\ v &= \frac{2d}{t} \\ d &= \frac{v \times t}{2} \\ &= \frac{336 \times 3}{2} \\ d &= 504 \text{ m} \end{aligned}$$

(b)

$$\begin{aligned} \text{new time } = 3 + 1.5 &= 4.5\text{sec.} \\ \text{New distance} &= \frac{V \times f}{2} \\ &= \frac{336 \times 4.5}{2} \\ &= 756 \text{ m.} \\ \text{Dintarce moved} &= 756 - 504 \\ &= 252 \text{ m} \end{aligned}$$

(ii) **(a)** A radioactive nucleus X emits an alpha particle followed by two beta particles and forms a nucleus Y. What is the general name of the elements X and Y ? **[3]**

(b) If the atomic number of Y is 80 then what is the atomic number of X ?

(c) If the atomic mass number of Y is 189 then what is the atomic mass number of X ?

Answer.

(a)

$$_{Z}X^{A} \xrightarrow{-\alpha} {}_{Z-2}\beta^{A-4} \xrightarrow{-2\beta} {}_{Z}Y^{A-4}$$

x and y are isotopes.

(b) 80 isotopes rave same atomic number.

(c) $A - 4 = 189$

$A = 189 + 4 = 193.$

(iii) A boy tunes a radio channel to a radio station 93.5MHz **[4]**

(a) Name and define the scientific wave phenomenon involved in tuning the radio channel.

(b) Now, what is the frequency of the channel? Convert this frequency into S.I. unit.

Answer.

(a) The phenomenon involved is resonance.

(b) $f = 93.5\text{MH}_z$

$$\text{S.I} \Rightarrow f = 93.5 \times 10^6 \text{ Hz.}$$

Question 8.

(i) **(a)** What is the meaning of the statement 'the power rating of an appliance is 60 W,220 V? **[3]**

(b) In which wire is the fuse connected in a circuit?

(c) State the function of the main switch in an electric circuit.

Answer.

(a) The bulb will consume 60J of Energy per second when connected across the main supply of voltage 220 V.

(b) Live wire.

(c) The purpose of a switch in a sense circuit is to make it easy to open or close the electrical circuit.

(ii) **(a)** Copy and complete the following nuclear reaction. **[3]**

$$_{86}R_n \longrightarrow \frac{218}{} P_0 + {}^4_2\alpha$$

(b) What will be the effect on the radiation emitted in the above reaction when it is allowed to pass through an electric field? [Be specific in your answer]

Answer.

(a)

$$\frac{222}{86}\text{Rn} \rightarrow \frac{218}{84}\text{Po} + \frac{4}{2}\propto$$

(b) When the radiation coming out from a radioactive substance is passed through an electric field the alpha particle slightly deviated toward the negatively charged plate

(iii) Observe the given circuit diagram and answer the questions that follow: **[4]**

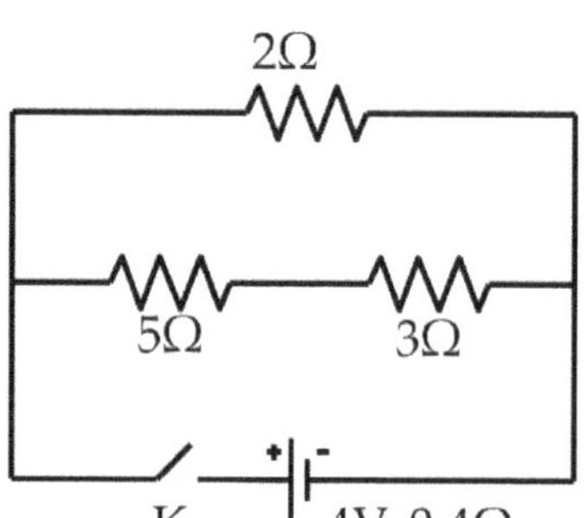

(a) Calculate the resistance of the circuit when the key K completes the circuit.

(b) Calculate the current through 3Ω resistance.

Answer.

(a)

$$R_{eq} = \frac{R_1 R_2}{R_1 + R_2}$$
$$= \frac{8 \times 2}{8 + 2}$$
$$= \frac{16}{10} = 1.6\Omega$$

(b)

Total consent $= \frac{4}{1\cdot6+0.4} = 2$ A voltage across Resistance combination.

$$V = IR = 2 \times 1.6 = 3.2 \text{ V}$$

current in 3Ω

$$I = \frac{3 \cdot 2}{5 + 3} = 0.4 \text{ A.}$$

Question 9.

(i) A metal piece present at 120°C is quickly dropped in a calorimeter of mass 80 g containing 200 g of water at 30°C. The final temperature attained by the mixture is 40°C. Calculate the thermal capacity of the metal piece. [Specific heat capacity of water = $4.2 \text{Jg}^{-1}\,{}^{0}\text{C}^{-1}$, Specific heat capacity of a calorimeter = $0.4 \text{Jg}^{-1}\,{}^{0}\text{C}^{-1}$] **[3]**

Answer. Heat has given by the metal piece

$$= C' \times (120 - 40)$$

The heat is taken by water and a calorimeter

$$= 200 \times 4.2(40 - 30) + 80 \times 0.4(40 - 30)$$
$$= 200 \times 42 + 80 \times 4$$
$$= 8400 + 320 \Rightarrow 8720 \text{ J.}$$

Acc. to principle of calorimeter

Heat loss = Heat gain

$$80 \times C' = 8720$$
$$C' = \frac{8720}{80} = 109 \text{ J/g.}$$

(ii) The diagram below shows a cooling curve for a substance: **[3]**

(a) State the temperatures at which the substance condenses and solidifies respectively.

(b) The temperature range in which the substance is in a liquid state.

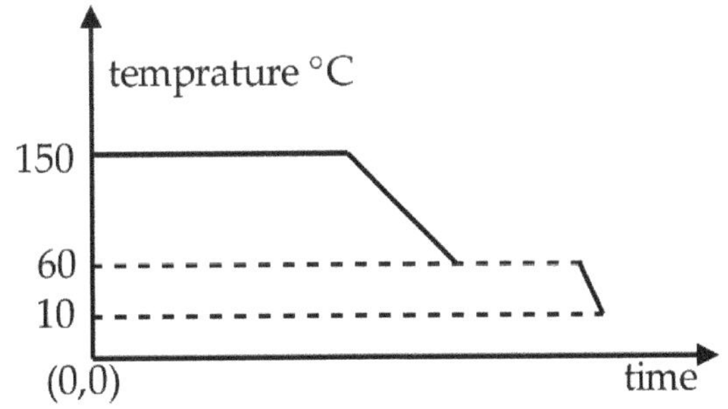

(c) Why do we prefer ice to ice-cold water for cooling a drink?

Answer.

(a) **(a)**condenses at 150°C

solidifies at 60°C

(b) 150 − 60 = 90°C

(c) Because ice takes heat equal to its Latent heat without raising the temperature.

(iii) The diagram below shows a magnet placed between two coils A and B. The magnet is moved along the axis towards coil B. **[4]**

(a) State the polarities induced at the ends Q and R of the coil due to the motion of the magnet.

(b) Name the phenomenon due to which the current is induced in the coils.

(c) Name the law which helps to find the polarities at the ends Q and R.

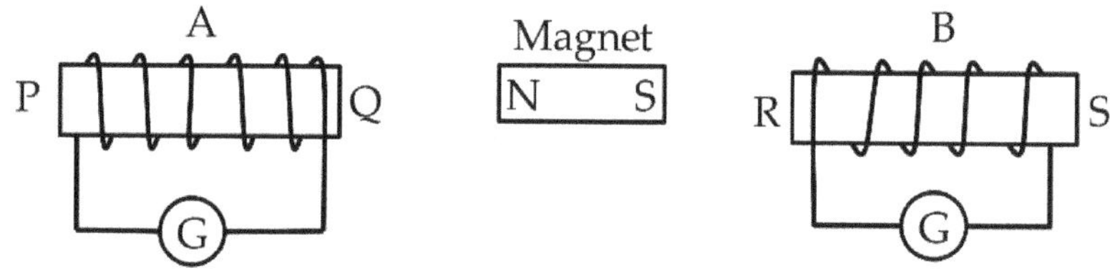

Answer.

(a) Q → South pole

R → South Pole

(b) E.M.I.

2 Lenz law

ICSE 2023 EXAMINATION
SAMPLE PAPER-1
PHYSICS
(SCIENCE PAPER - 1)

Maximum Marks: 80

Time allowed: Two hours

Answers to this Paper must be written on the paper provided separately.

You will not be allowed to write during first 15 minutes.

This time is to be spent in reading the question paper.

The time given at the head of this Paper is the time allowed for writing the answers.

SECTION A is compulsory. Attempt any four questions from SECTION B.
The intended marks for questions or parts of questions are given in brackets [ ].

SECTION – A (40 Marks)
(Answer all the questions from this SECTION)

Question 1.

(i) A magnetic field deflects.

(a) α and β particles
(b) α, β, and γ rays
(c) γ rays
(d) α and γ rays
Answer. (a)

(ii) When ice melts at 0°C, its volume

(a) Decreases
(b) Increases
(c) Remains unchanged
(d) None of the above
Answer. (a)

(iii) The SI unit of specific heat capacity is

(a) cal g^{-1}
(b) J^0C^{-1}
(c) J Kg^{-1} $°C^{-1}$
(d) k cal $°C^{-1}$
Answer. (c)

(iv) The direction of induced emf is obtained by

(a) Right-hand thumb rule

(b) Corkscrew rule

(c) Fleming's right-hand rule

(d) Flemings left hand rule

Answer. (c)

(v) A dynamo works on the principle of

(a) Electrostatic induction.

(b) Optical induction.

(c) Electromagnetic induction.

(d) None of these.

Answer. (c)

(vi) The main fuse is connected in

(a) Earth wire

(b) Neutral wire

(c) Live wire

(d) None of the above

Answer. (c)

(vii) What is the current in the given circuit?

(a) 3 A

(b) $\frac{2}{3}$ A

(c) $\frac{3}{2}$ A

(d) $\frac{3}{2}$ A

Answer. (a)

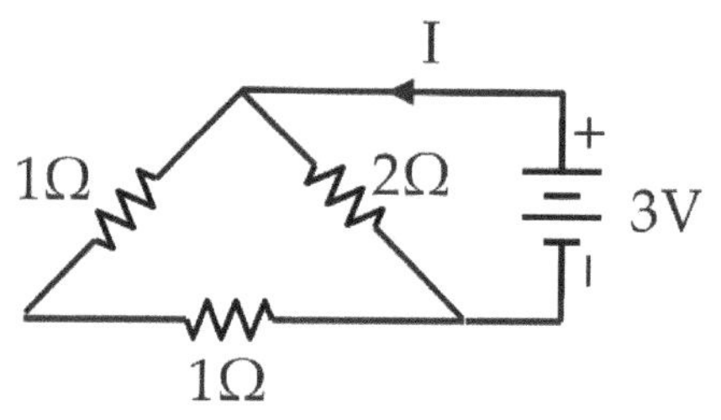

(viii) The critical angle for diamonds is about

(a) 42°

(b) 30°

(c) 24°

(d) 10°

Answer. (c)

(ix) Which of the following statement is not true for a machine?

(a) A machine can also be used as a speed multiplier

(b) A machine can have M.A. > V.R.

(c) η of a machine is always less than 100%

(d) M.A. of a machine is less than 1.

Answer. (b)

(x) A couple produces

(a) Linear motion

(b) Rotational motion

(c) Both (a) and (b)

(d) Neither (a) nor(b)

Answer. (b)

(xi) $kgm^2\ s^{-3}$ is associated with

(a) Kinetic energy

(b) Force

(c) Work

(d) Power

Answer. (d)

(xii) For stable equilibrium, the center of gravity of a body must be

(a) Least

(b) Maximum

(c) In the middle

(d) Outside the body

Answer. (a)

(xiii) A person standing between two vertical cliffs produces a sound. Two successive echoes are heard at 4s and 6s Calculate the distance between the cliffs, take the speed of sound in air = $320\ ms^{-1}$.

(a) 1000 m

(b) 1200 m

(c) 1400 m

(d) 1600 m

Answer. (d)

(xiv) The distance between a crest and the next trough in a transverse wave is

(a) $\frac{\lambda}{2}$

(b) $\frac{\lambda}{4}$

(c) λ

(d) 2λ

Answer. (a)

(xv) The heater of power P watt raises the temperature of mkg of a liquid by ΔTK in time t. The specific heat capacity of the liquid in terms of the above data is given by

(a) $c = \frac{Pt}{m\Delta T}$

(b) $-Pm\Delta T$

(c) $c = \frac{P^2t}{m\Delta I}$

(d) $c - \frac{Ptm}{\Delta I}$

Answer. (a)

Question 2.

(i) Calculate the speed and wavelength of light **[3]**

(a) In glass

(b) In the air, when light waves of frequency 6×10^{14} Hz travel from air to glass of n = 1.5.

Answer. Frequency $(f) = 6 \times 10^{14}$ Hz

(a)

$$n = \frac{\text{speed of light inair}}{\text{speed of light in glass}}$$

$$1.5 = \frac{3 \times 10^8}{\text{Vgless}}$$

$$\text{Vglass } = \frac{3 \times 10^8}{1.5} = 2 \times 10^8 \text{ m/s}$$

$$\text{Wave length in glass } (\lambda) = \frac{c}{f}$$

$$= \frac{2 \times 10^8}{6 \times 10^{14}}$$

$$\lambda = \frac{1}{3} \times 10^{-6} \text{ m.}$$

(b)

$$V_{\text{air}} = 3 \times 10^8 \text{ m/s}$$

$$\text{Wavelength of light in air} = \frac{C}{f}$$

$$= \frac{3 \times 10^8}{6 \times 10^{14}} = \frac{1}{2} \times 10^{-6} \text{ m}$$

$$= 0.5 \times 10^{-6} \text{ m. Ans.}$$

(ii) (a) What do you mean by kilogram force? **[2]**

(b) Write the relation between kilogram-force and newton.

Answer.

(a) One Kilogram-force = 1kgf is the force required to lift an object having a mass 1 kg.

(b) $1\ kgf = 9.8\ N$

(iii) Observe the diagram given below which shows a ray of light incident on the face AC of a glass prism and answer the questions that follow:

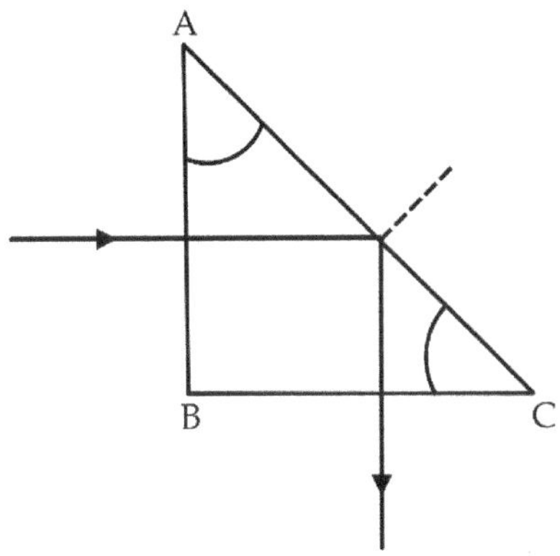

(a) Name the prism.

(b) What is the angle of incidence on face AC of glass prism?

Answer.

(a) It is right angled isosceles prism also known as totally reflecting prism.

(b) The angle of incidence at face AC is 45°.

(iv) Differentiate between centripetal and centrifugal force. **[2]**

Answer.

Centtipetal force	**Centrifugal force**
1. This type of force is directed towards the center.	This type of force is directed away from the center.
2. For example, planets orbiting around the sun.	For example, mud flying out of the revolving wheel

(v) 'What is the main difference between a linear and a circular motion? **[2]**

Answer.

Linear motion	**Circular motion**
1. Velocity is constant	Velocity is variable
2. It is an unaccelerated motion.	It is an accelerated motion.

(vi) What should be the angle between the force and displacement in order to get:

(a) The maximum work.

(b) The minimum work.

Answer.

(a) As we know, $W = f.s \cos\theta$

The maximum value of $\cos\theta$ is at $\theta = 0°$

Therefore, maximum work is attained at $\theta = 0°, W = Fs\ cos0° = f.d$

(b) The minimum value of $\cos\theta\ is\ at\ \theta = 90°$

Therefore, maximum work is attained at $\theta = 90°, W = Fs\ cos90° = 0$

(vii) A man weighing 800 N carries a load of 80 N up a flight of stairs 3 m high in 11 sec. What is his power? **[2]**

Answer.

Total force $F = 800 + 80 = 880\ N,$

Distance, $d = 3m$

Power, $P = \frac{W}{T} = \frac{880 \times 3}{11} = \frac{2640}{11} = 240$ W

Question 3.

(i) Write two uses of echoes.

Answer. The two uses of echoes are:

1. Echoes are used by bars in finding their way during the night.

2. Echoes are used in radars in order to estimate the position of a far-off object.

(ii) State work-energy theorem. **[2]**

Answer.

Work energy theorem ⇒According to the work energy theorem work done by a force acting in the direction of the moving body is equal to the increase in kinetic energy of a moving body.

(iii) A uniform meter scale is in equilibrium as shown below. Calculate the mess of the ruler. **[2]**

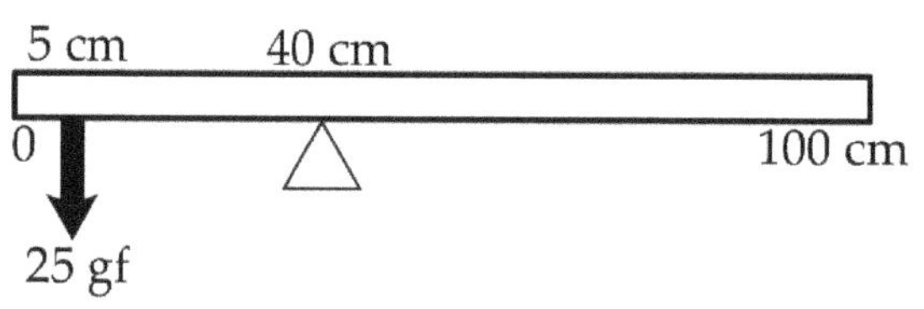

Answer. Mass = m

Therefore, $25 \times (40 - 5) = m \times (50 - 40)$

$m = 87.5\ gf$

(iv) Explain the principle of reversibility of light. **[2]**

Answer.

According to the principle of reversibility of light, if a light ray travel from air to water along a certain path and the path is reversed from water to air, then the ray will trace the previous path.

(v) **(a)** What is a fuse?

(b) In which part of the wiring is a fuse connected? **[2]**

Answer.

(a) A fuse is a safety device that cut off the circuit connecting the electric appliance if the current flowing through the live wire gets too large.

(b) A fuse is connected in series with the live wire.

SECTION – B (40 Marks)
(Attempt any four questions)

Question 4.

(i) **(a)** How does a trawlerman catch fish in deep water? **[3]**

(b) If the amplitude of a wave is doubled, what will be the effect on its loudness?

Answer.

(a) The trawlerman uses sound detection methods to catch fish in deep water. He sends ultrasonic waves to detect the fish which are then reflected back on striking with the fish and the depth of the shoal of fish is detected.

(b) Loudness depends on the square of the amplitude of the wave. Thus, when the amplitude of the wave is doubled, the loudness becomes four times.

(ii) Ria fires a gun toward a hill and bears its echo after 6 seconds. She then moves 350 m towards the hill and fires again. This time she hears the echo after 4 seconds. Calculate the speed of sound. **[3]**

Answer.

Consider the distance of the cliff from the original position be d and the speed of sound is v,

then the time t_1 after which the first echo was heard is given by

$$t_1 = \frac{2d}{v} \quad \text{......(i)}$$

In the second case, the time t_2 is given by $t_2 = \frac{2(d-350)}{v}$ ....(ii)

Dividing Eq. (ii) by Eq. (i), we get

$$\frac{t_2}{t_1} = \frac{2(d-350)}{d}$$

$$\frac{4}{6} = \frac{(d-350)}{d}$$

$$d = 1050 \text{ m}$$

$$v = \frac{2d}{t} = 2 \times \frac{1050}{3} = 350 \text{ m s}^{-1}$$

(iii) **(a)** Differentiate between forced vibrations and resonance.

(b) Why is a loud sound heard at acoustic resonance? **[4]**

Answer.

(a)

Force vibrations	Resonance
1. The vibration the take place under the influence of external periodic forces are called forced vibration.	Resonance The phenomena of setting a body into oscillations with its natural frequency by another vibrating body with the same frequency are called resonance or acoustic resonance.

2. The external frequency may or may not be equal to the natural frequency of the body.	The external frequency has the same frequency as the natural frequency of oscillation of the given oscillatory system.

(b) At acoustic resonance, the amplitude of vibration of the body becomes very large producing loud sound, as loudness is proportional to square of the amplitude.

Question 5.

(i) Answer the following questions on the basis of an electric plug that consists of three pins: **[3]**

(a) How would you identify the earth pin?

(b) In which of the three connecting wires should the electric switch be connected?

(c) Explain why a switch should not be touched with wet hands.

Answer.

(a) The earth pin is thicker and longer than the other two pins

(b) The electric switch should be connected in the Live wire.

(c) A wet hand is a good conductor of electricity and there is a chance of getting an electric shock. Hence, the switch should not be touched with wet hands.

(ii) **(a)** Mention two Factors on which the internal resistance of a cell depends.

(b) Write an expression for the resistance of a conducting wire in terms of its length and area of cross-section.

(c) State Ohm's law **[3]**

Answer.

(a) The factors on which the internal resistance of a cell depends are :

I. The nature of the electrolyte used.

II. The area of two electrodes and the distance of separation between them.

(b) If R is the resistance of a wire of length L and A be its area of cross-**SECTION** then $R = \rho \frac{L}{A}$ where ρ is the resistivity or specific resistance of the material of the wire.

(c) Ohm's Law states that the current flowing in a conductor is directly proportional to the potential difference across its ends provided the physical conditions and temperature of the conductor remain the same.

(iii) Four cells each of 3 V and internal resistance of 0.15 ohm are connected in series. The combination is connected to an ammeter of negligible resistance, a 2-ohm resistor, and an unknown resistor R. The current in the circuit is 4 A. **[4]**

(a) Draw a labeled circuit diagram for the above arrangement

(b) Calculate:

I. The total resistance of the circuit and total emf

II. The value of R_1, and

III. The potential difference across R_1,

Answer.

(a) The circuit diagram is as shown below:

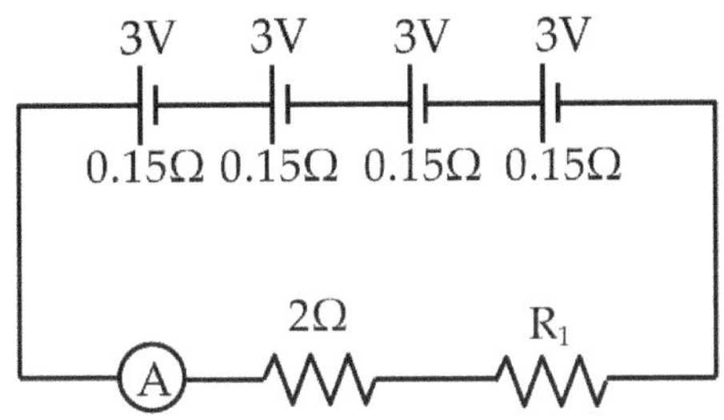

(b) I. Total internal resistance = $4 \times 0.15 = 0.6\Omega$

Total resistance = $2 + 0.6 + R_1$

$= (2.6 + R_1)\Omega$

Total emf = $3 + 3 + 3 + 3 = 12$ V

II. Using $I = \frac{\text{Total emf}}{\text{Total resistance}}$

$$\Rightarrow 4 = \frac{12}{(2.6 + R_1)}$$

$\Rightarrow R_1 = 0.4\Omega$

III. Potential difference across $(R_1) = IR_1 = 2 \times 0.4 = 1.6$ V

Question 6.

(i) **(a)** Give one example of each where high specific heat capacity of water is used

I. In cooling and

II. As heat reservoir.

(b) Define calorimetry. **[3]**

Answer.

(a) I. Water is used to cool the radiators of engines of cars.

II. As a heat reservoir, water is used in hot water bottles for fomentation or in hot water pipes for heating rooms in cold countries.

(b) The measurement of quantity of heat is known as calorimetry.

(ii) (a) Define specific latent heat of vaporization **[3]**

(b) Differentiate between heat and temperature

Answer.

(a) The specific latent heat of vaporization of a liquid is defined as the heat required to convert one kilogram of the liquid into vapor at its boiling point without any change in its temperature.

(b)

Heat	Temperature
1. Heat is a form of energy	Temperature is a degree of hotness or coldness
2. Its S.I. unit is joule (J)	Its S.I. unit is kelvin (K)

(iii) In an experiment to determine the specific latent heat of vaporization of steam L, the following measurements were taken: **[4]**

Mass of calorimeter + stirrer = $x$kg

Mass of water = $y\ kg$

The initial temperature of water = L°C

Final temperature of the mixture t_2 °C

Given: Specific heat capacity of calorimeter and water are S_1 and S_2 respectively Express L in terms of the above data. Mass of condensate (steam condensed) = m kg.

Answer. Heat lost by steam to condense = $m \times L$

Heat lost by water to lower its temperature to $t_2 = m \times S_2(100 - t_2)$

Total heat lost = $m \times L + m \times S_2(100 - t_2)$

Heat gained by water = $y \times S_2(t_2 - t_1)$

Heat gained by calorimeter = $x \times S_1(t_2 - t_1)$

Total heat gained = $y \times S_2(t_2 - t_1) + x \times S_1(t_2 - t_1)$

By the Principle of Calorimetry,

Heat lost = Heat gained, we get

$$mL + mS_2(100 - t_2) = yS_2(t_2 - t_1) + xS_1(t_2 - t_1)$$

$$L = \frac{\{(xS_1 + yS_2)(t_2 - t_1) - mS_2(100 - t_2)\}}{m}$$

Question 7.

(i) **(a)** Define Radioactivity.

(b) 'What happens inside the nucleus that causes the emission of beta particles?

(c) Express the above change in the form of an equation.

Answer.

(a) The process of spontaneous emission of alpha, beta and gamma radiations from nuclei of atoms during their decay is termed as radioactivity.

(b) A change of a neutron into a proton inside the nucleus causes the emission of beta particle.

(c) ${}^1_0n \longrightarrow {}^1_1p + {}^{0}_{-1}e$

(ii) A radioactive nucleus ${}^A_Z$X first emits a β particle and then an α particle and the resulting nucleus is represented by QY. What are the values of P and Q in terms of A and Z ? **[3]**

(iii) **(a)** A radioactive substance is oxidized. What change would you expect w take place in the nature of its radioactivity? Give reason for your answer.

(b) Explain how β - emission changes the nucleus of an unstable element. **[4]**

Answer.

(a) Oxidation takes place between the electrons and has no effect on the nucleus but unlike oxidation, radioactivity is a nuclear phenomenon due to which it remains unaffected.

(b) The mass number of the nucleus in case of a β-emission remains same but the number of neutrons decrease by one and number of protons increase by one which implies, atomic number increases by one due to which the element moves one place forward in the periodic table.

Question 8.

(i) **(a)** State two ways by which the magnetic field of a solenoid can be made stronger.

(b) What material is used for making the armature of an electric bell? Give a reason for using this material. **[3]**

Answer.

(a) By increasing the number of turns of winding in the solenoid

By increasing the current through the solenoid.

(b) The material used for making the armature of electric bell is soft iron core.

reason for using material is it can be magnetized and demagnetized very easily.

(ii) On what factors the magnitude of the force on a current-carrying conductor placed in a magnetic field depends? **[3]**

Answer.

(a) Current flowing in the conductor.

(b) Length of the wire

(c) Strength of magnetic field

(iii) Draw field lines due to

(a) Current flowing into a circular coil

(b) Solenoid carrying current.

Answer.

(a)

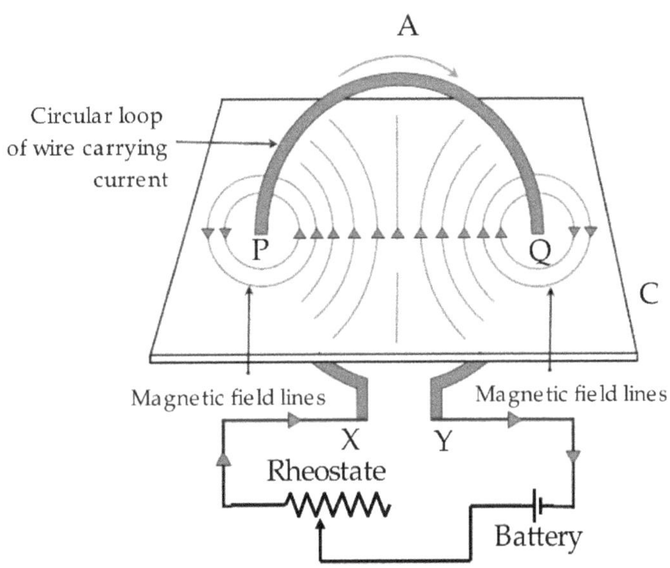

(b)

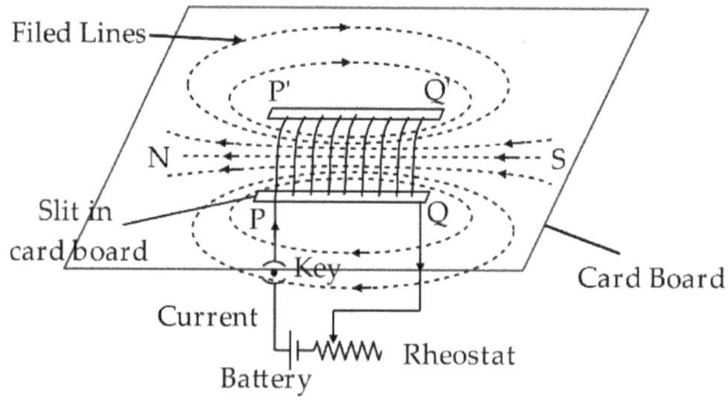

Question 9.

(i) A lens forms a real image 3 cm high of an object 1 cm high. If the separation of object and image is 15 cm, find the focal length of the lens. **[3]**

Answer.

$$u = -3.75 \text{ cm}$$
$$v = 15 + u = 15 + (-3.75)$$
$$v = 11.25 \text{ cm}$$
$$\frac{1}{f} = \frac{1}{v} - \frac{1}{u}$$
$$h_i = -3 \text{ cm}$$
$$-u + v = 15$$
$$f = ?$$
$$\frac{h_i}{h_0} = \frac{V}{u}$$
$$-\frac{3}{i} = \frac{15 + u}{u}$$
$$-3u = 15 + u$$
$$-3u - u = 15$$
$$-4u = 15$$
$$u = -15/4$$

$$\frac{1}{f} = \frac{1}{11.25} - \frac{1}{(-3.75)}$$
$$f = 2.82 \text{ cm}$$

(ii) **(a) I.** What is meant by the refraction of light?

II. What is the cause of the refraction of light?

(b) 'The refractive index of diamond is 2.42°.

What is meant by this statement? **[3]**

Answer.

(a)

I. Bending ability of light when it goes from one medium to another medium.

II. Speed of light is different in different medium.

(b) Speed of light in diamond will reduce by a factor of 2.42 as compared to its speed in air

(iii) A prism deviates a monochromatic ray of light through an angle $'\delta'$ when the angle of incidence on the surface of the prism is ' i '

(a) Draw a graph showing the variation of " δ' with. On your graph show the angle of minimum deviation.

(b) What is the relation between the angle of incidence and the angle of emergence when the ray suffers minimum deviation? **[4]**

Answer.

(a)

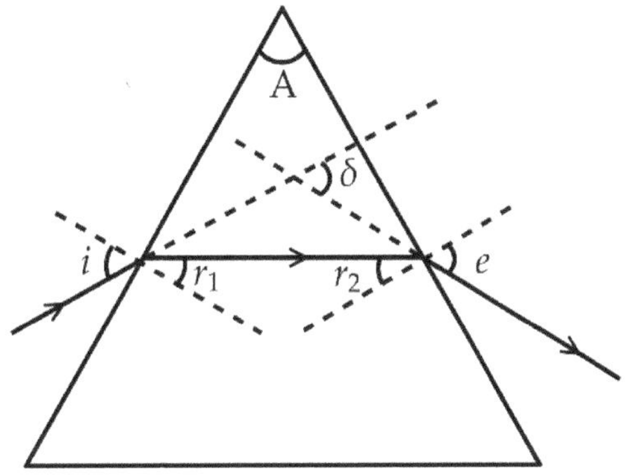

(b)

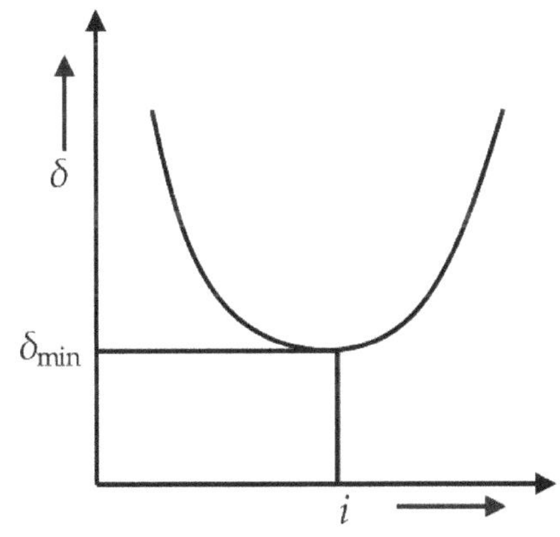

$$i + e = A + \delta$$

for minimum deviation

$$i = e$$
$$2i = A + \delta$$
$$\delta_{min} = 2i - A$$

ICSE 2023 EXAMINATION
SAMPLE PAPER-2
PHYSICS
(SCIENCE PAPER - 1)

Maximum Marks: 80

Time allowed: Two hours

Answers to this Paper must be written on the paper provided separately.

You will not be allowed to write during first 15 minutes.

This time is to be spent in reading the question paper.

The time given at the head of this Paper is the time allowed for writing the answers.

SECTION *A* is compulsory. Attempt any four questions from SECTION *B*.

The intended marks for questions or parts of questions are given in brackets [ ].

SECTION – A (40 Marks)
(Answer all the questions from this SECTION)

Question 1.

(i) Carbon dating is used to

(a) Assess the amount of radioactivity

(b) Assess the age of fossils

(c) Assess the rate of radioactivity

(d) None of the above

Answer. (b)

(ii) The S.I. unit of specific latent heat is

(a) $J\ Kg^{-1}$

(b) $J\ Kg^{-1}\ K^{-1}$

(c) $cal\ G^{-1}$

(d) $cal\ G^{-1}\ K^{-1}$

Answer. (a)

(iii) A temperature of 100°F is almost exactly

(a) 38°C

(b) 56°C

(c) 122°C

(d) 212°C

Answer. (a)

(iv) The quantity of heat required to raise the temperature of a unit mass of a substance by 1°C. Is called

(a) Specific heat capacity

(b) Heat of fusion
(c) Latent heat
(d) Neither specific heat nor latent heat
Answer. (a)

(v) The S.I unit of a magnetic field is
(a) $N^{-1}AM$
(b) NAM
(c) $NA^{-1}M^{-1}$
(d) $N^{-1}\ A^{-1}\ m$
Answer. (c)

(vi) Magnetic lines of force
(a) Cannot intersect at all.
(b) Intersect within the magnet.
(c) Intersect only at the south and north poles.
(d) Intersect at neutral points only.
Answer. (a)

(vii) One watt-hour is equal to
(a) 36 J
(b) 360 J
(c) 3600J
(d) 36000 J
Answer. (c)

(viii) What is the resistance between P and Q ?
(a) $\frac{3}{4}\Omega$
(b) $\frac{4}{3}\Omega$
(c) $\frac{16}{3}\Omega$
(d) Infinity
Answer. (c)

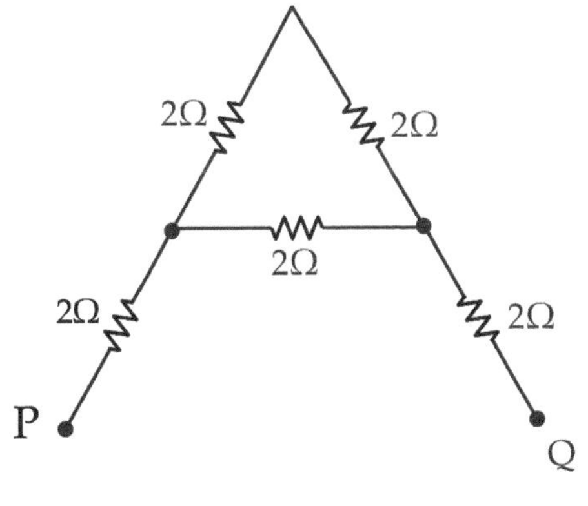

(ix)Which of the following shows the bending of light from rarer (R) into denser (D) medium?

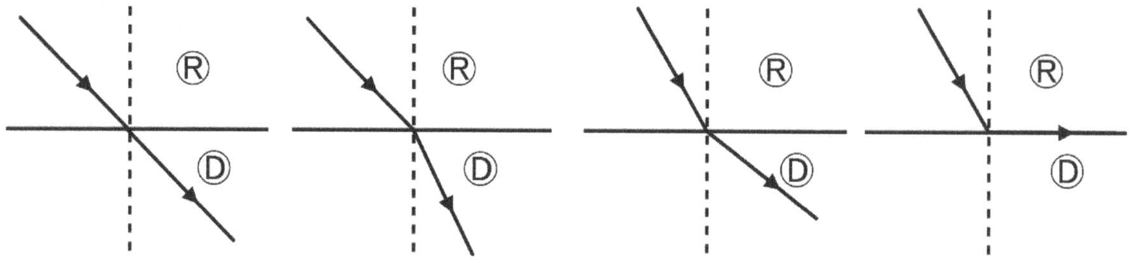

(a) (b) (c) (d)

Answer. (b)

(x) Mechanical advantage (MA), load (L), and effort (E) are related as

(a) MA = L × E

(b) L = MA × E

(c) E = MA × L

(d) None of these.

Answer. (b)

(xi)Two forces each of magnitude 10 N act vertically upwards and downwards respectively on the two ends of a uniform rod of length 4 m, freely pivoted at its mid-point as shown in Then the magnitude of the resultant moment of forces about the pivot O is

(a) 40Nm (clockwise)

(b) 40Nm (anticlockwise)

(c) 20Nm (clockwise)

(d) 10Nm (anticlockwise)

Answer. (b)

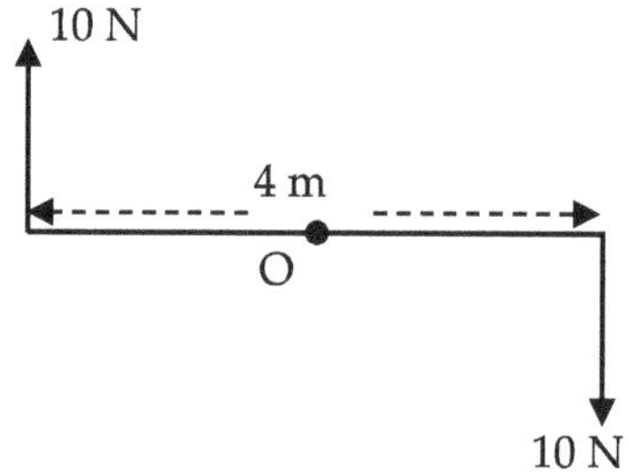

(xii) Two bodies of masses m and $4m$ are moving with equal kinetic energy. The ratio of the velocities with which they are moving is

(a) 2: 1

(b) 1: 2

(c) 4: 5

(d) 3: 4

Answer. (a)

(xiii) Sound waves cannot travel through

(a) Air
(b) Water
(c) Vacuum
(d) All of these
Answer. (c)

(xiv) A motor converts______ energy into_______ energy.

(a) Electrical, mechanical
(b) Mechanical, electrical
(c) Thermal, mechanical
(d) None of these
Answer. (a)

(xv) Specific latent heat of vaporization of steam is

(a) 2.26 J kg^{-1}
(b) 22.6 J kg^{-4}
(c) 226 J kg^{-1}
(d) 2260 J kg^{-1}
Answer. (d)

Question 2.

(i) An electric heater is marked $500KW, 220v$. If the heater is operated for 1 hour, calculate the energy consumed in kWh and in f. **[3]**

Answer. $P = 500\text{KW}$

$V = 220\text{ V}$

$T = 1h$

$\varepsilon = P \times T$

$\varepsilon = 500 \times 1$

$\varepsilon = 500\text{KWR}$

In terms of joule

$\varepsilon = 500 \times 3.6 \times 10^6\text{J}$

$\varepsilon = 1.8 \times 10^9\text{J}$

(ii) **(a)** Which type of pulley is often used as a machine even though it does not give any gain in mechanical advantage?

(b) What is the use of the above-mentioned type of pulley system?

Answer.

(a) It is a single fixed pulley system.

(b) A single fixed pulley system is used to change the direction of fore.

(iii) Calculate the speed of light in water when the refractive index of water is 3×10^8 m/s.

Answer. 30 Speeds of light in a vacuum

Speed of light in water (medium) $= \frac{3\times10^8}{\frac{4}{3}}$

$$= 2.25 \times 10^8 m/s$$

(iv) **(a)** State any two characteristics of a wave motion.

(b) On which principle does SONAR base?

Answer.

(a) Some of the characteristics of wave motion are:

I. It is a periodic disturbance.

II. Energy transfer takes at a constant speed.

(b) Sonar is based on the principle of echo.

(v) Two fuse wires of the same length are 5 A and 20 A. Which of the false is thicker and why?

Answer. The fuse ware rated 20 A is thicker. As the thickness of the wire increases, the assistance of the wire decrease because of which leas heat is produced, and the wire is capable to carry larger values of current through it before its breakdown.

(vi) **(a)** If an a-particle absorbs an electron, what does it change to?

(b) Identify & X in the given fusion reaction.

$${}_1^2H + {}_1^2H \rightarrow {}_2^4He + X$$

Answer.

(a) ${}_2^4He + {}_{-1}^{0}e \longrightarrow {}_1^3H + {}_0^1n$

(b) In the above fusion reaction, two hydrogen atoms are fused to form one helium atom thereby releasing energy which is 24MeV as represented by X.

(vii) Observe the circuit given below and find the equivalent resistance. **[2]**

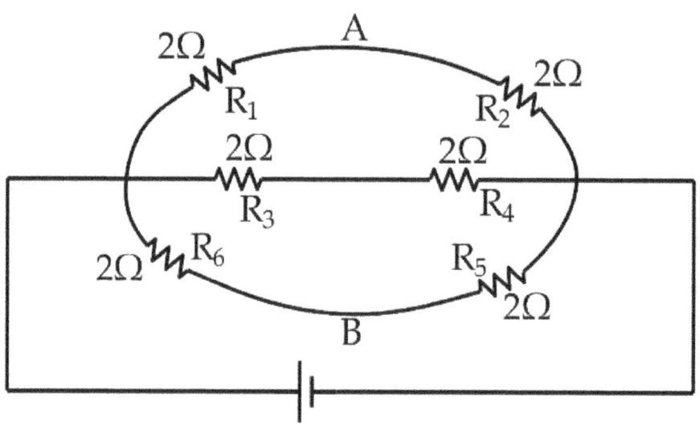

Answer. Here, R_1, R_2, R_3, R_4., and R_5, R_6, are a series combination.

Therefore, $R_{S1} = R_1 + R_2 = 2 + 2 = 4\Omega$

$$R_{S2} = R_3 + R_4 = 2 + 2 = 4\Omega$$

$$R_{S3} = R_5 + R_6 = 2 + 2 = 4\Omega$$

Now, the circuit is simplified.

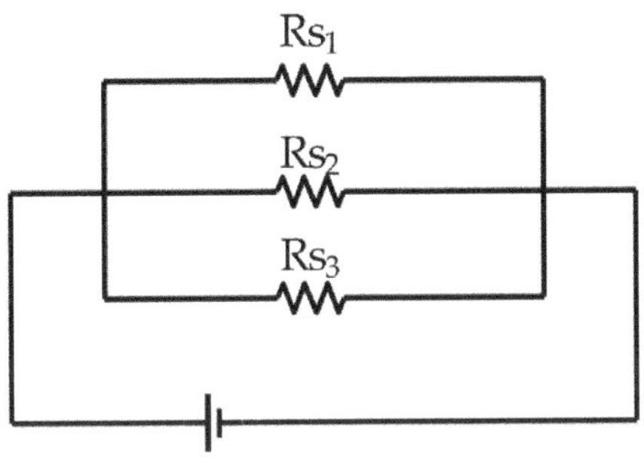

Equivalent resistance, $\frac{1}{R} = \frac{1}{Rs_1} + \frac{1}{Rs_2} + \frac{1}{Rs_3}$

$$\frac{1}{R} = \frac{1}{4} + \frac{1}{4} + \frac{1}{4}$$
$$R = 1.33\Omega$$

Question 3.

(i) Why does a stone lying in the sun get heated up much more than water lying for the same duration of time?

Answer. The specific heat capacity of water is very much higher than that of stone because of which it heats up very slowly compared to stone.

(ii) (a) What is the function of carbon brushes in DC motors? **[2]**

(b) What is the function of laminated core in DC motor? **[2]**

Answer.

(a) Carbon brushes supply continuous current to the revolving commutator.

(b) The strongly magnetized laminated core helps in setting up a strong deflecting couple.

(iii) The refractive index of dense flint glass is 1.65 and for alcohol is 1.36 w.r.t air. Find the refractive index of dense flint glass with respect to alcohol. **[2]**

Answer.

$$a\mu f = 1.65$$
$$a\mu al = 1.36$$
$$al\mu f = \frac{a\mu f}{a\mu al}$$
$$= 1.65/1.36$$
$$al\mu f = 1.21$$

(iv) Radar can detect the reflected waves from an airplane belonging to an enemy after a time interval of 0.2 milliseconds. Calculate the distance of the airplane from the radar. Take velocity of the wave as $3 \times 10^8 ms^{-1}$.

Answer. speed of wave $= 3 \times 10^8$ m/s

Time = $0.2\ msec.$

$t = 0.2 \times 10^{-3} m/s$

$V = 2d/t$

$$2d = V \times T$$
$$2d = 3 \times 10^8 \times 0.2 \times 10^{-3}$$
$$2d = 0.6 \times 10^5$$
$$d = 0.6/2 " \times " 10^5$$
$$d = \frac{0.3}{10 \times 10^5}$$
$$d = 30000m$$
$$d = 30Km$$

(v) If the power of a motor is 40 kW, at what speed does it raise a load of 20,000 N ? **[2]**

Answer. $P = 40KW$

$$F = 20{,}000N$$
$$P = F.V$$
$$40{,}000 = 20{,}000.V$$
$$V = 2m/s$$

SECTION – B (40 Marks)
(Attempt any four questions from this SECTION)

Question 4.

(i) What is the effect of frequency and amplitude on a musical note? **[3]**

Answer. The frequency and pitch of a sound are directly proportional to each other, therefore, increase its frequency increases the pitch of a musical note linearly. An increase in the amplitude of a sound increases. the loudness and so the intensity of note changes.

(ii) Define: **[3]**

(a) Work

(b) Power

(c) Energy

(d) Velocity ratio

Answer.

(a) Work is said to be done when a force applied to a body produces some displacement in the direction of the force applied.

(b) Power is defined as the state of doing work.

(c) Ability of a body to do certain work is called energy.

(d) The ratio of the velocity of effort to the velocity of the load is called the velocity ratio of the machine.

(iii) **(a)** Draw a neat diagram of a pulley system having a velocity ratio of 4.

(b) If the pulley system mentioned above is 60% efficient and lifts a load of 2000 N, find the effort required.

Answer.

(a) Pulley system of velocity ratio 4 is as shown alongside.

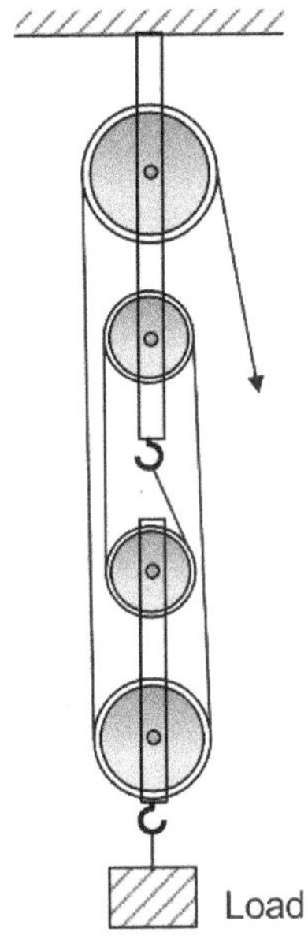

(b) $VR = 4,$

$\eta = 0.6$ L=2000N, the effort required to be E.

$$\text{As we know}, n = \frac{MA}{VR}$$

$$0.6 = \frac{MA}{4} \Rightarrow MA = 2.4$$

$$MA = \frac{L}{E} \Rightarrow E = \frac{L}{MA} = \frac{2000}{2.4}$$

$$= 833.33N$$

Question 5.

(i) Is it possible to burn a piece of paper using a convex lens in daylight without using matches or any direct flame? Draw a ray diagram to illustrate your answer.

Answer.

Yes, it is possible to burn a piece of paper by using a convex lens. The sunlight coming from infinity is made to pass through a convex lens. These rays make the image of the sun at the focus of the lens and the piece of paper burns without matches or any direct flame.

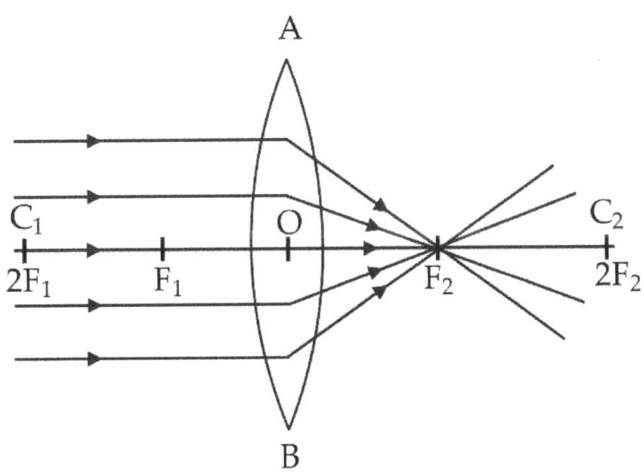

(ii) **(a)** Why does the rising sun appear bigger?

(b) Which component of light rays produces a heating sensation?

Answer.

(a) It is due to the atmospheric refraction of sunlight as it travels through Earth's atmosphere. During sunrise and sunset, light rays have to travel a longer distance through the atmosphere due to which they undergo multiple refractions by different layers of the atmosphere making the sun appear bigger and flattened.

(b) Infrared rays are responsible for the heating sensation of light rays.

(iii) **(a)** What do you understand by the refraction of light?

(b) State Snell's law.

(c) Mention one difference between the reflection of light from a plane mirror and the total. Internal reflection of light from a prism. **[4]**

Answer.

(a) The phenomenon of change in the path of a ray of light when it moves from one medium to another is called refraction.

(b) Snell's law states that "The ratio of the sine of an angle of incidence to the sine of the angle of refraction is always constant".

(c)

Reflection from a plane mirror	Total internal reflection from a prism
1. The reflection of light incident on the mirror takes place for all angles of incidence. 2. A lot of light energy is absorbed in ordinary reflection	The incident ray is reflected back from the other surface only if an incident angle is greater than the critical angle. No light is absorbed during total internal reflection.

Question 6.

(i) **(a)** A sound wave propagates via compression and rarefaction through the air. How will the distance between successive rarefactions- vary, if the sound is of higher pitch comparatively?

(b) What are damped vibrations?

Answer.

(a) As the pitch of a sound increases, the frequency of the vibration also increases which implies the number of sound waves increases for that time period. So the distance between successive compressions and rarefactions decreases for a particular time period.

(b) The periodic vibration whose amplitude is decreasing continuously is called damped vibrations.

(ii) Daniel standing between two vertical cliffs and 660 m away from the nearest cliff shouted. He heard the first echo after 4 seconds and the second echo 3 seconds later. Calculate:

(a) The velocity of sound in air and

(b) The distance between the cliffs.

Answer.

(a) For the first echo,

Time to reach the nearest cliff = $t_1 = 2\ s$,

Distance, s = $600m$

Velocity of sound, $v = \frac{s}{t_1} = \frac{660}{2} = 330\ m\ s^{-1}$

(b) Let x be the distance of the second cliff,

$$\text{Time} = t_2 = \frac{(4+3)}{2} = 3.5s$$

$$x = v \times t_2 = 330 \times 3.5 = 1155\ m$$

Distance between two cliff

$$= 660 + 1155 = 1815m$$

(iii) **(a)** Distinguish between loudness and pitch.

(b) Draw a displacement-time graph for damped and undamped vibrations. **[3]**

Answer.

(a)

Loudness	**Pitch**
It is determined by the amplitude of sound waves. It is proportional to the square of the amplitude.	It is determined by the frequency of sound waves. Pitch and frequency bear a linear relationship.

(b)

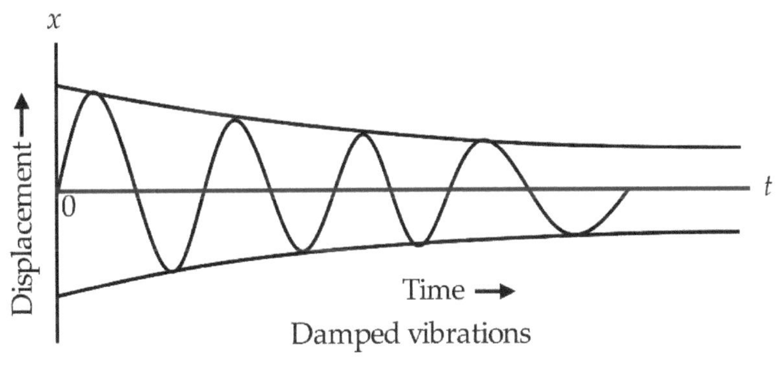

Damped vibrations

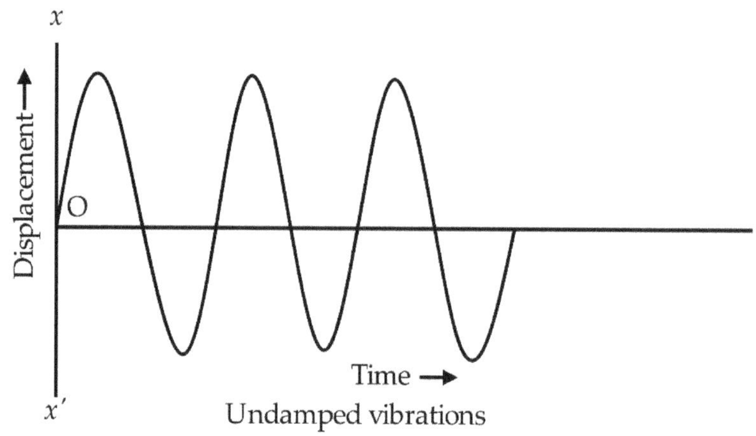

Undamped vibrations

Question 7.

(i) **(a)** 'Why is Tungsten used for the filament of electric bulbs?

(b) 'Which part of an electric appliance is earthed? Why? **[3]**

Answer.

(a) The high resistivity and high melting of Tungsten make it the best candidate for filaments of electric bulbs.

(b) The metallic body of an electrical appliance is earthed in order to avoid any incident due to leakage of current.

(ii) **(a)** What is the necessary condition for a conductor to obey Ohm's law?

(b) 'What do you understand by Emf of a cell? Give its units.

Answer.

(a) The necessary condition for a conductor to, obey Ohm's law is that the ratio of $\frac{V}{I}$ must be constant for all values of V or I.

(b) Emf of a cell is the amount of work done in carrying a unit positive charge from the negative terminal to the positive termital of a battery. Its S.I. unit is volt (V).

(iii) Observe the circuit given below which shows three resistors of 2,4 and x connected to a battery of emf 2 V and internal resistance 3. The main current of 0.25 A flows through the circuit. Find:

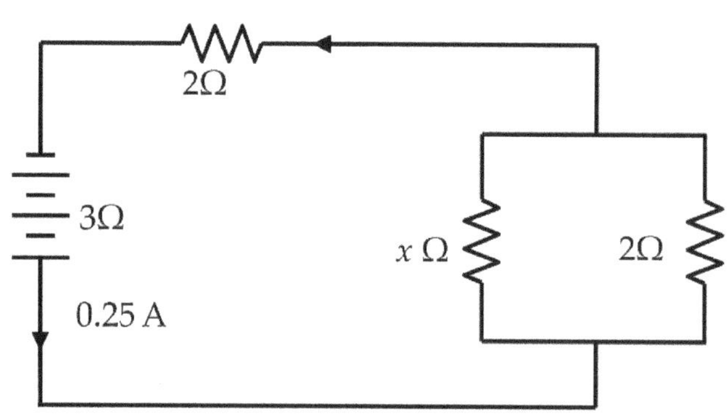

(a) The value of x.

(b) The potential difference across 4 resistors.

(c) The potential difference across x and 2 resistors.

(d) The potential difference across the internal resistance of the battery.

Answer.

(a) The equivalent resistance of the circuit,

$$R = \frac{V}{I} = \frac{2}{0.25} = 8\Omega$$

$$R = \frac{2x}{2+x} + 4 + 3 = 8$$

Equivalent resistance of the circuit using parrel and series combination)

On solving, we get, $x = 2\Omega$

Question 8.

(i) **(a)** State the factors on which the head is absorbed by a body depends. **[3]**

(b) Why is it not advisable to wear damp clothes?

Answer.

(a) The heat absorbed by a body depends upon

I. Mass of the body.

II. Increase in temperature

III. Specific heat capacity,

(b) Damp clothes contain a large number of water molecules which get evaporated at a high rate consuming the latent heat of the body due to which the body gets much cooler making the body prone to infections such as cough and cold.

(ii) **(a)** Define the term specific heat capacity of a substance. Give its SI. unit. **[3]**

(b) Why copper is preferred over other metal for making calorimeters? Give two reasons.

Answer.

(a) The amount of heat required to raise the temperature of one kilogram of a substance by 1°C is known as its specific heat capacity. Its SI unit is $Jkg^{-1}C$.

(b) Copper is preferred over other metals for making calorimeter because:

I. Being a good conductor of heat, a calorimeter made of copper acquires the temperature of its contents.

II. The thermal capacity of the calorimeter is low as the specific heat capacity of copper is low.

(iii) An immersion water heater having a resistance 40Ω is connected to a 220 V mains. How much time (Given; Specific heat capacity of water $4 \times 10^3 J/kg^0C$). **[4]**

Answer. As we know, $I = \frac{V}{R} = \frac{220}{40} = 5.5A$

For certain times T,

The heat required = Heat produced

mC $\theta = I^2 RT$

$13 \times 4 \times 10^3 \times (100 - 20) = 5.5^2 \times 40 \times T$

$t = 793.39$ s $= 13.2$ min

Question 9.

(i) **(a)** Why should radioactive substances not be touched by hand? **[3]**

(b) Give the equation which represents the process involved in the generation of energy in the sun name and the process.

Answer.

(a) Radioactive substances continuously undergo radioactive decay thereby emitting alpha, beta, and gamma rays. These rays are very harmful and can destroy the living cells and cause massive health hazards. Therefore, it is not advisable to touch radioactive substances by bare land.

(b) The representative equation is as given below:

$4^2H \longrightarrow {}_2^4He + 2_1e^e + Energy$

The process responsible is known as nuclear fusion.

(ii) **(a)**Give the composition of α, β, and γ rays. **[3]**

(b) What changes take place within the nucleus when beta particles are emitted by a radioactive substance?

Answer.

(a) The composition of alpha, beta, and gamma particles is as given in the table below:

α - particles	β – particles	γ -particles
They are helium nuclei	They are streams of electrons	They are photons
Mass is $6.645 \times 10^{-27} Kg.$	Mass is $9.11 \times 10^{-31} Kg$	Their rest mass is zero
Charge is 3.2×10^{-19}C	Charge is 1.6×10^{-19}C	They have no change

(b) When a beta particle is emitted by a radioactive substance, its mass number remains unchanged, and the atomic number increases by one.

(iii) X is an atomic nudeus consisting 84 proton land 128 neutrons, it undergoes radioactivity and emit alph at particles thereby forming Y **[3]**

(a) What is the composition of the nucleus Y ?

(b) What is the mass number of X?

(c) If the nucleus Y further undergoes radioactive decay emitting beta particle and forms Z, what would be the composition of Z ?

Answer.

(a) The composition of nucleus Y is $\frac{208}{82}Y$.

(b) The mass number of X is 212.

(c) The composition of Z is ${}_{83}^{208}Z$.

UNSOLVED SAMPLE PAPER

ICSE 2023 EXAMINATION

SAMPLE PAPER - 1

PHYSICS

(SCIENCE PAPER - 1)

Maximum Marks: 80

Time allowed: Two hours

Answers to this Paper must be written on the paper provided separately.

You will not be allowed to write during first 15 minutes.

This time is to be spent in reading the question paper.

The time given at the head of this Paper is the time allowed for writing the answers.

SECTION *A* is compulsory. Attempt any four questions from SECTION *B*.
The intended marks for questions or parts of questions are given in brackets [ ].

SECTION – A (40 Marks)

(Answer all the questions from this SECTION)

Question 1.

(i) Which of the following radiations has the highest penetrating power?

(a) X-rays
(b) β-rays
(c) γ-rays
(d) α-rays
Answer. (c)

(ii) S.I. unit of heat capacity is

(a) Cal^0C^{-1}
(b) $J\ K^{-1}$
(c) JKg^{-1}
(d) $JKg^{-1}\ K^{-1}$
Answer. (b)

(iii) One gram of ice at 0°C is added to 5 g of water at 10°C The final temp. Of the mixture is

(a) $-5°C$
(b) $5°C$
(c) $0°C$
(d) None of these
Answer. (a)

(iv) The presence of magnetic field at a point can be detected by

(a) A magnetic needle
(b) A generator

(c) A dynamo
(d) A current carrying conductor
Answer. (a)

(v) The alternating current produced in India changes its direction every
(a) 100 seconds
(b) 1/10 second
(c) 1/100 second
(d) 50 seconds
Answer. (c)

(vi) The mathematical representation of ohm's law is
(a) V = IR.
(b) $I = VR$
(c) R = VI
(d) $V = \frac{1}{R}$
Answer. (a)

(vii) The rating of a fuse connected in the lighting circuit is
(a) 5 A
(b) 10 A
(c) 15 A
(d) 20 A
Answer. (a)

(viii) A ray of light does not bend at the boundary in passing from one medium to another medium if the angle of incidence is
(a) 15°
(b) 30°
(c) 60°
(d) 0°
Answer. (d)

(ix) A convex lens forms a virtual image if the object is placed:
(a) Between f and $2f$
(b) At infinity
(c) Between the lens and its focus
(d) On the focus of the lens
Answer. (c)

(x) Mechanical advantage (M.A.), load (L) and effort (E) are related as
(a) M.A. × E = L
(b) M.A. = L × E

(c) M.A. × L = E
(d) None of the above
Answer. (a)

(xi) The moment of a force about a given axis depends:
(a) Only on the magnitude of the force
(b) Only on the distance from the axis
(c) Neither on the force nor on the perpendicular distance of force from
(d) Both on the force and its perpendicular distance from the axis
Answer. (d)

(xii) Kilowatt hour is the unit of
(a) Energy
(b) Power
(c) Linear momentum
(d) None of these
Answer. (a)

(xiii) Compression is a region of
(a) Low pressure
(b) Normal pressure
(c) High pressure
(d) No pressure
Answer. (c)

(xiv) During the change of state of substance
(a) Potential energy of its molecules increases
(b) Kinetic energy of its molecules increases
(c) Both potential as well as kinetic energy of its molecules remains constant
(d) None of the above
Answer. (b)

(xv) The power of two lenses is $+6D$ and $-4D$ the power of two lenses is:
(a) $+2D$
(b) $+6D$
(c) $-4D$
(d) $24D$
Answer. (a)

Question 2.

(i) (a) (i) Define the term momentum. **[3]**
(ii) How is force related to the momentum of a body?
(iii) State the condition when the change in momentum of a body depends only on the

change in its velocity.

(b) A body of mass 50kghas a momentum of 3000kgms^{-1}. Calculate

(i) The kinetic energy of a body

(ii) The velocity of the body

Answer.

(i) $90{,}000J$

(ii) $60m/s$

(ii) The speed of a moving body is halved. What change takes place in its kinetic energy? **[2]**

(iii) Define M.A., V.R., and η of the machine. Find the relation between them. **[2]**

(iv) Distinguish between a real and a virtual image. **[2]**

(v) The critical angle for glass is $42°$. A ray of light enters a glass slab PQRS as shown in Fig. Complete the path of the ray till it emerges from the glass slab PQRS. **[2]**

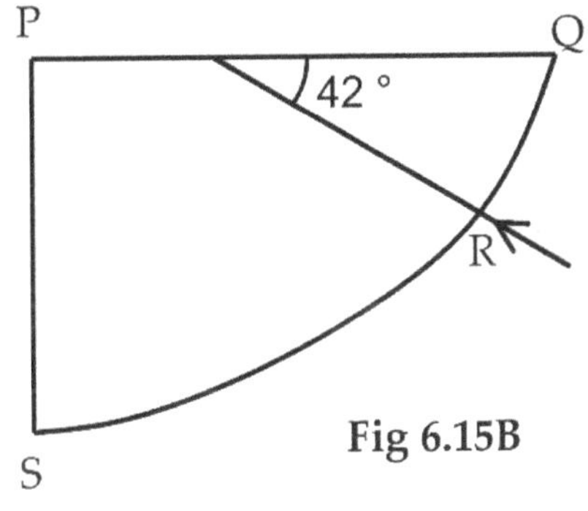

Fig 6.15B

(vi) Name the material used for making a fuse wire. State two properties of this material which make it suitable for use as fuse wire. **[2]**

(vii) If the amplitude of a wave is doubled, what will be the effect on its loudness? **[2]**

Question 3.

(i) On what factors does heat energy absorbed by a body depend? **[2]**

(ii) A boy of mass 40 kg runs up a flight of 15 steps each 0.15 m high in 10 s find the work done and the power developed by him. (Take g = 10 ms^{-2}) **[2]**

Answer. $W = 900J$ $P = 90W$

(iii) What are the factors on which the resistivity of a material depends? **[2]**

(iv) Copy and complete the following nuclear equations by filling in the correct values in them **[2]**

$$P^{92}_{238} \xrightarrow{\alpha} \ldots P_1 \xrightarrow{-\beta} \ldots P_2^- \xrightarrow{-\beta} \ldots P_3 \ldots$$

Answer.

$$\frac{90}{234}P_1 \xrightarrow{-\beta} \ldots \frac{91}{234}P_2^- \xrightarrow{-\beta} \ldots \frac{92}{234}P_3 \ldots$$

(v) A person standing at a distance 200 m from a hill blows a horn. After what time can he hear the echo? Take the velocity of sound in air as 300 ms^{-1}. **[2]**

SECTION – B (40 Marks)
(Attempt any four questions)

Question 4.

(i) Shows a right-angled prism with a ray of light incident on the side *AB*. (The critical angle for glass is 42°). **[3]**

(a) Copy the diagram and complete the path of the ray of light in and out of the glass prism.

(b) What is the value of the angle of deviation shown by the ray?

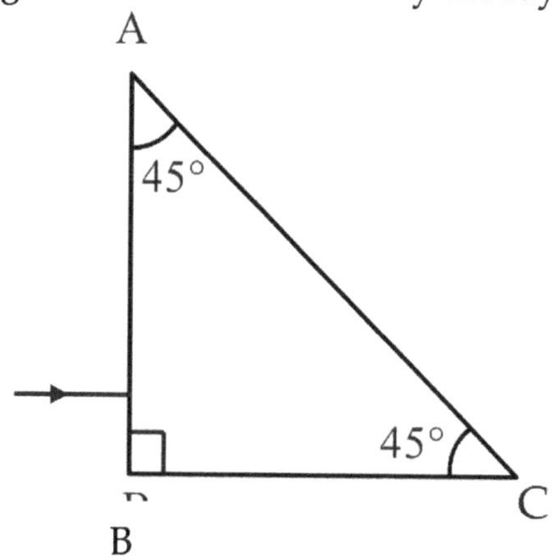

(ii) shows a system of five pulleys. The upper three pulleys are fixed and the lower two are movable. **[3]**

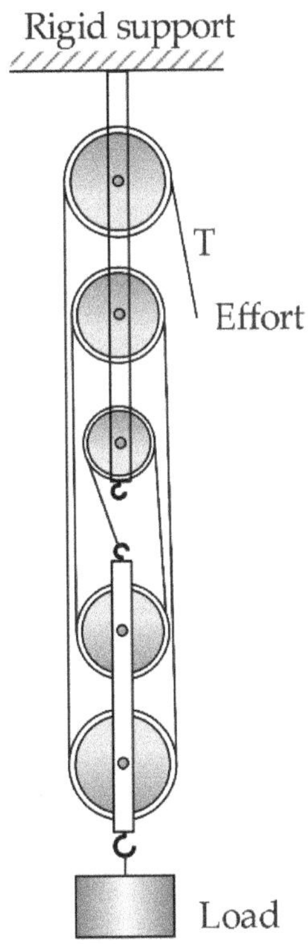

(a) Draw a string around the pulleys. Also, show the place and direction in which the effort is applied.

(b) What is the velocity ratio of the system?

(c) What is the mechanical advantage of the system?

(d) What assumption do you make in arriving at your answer in part (iii)?

Answer. $VR = 5, MA = 5$

(iii) Four cells each of e.m.f. 1.5 V and internal resistance 2.0ohm are connected in parallel. The battery of cells is connected to an external resistance of 2.5ohm Calculate: **[4]**

(a) The total resistance of the circuit.

(b) The current flowing in the external circuit and

(c) The drop in potential across the terminals of the cells.

Answer.

(a) $R = 3\Omega,$

(b) $I = 0.5A,$

(c) $V = 0.3V,$

Question 5.

(i) **(a)** Differentiate between heat and temperature **[3]**

(b)(i) Define calorimetry.

(ii)What is meant by energy degradation?

(ii) The wavelength of a sound wave is 66 m Calculate the frequency of the wave, if the velocity of sound is 330 ms^{-1}. Would this sound be audible to the human ear? **[3]**

Answer. 5Hz

(iii) An electric heater of power 600W raises the temperature of 4.0 kg of a liquid form 10.0°C to 15.0°C in 100s Calculate: **[4]**

(a) The heat capacity of liquid,

(b) The specific heat capacity of the liquid.

Answer.

(a) $C'=12000J/Kg,$

(b) $C = 3000J/Kg\ K,$

Question 6.

(i) A body P has a mass of 20 kg *and* is moving with a velocity of 5 ms^{-1}. Another body Q has a mass of 5 kg and is moving with a velocity of 20 ms^{-1}. Calculate **[3]**

(a) The ratio of the momentum of P and Q and

(b) The kinetic energy of in unit.

Answer.

(a) $1:1,$

(b) $1:4$

(ii) An object viewed through a glass prism with its vertex pointing upwards appears to be displaced upward. Draw the ray diagram. **[3]**

(iii) A bullet of mass 50 g is moving with a velocity of 500 ms^{-1}. It penetrates 10cm into a still target and comes to rest. **[4]**

(a) Calculate the KE possessed by the bullet.

(b) The average retarding force offered by the target.

Answer.

(a) $K.E. = 6250J,$

(b) $F = 62500N$

Question 7.

(i) The V-I graph for a series combination and for a parallel combination of two resistors is as shown in the figure:

Which of the two, A or B, represents the parallel combination? Give a reason for your answer. **[3]**

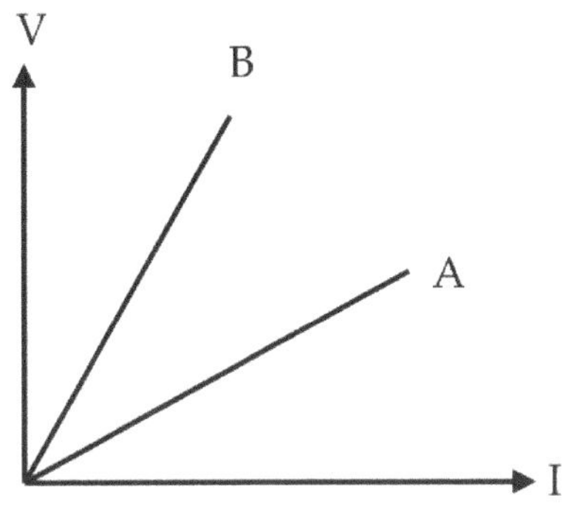

(ii) On what factors the magnitude of the force on a current-carrying conductor placed in a magnetic field depends? **[3]**

(iii) Draw field lines due to **[4]**

(a) Current flowing into a circular coil

(b) Solenoid carrying current.

Question 8.

(i) (a) What is meant by the term 'critical angle'? **[3]**

(b) How is it related to the refractive index of the medium?

(c) Does the depth of a tank of water appear to change or remain the same when viewed normally from above?

(ii) A water tank appears to be 2.7 mdeep. If the refractive index of water is 4/3, find the real depth of the water tank. **[3]**

Answer. $R.D. = 3.6m$

(iii) A block and tackle with 5 pulleys are found to have an M.A. = 4 when a load of 5 N is raised by it. Calculate **[4]**

(a) The effort (E) applied,

(b) V.R.

(c) η,

Answer.

(a) $E = 1.2N$,

(b) $VR = 5$, (c) $\eta = 0.8$

Question 9.

(i) Distinguish between **[3]**

(a) Intensity and loudness,

(b) Frequency and pitch,

(c) Timbre and waveform of sound.

(ii) State two important properties and two uses of: **[3]**

(a) Gamma rays

(b) X-rays

(c) UV rays

(iii) A man standing in a gorge between two large cliffs gives a short sharp shout. He hears two echoes, the first after 1 second and the next. after 1.5 seconds (after his shout). The speed of sound is 340 ms^{-1}. Calculate **[4]**

(a) The distance of the man from each cliff and

(b) The distance between the cliffs.

Answer.

(a) $d = 850m,$

(b) $d = 340m$

ICSE 2023 EXAMINATION
SAMPLE PAPER - 2
PHYSICS
(SCIENCE PAPER - 1)

Maximum Marks: 80

Time allowed: Two hours

Answers to this Paper must be written on the paper provided separately.

You will not be allowed to write during first 15 minutes.

This time is to be spent in reading the question paper.

The time given at the head of this Paper is the time allowed for writing the answers.

SECTION *A* is compulsory. Attempt any four questions from SECTION *B*.
The intended marks for questions or parts of questions are given in brackets [ ].

SECTION – A (40 Marks)
(Answer all the questions from this SECTION)

Question 1.

(i) A current carrying a straight conductor produces

(a) Only electric field

(b) A magnetic field

(c) Nuclear field

(d) None of the above.

Answer. (b)

(ii) If the current flows always in the same direction, it is called

(a) Alternating current

(b) Direct current

(c) Induced current

(d) None of these

Answer. (b)

(iii) Which one of the following is an example of isobars?

(a) ${}^{13}_{6}C$, ${}^{13}_{7}N$

(b) ${}^{14}_{7}N$, ${}^{15}_{7}N$

(c) ${}^{31}_{14}Si$, ${}^{32}_{15}P$

(d) None of the above

Answer. (a)

(iv) S.I. unit of specific heat capacity is

(a) $JKg^{-1}\ K^{-1}$

(b) JKg^{-1}

(c) JKg^{-1}
(d) cal Kg^{-1} $°C^{-1}$
Answer. (a)

(v) Which of the following graph represents an ohmic conductor?

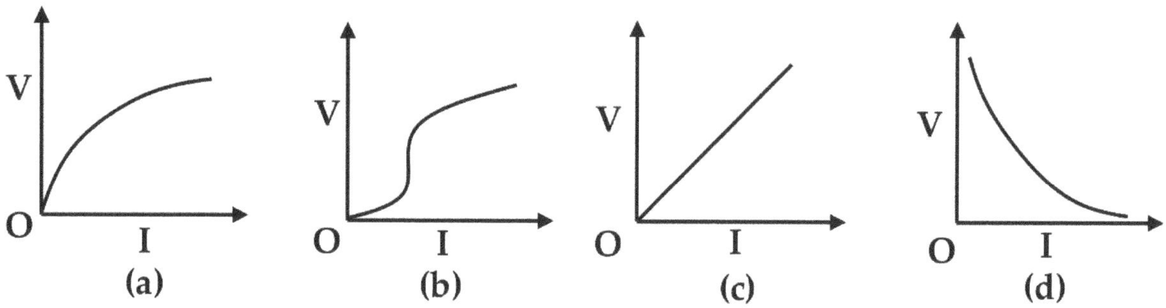

Answer. (c)

(vi) Which of the following combinations of resistances is different from the others?

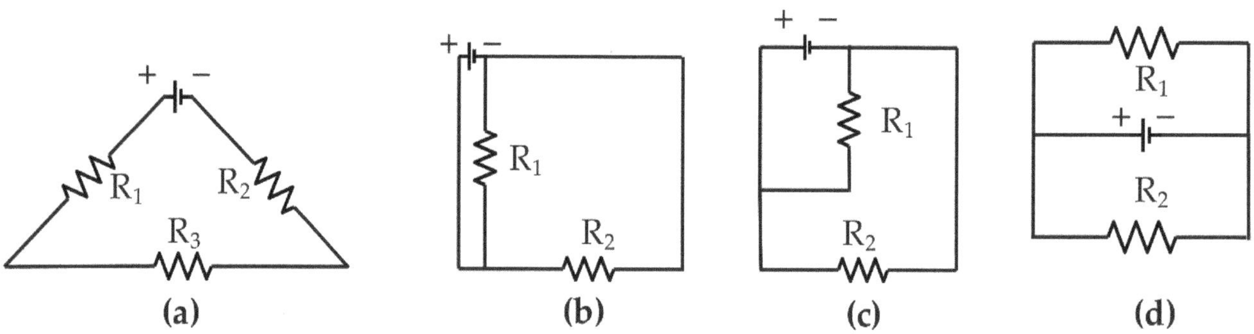

Answer. (a)

(vii) The refractive indices of four materials $P, Q, R,$ and S are 1.33, 1.43, 1.71, and 1.52 respectively. Light rays pass from air into these materials, they refract the maximum in:
(a) S
(b) R
(c) P
(d) Q
Answer. (b)

(viii) The power of a concave lens of a focal length of 20 cm is
(a) $-5D$
(b) $-4D$
(c) $-6D$
(d) $-2D$
Answer. (a)

(ix) The relationship between V.R., distance moved by the load (d_L) and distance moved by the effort (d_E) is

(a) V.R. $= \frac{d_E}{d_L}$

(b) V.R. $= d_E \times d_L$

(c) V.R. $= d_E + d_L$

(d) V.R. $= \frac{d_L}{d_E}$

Answer. (a)

(x) While opening a tap with two fingers, the forces applied are

(a) Opposite in direction

(b) Equal in magnitude

(c) Parallel to each other

(d) All the above

Answer. (d)

(xi) 1kWh equals

(a) 3.6 J

(b) 3.6MJ

(c) 3.6 kJ

(d) 3.6×10^6 M

Answer. (b)

(xii) Wave motion transfers

(a) Matter

(b) Momentum

(c) Energy

(d) Both (b) and (c)

Answer. (d)

(xiii) The image formed of an object placed between the optical center and focal of a convex lens is

(a) Virtual and diminished

(b) Virtual and enlarged

(c) Real and enlarged

(d) Real and diminished

Answer. (b)

(xiv) Fleming's left-hand rule is applied when

(a) Electrical energy changes into chemical energy

(b) The direction of force on a current carrying conductor placed in a magnetic field is to be determined

(c) Mechanical energy changes into electrical energy

(d) Electrical energy changes into heat energy

Answer. (b)

(xv) A boy hears an echo from a distant hill after one second. If the speed of sound in air is 350 ms^{-1}. The distance of the hill from the try is

(a) 175 m

(b) 150 m

(c) 87.5 m

(d) 700m

Answer. (a)

Question 2.

(i) Write the energy changes in the following cases while in use: **[3]**

(a) Burning coal

(b) Loudspeaker

(c) An electric bulb

(ii) If ' m ' is the mass of the body, ' v ' its velocity, and ' p ' the momentum, then write a relationship between the change in momentum, mass, and velocity of the body, when **[2]**

(a) is almost equal to, the velocity of light

(b) is very-very less compared to, the velocity of light.

(iii) **(a)** Define one newton. **[2]**

(b) Write the relation between the SI unit and the CGS unit of force.

(iv) A small object is so placed in front of a convex lens of 5 cm focal length that a virtual image is formed at a distance of 25 cm. Find the magnification. **[2]**

Answer. $m = 6$

(v) Draw a labeled diagram of a combination of three movable pulleys with one fixed pulley showing the direction of load, effect, and tension in each strand. **[2]**

(vi) Define specific heat capacity and write its units. **[2]**

(vii) Two bulbs are marked 60W 220Vand 60W 110V. Calculate the ratio of their resistance. **[2]**

Answer. $R_1 : R_2 = 4 : 1$

Question 3.

(i) The refractive index of water w.r.t. Air is ${}_a\mu_w$ and of glass w.r.t. Air is ${}_a\mu_g$. What will be the refractive index of glass w.r.t. Water? **[2]**

(ii) State three properties that are common to all types of electromagnetic radiation. **[2]**

(iii) What is an echo? What is the condition for hearing a distinct echo? **[2]**

(iv) Write the penetration range of $\alpha, \beta,$ and γ radiations in air. **[2]**

(v) Give two factors on which the strength of the magnetic field produced by a current-carrying solenoid depends. **[2]**

SECTION – B (40 Marks)
(Attempt any four questions)

Question 4.

(i) Calculate the value of the resistance which must be connected to a 15Ω resistance to provide an effective resistance of 6Ω **[3]**

Answer. $X = 10\Omega$

(ii) 40g of ice at 0°C is added to 160g of water at 40°C. Calculate the final temperature. Specific latent heat of ice = 336Jg^{-1} and specific heat capacity of water = $4.2 \text{Jg}^{-1}\,\text{K}^{-1}$. **[3]**

Answer. $t = 16^0 C$

(iii) **(a)** Define heat capacity and obtain its relationship with specific heat capacity. **[4]**

(b) Define the specific heat capacity of a material

Question 5.

(i) Differentiate between resonance and forced vibrations **[3]**

(ii) Shows two forces $F_1 = 5$ N and $F_2 = 3$Nacting at A and B respectively of a rod pivoted at the point 0 such that 0A = 2 m and 0B = 4m **[3]**

(a) The moment of the force 5 N about 0,

(b) Moment of the force 3 N about, and

(c) Total moment of the two forces about.

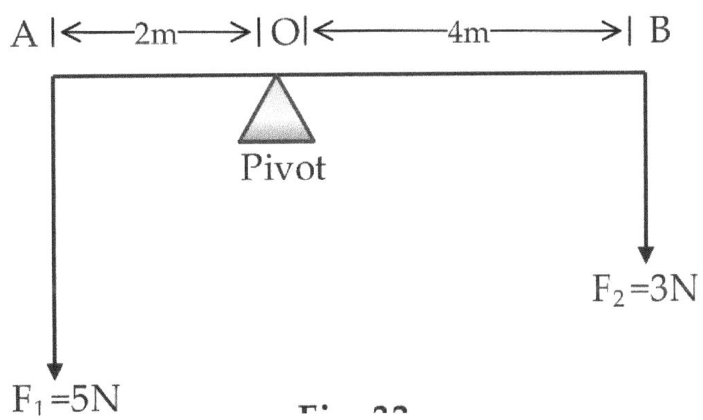

Answer.

(a) $\tau = 10Nm[A.C.W.]$

(b) $\tau = 12Nm[C.W.]$

(c) $\tau_{net} = 2Nm[C.W.]$

(iii) A pendulum has a frequency of 5 vibrations per second. An observer starts the pendulum and fires a gun simultaneously. He hears the echo from the cliff after 8 vibrations of the pendulum. If the velocity of sound in air is 340 ms^{-1}, what is the distance between the cliff and the observer? **[4]**

Answer. $d = 272m$

Question 6.

(i) Draw a neat diagram of a block and tackle system of pulleys having a $V.R. = 5$. Show the points of application direction of load and effort and mark the tension in each strand. **[3]**

(ii) A body, when acted upon by a force of 10 kgf, gets displaced by 0.5 m Calculate the work done by the force when the displacement is **[3]**

(a) At an angle of 60° with the force,

(b) In the direction of force, and

(c) Normal to the force. Take $g = 10\text{nkg}^{-1}$.

Answer.

(a) $W = 25J$

(b) $W = 50J$

(c) $W = 0$

(iii) In the diagram is an incident ray making an angle of 30° With the side AC of the prism. $\angle AOP = 90°$. Complete the path of the ray from Ponwards. Explain briefly. **[4]**

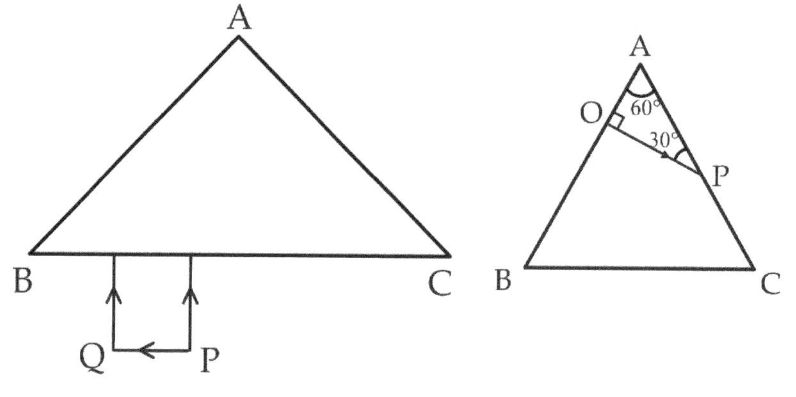

Question 7.

(i) Three 250W heaters are connected in parallel to a 100 V supply. Calculate **[3]**

(a) Total current drawn from the supply,

(b) Resistance of each heater and

(c) Energy is consumed by the three heaters in five hours.

Answer.

(a) $I = 7.5A$

(b) $R = 40\Omega$

(c) $E = 3.75kWh$

(ii) In a three-pin plug. Why is the earth pin made longer and thicker than the other two pins? **[3]**

(iii) Three resistors are connected to a 12Vbattery as shown in the figure given below: **[4]**

(a) What is the current through the 8-ohm resistor?

(b) What is the potential difference across the parallel combination of 6 ohm and 12ohm resistors?

(c) What is the current through the 6-ohm resistor?

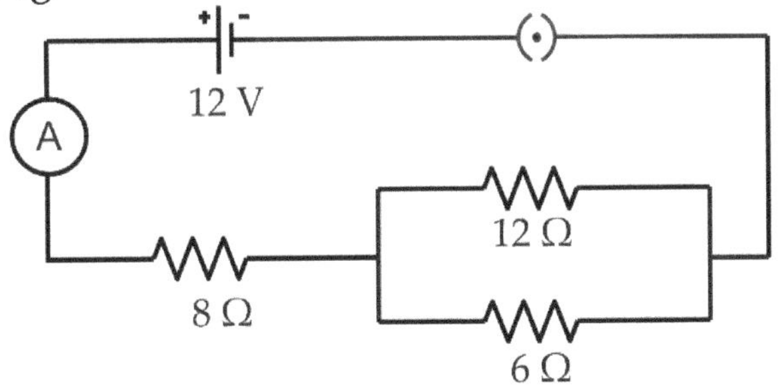

Answer.

(a) $I = 1A$

(b) $4V$

(c) $I_1 = 0.66\text{A}$

Question 8.

(i) Draw a labeled temperature-time sketch (graph) of water, starting from ice at 0 °C to water boiling at 100°C (only sketch showing variation in slopes). What do the flat segments of this graph signify? **[3]**

(ii) Hot water at 100°C is added to 300 g of water at 0°C until the final temperature is 40°C Calculate the mass of the hot water assuming no loss of heat. **[3]**

Answer. $m = 200gm$

(iii) **(a)** Differentiate between heat and temperature. **[4]**

(b) What is meant by energy degradation?

(c) 200 g of hot water at 80°C is added to 300 g of cold water at 10°C calculate the final temperature of the mixture of water. Consider the heat taken by the container to be negligible. [specific heat capacity of water is $4200\text{Jkg}^{-1}\text{C}^{-1}$].

Answer.$\text{t} = 38^0\text{C}$

Question 9.

(i) State Fleming's right-hand rule to find the direction of induced emf. **[3]**

(ii) Define isotope, isobar, and isotone. **[3]**

(iii) The diagram below shows a coil connected to a center zero galvanometer G. The galvanometer shows a deflection to the right when the N pole of a powerful magnet is moved to the right as shown. **[4]**

(a) Explain why the deflection occurs in the galvanometer.

(b) Does the direction of current in the coil appear clockwise or anticlockwise when viewed from end *A* ?

(c) State the observation in G when the coil is moved away from N.

(d) State the observation in G when, both the coil and the magnet, are moved to the right at the same speed.

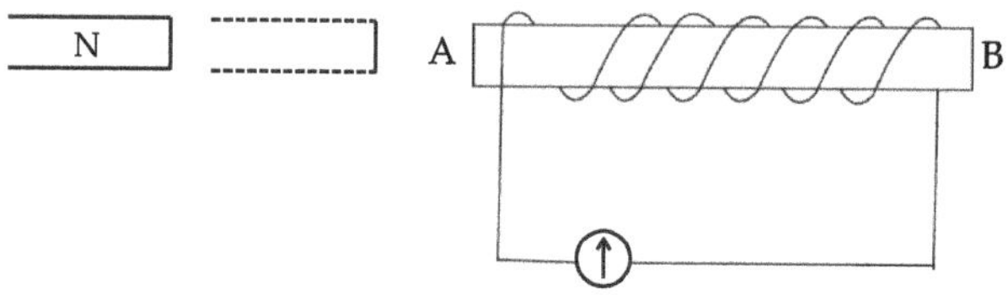

ICSE 2023 EXAMINATION
SAMPLE PAPER - 3
PHYSICS
(SCIENCE PAPER - 1)

Maximum Marks: 80

Time allowed: Two hours

Answers to this Paper must be written on the paper provided separately.

You will not be allowed to write during first 15 minutes.

This time is to be spent in reading the question paper.

The time given at the head of this Paper is the time allowed for writing the answers.

SECTION *A* is compulsory. Attempt any four questions from SECTION *B*.
The intended marks for questions or parts of questions are given in brackets [ ].

SECTION – A (40 Marks)
(Answer all the questions from this SECTION)

Question 1.

(i) A radioactive substance emits

(a) α, β, and γ radiations simultaneously

(b) Only α radiations

(c) Only β radiations

(d) α and β only

Answer. (a)

(ii) With the increase of pressure, the melting point of ice

(a) Decreases

(b) Increases

(c) Remains unchanged

(d) None of the above

Answer. (a)

(iii) Heat gained by 10 gm of water when heated from 0°C to 100°C

(a) 1000cal

(b) 100cal

(c) 10cal

(d) 4200cal

Answer. (d)

(iv) 540 g of ice at 0°C is mixed with 540g of water at 80^0C. The final temp. Of the mixture is

(a) 0°C

(b) 40°C
(c) 80°C
(d) 100°C
Answer. (a)

(v) The direction of lines of force of the magnetic field ε produced by a straight wire carrying current can be obtained by using
(a) Maxwell's right-hand grip rule
(b) Maxwell's right-hand rule
(c) Maxwell's left-hand rule
(d) Lenz's law
Answer. (b)

(vi) There are three resistors of values $2\Omega, 3\Omega$, and 5Ω respectively. To get total resistance less than 2Ω these resistances wall must join in
(a) Series
(b) Parallel
(c) Series as well as parallel
(d) None of the above
Answer. (b)

(vii) Three resistances R_1, R_2, R_3 are connected in series. The total resistance is
(a) $R_s = R_1 + R_2 + R_3$
(b) $R_s = \frac{1}{R_1} + \frac{1}{R_2} + \frac{1}{R_3}$
(c) $R_s = \frac{R_1+R_2}{R_3}$
(d) $R_s = \frac{R_2}{R_1+R_2}$
Answer. (a)

(viii) When is a ray of light enters from air into a denser medium, it
(a) Passes undefeated
(b) Reflected back
(c) Bends away from the normal
(d) Bends toward the normal
Answer. (d)

(ix) An illuminated object is placed at a distance of 20 cm from a convex lens of focal length 15 cm the image formed on the screen is:
(a) Inverted and diminished
(b) Inverted and magnified
(c) Upright and magnified
(d) Upright and diminished
Answer. (b)

(x) For an ideal machine, the ratio of M.A. to V.R. is

(a) Less than 1

(b) Greater than 1

(c) Equal to 1

(d) Can have any value other than 1

Answer. (c)

(xi) The moment of a force of 10 N about a fixed-point O is 5Nm. The distance of the point from the line of action of the force is two unequal forces at two ends but in the same direction

(a) 5 m

(b) 0.5 m

(c) 2 m

(d) 50 m

Answer. (b)

(xii) If m, p, and k respectively denote mass, linear momentum, and kinetic energy, then we can write,

(a) $p = 2mk$

(b) $p = \sqrt{2mk}$

(c) $p = \frac{2m}{k}$

(d) $p = \frac{k}{2m}$

Answer. (b)

(xiii) Which of the following is a mechanical wave

(a) Lightwave

(b) Sound wave

(c) x-ray

(d) Ultraviolet

Answer. (b)

(xiv) Specific latent heat of vaporization of steam is

(a) 2.26 J kg^{-1}

(b) 22.6 J kg^{-4}

(c) 226 J kg^{-1}

(d) 2260 J kg^{-1}

Answer. (d)

(xv) A uniform circular motion is an

(a) Accelerated motion with variable speed

(b) Accelerated motion with a constant speed

(c) Linear motion

(d) None of the above

Answer. (b)

Question 2.

(i) The figure below shows an electromagnet:

(a) What will be the polarity at the end X ?

(b) Suggest a way by which the strength of the electromagnet referred to in the question may be increased. **[3]**

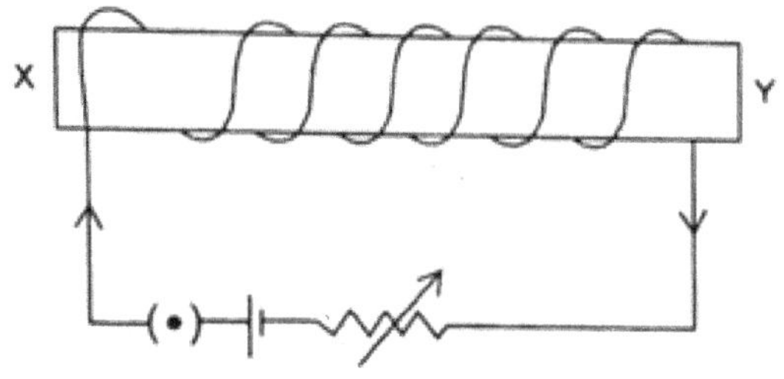

(ii) An object of height 4 cm is placed at a distance of 15 cm in front of a concave lens of power, −10 dioptres. Find the size of the image. **[2]**

Answer. Size of image = 1.6cm

(iii) What should be the angle between force and displacement to get the **[2]**

(a) Minimum work,

(b) Maximum work

Answer.

(a) $\theta = 90^o$

(b) $\theta = 0^o$

(iv) Write an example for each of the following use of a machine **[2]**

(a) To obtain gain in force

(b) To change the point of application of force

(c) To change the direction of force

(v) Derive the relation between newton and dyne. **[2]**

(vi) What is meant by acoustic resonance? Give one example. **[2]**

(vii) What is meant by the scattering of light? **[2]**

Question 3.

(i) A heater of power P watts raises the temperature of m kg of a liquid by Δ K in t seconds. Write the expression for the specific heat capacity of the liquid in terms of the above data. **[2]**

(ii) What is resistance? What are the factors on which the resistance of a conductor depends? **[2]**

(iii) What is a fuse? In which part of the wiring is it connected? **[2]**

(iv) Why has the surrounding of a lake become pleasantly warm when the water in it starts freezing? **[2]**

(v) Calculate the electrical energy (in SI units) consumed by a 100W bulb and a 60W fan connected in parallel for 5 minutes. **[2]**
Answer. $E = 48000J$

Question 4.

(i) Shows a uniform meter scale weighing 100gf. pivoted at its Centre O. Two weights 150 g and 250 gf hang from the meter scale as shown. Calculate: **[3]**
(a) The total anticlockwise moment is about O
(b) The total clockwise moment is about,
(c) The difference of the anticlockwise and clockwise moment, and
(d) The distance from where a 100gf weight should be placed to balance the meter scale.

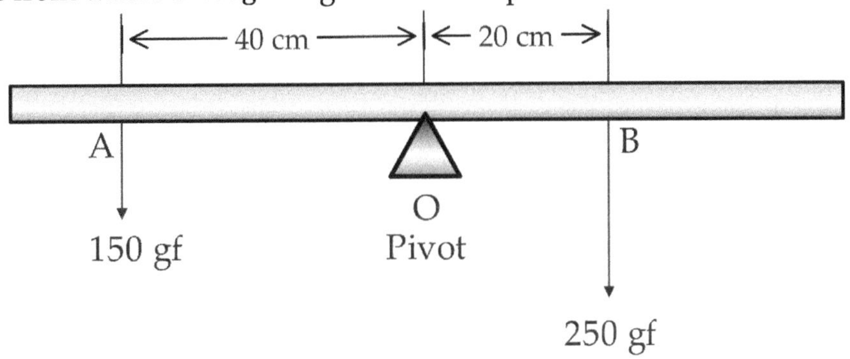

Answer.
(a) 6000gfcm
(b) 5000gfcm
(c) 1000gfcm
(d) 10cm on right side of 'O'

(ii) A block and tackle pulley system has $V.R. = 3$, **[3]**
(a) Draw a labeled diagram of this system. In your diagram. indicate clearly the points of application and the direction of the load and effort.
(b) Why should the lower block of this pulley system be of negligible weight?

(iii) **(a)** A man stands at a distance of 68 m from a cliff and fires a gun. After what time interval will he hear the echo, if the speed of sound in the air is 340 ms^{-1} ? **[4]**
Answer. 0.4sec.

(b) If the man had been standing at a distance of 12 m from the cliff, would he have heard a clear echo?

Question 5.

(i) Explain the phenomenon of total internal reflection. **[3]**

(ii) A ray of light of wavelength (λ) 5400 A^0 suffers refraction from air to glass. Given $\mu_E = 3/2$, find the wavelength of light in glass. **[3]**

Answer. $\lambda = 3600\ A^0$

(iii) A man standing in front of a vertical cliff fires a gun. He hears the echo after 3 s. On moving closer to the cliff by 82.5 m he fires again and hears the echo after 2.5 s Find : **[4]**

(a) The distance of cliff from the initial position of man, and

(b) The speed of sound.

Answer.

(a) $\text{d} = 495\text{m}$

(b) $\text{v} = 330\text{m/s}$

Question 6.

(i) A geyser has a label 2 kW, 240 V. What is the cost of running it for 30 minutes, if the cost of electricity is 3.00 per units? **[3]**

Answer. $Rs.\,3$

(ii) A radioactive nucleus ^A_ZX first emits a beta particle and then an alpha particle and the resulting nucleus is represented by ^P_QY. What are the values of P and Q in terms of A and Z ? **[3]**

(iii) Three resistors R_1, R_2 and R_3 are connected with a battery such that **[4]**

(a) The same current flows in each resistor.

(b) P.d. Is the same across each resistor.

(c) The equivalent resistance is more than either of the three resistances.

(d) The equivalent resistance is less than either of the three resistors.

How are these resistances connected in each of the above cases?

Question 7.

(i) A piece of ice at $-10°\text{C}$ is heated at a constant rate. The variation of temperature with heat input is shown in the graph below: **[3]**

(a) What is represented by AB and CD?

(b) What conclusion can you draw regarding the nature of ice from the given graph?

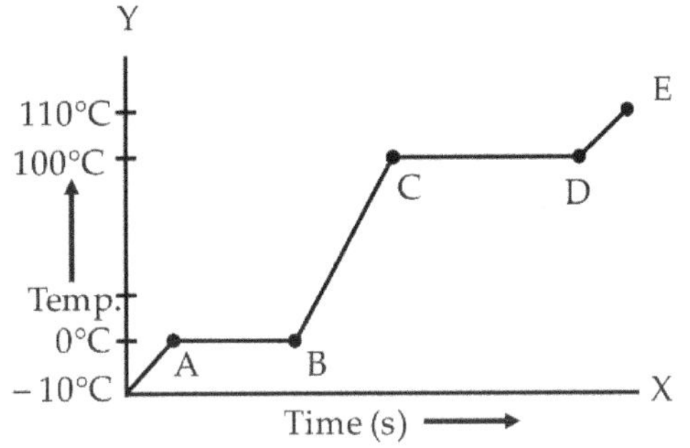

(ii) The temperature of 600 g of cold water rises by 15°C when 300 g of hot water at 50°C is added to it. Find the initial temperature of the cold water. **[3]**

Answer. $t_2 = 5^0C$

(iii) A calorimeter of mass 50g and specific heat capacity $0.42J/g^0C$ contains some mass of water at 20^0C. A metal piece of mass 20g at 100^0C is dropped into the calorimeter after stirring, the final temperature of the mixture is found to be 22^0C. Find the mass of water used in the calorimeter.

Specific heat capacity of metal= $0.3J/g^0C$

Specific heat capacity of water= $4.2J/g^0C$ **[4]**

Answer. $m = 50.7g$

Question 8.

(i) The speed of light in air is 3×10^8 m/s. In medium X its speed is 2×10^8 m/s and in medium Y the speed of light is 2.5×10^8 m/s. Calculate: **[3]**

(a) $_{air}n_X$

(b) $_{air}n_Y$

(c) $_Xn_Y$

Answer.

(a) 1.5

(b) 1.2

(c) 0.8

(ii) **(a)** State two ways by which the magnetic field of a solenoid can be made stronger.

(b) What material is used for making the armature of an electric bell? Give a reason for using this material. **[3]**

(iii) **(a)** A straight wire conductor passes vertically through a piece of cardboard sprinkled with iron Copy the diagram and show the setting of iron filings when a current is passed through the wire in the upward direction and the cardboard is tapped gently. Draw arrows to represent the direction of the magnetic field lines. **[4]**

(b) Name the law which helped you to find the direction of the magnetic field lines

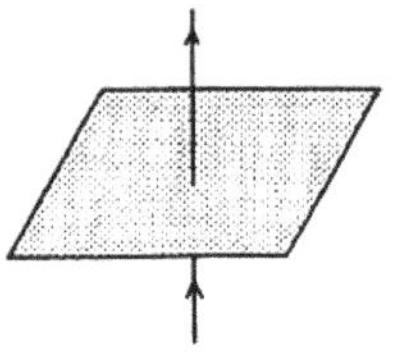

Question 9.

(i) The power of a combination of two lenses X and Y is $5D$. If the focal length of the lens X be 15cm **[3]**

(a) Calculate the focal length of the lens Y.

(b) State the nature of lens Y.

Answer.

(a) $F_y = -60\text{cm}$

(b) Concave lens

(ii) 0.5 kg of lemon squash at 30°C is placed in the refrigerator which can remove heat at an average rate of $30J^{-1}$. How long will it take to cool the lemon squash to 5°C ? Take the specific heat capacity of squash = $4200 Jkg^{-1} K^{-1}$: **[3]**

Answer. T = 29min10sec.

(iii) State ohm's a law and draws a labeled circuit diagram to verify it. Draw a graph between the potential difference (V) and a current flowing in a conductor. What does the slope of this graph represent? **[4]**

ICSE 2023 EXAMINATION

SAMPLE PAPER - 4

PHYSICS

(SCIENCE PAPER - 1)

Maximum Marks: 80

Time allowed: Two hours

Answers to this Paper must be written on the paper provided separately.

You will not be allowed to write during first 15 minutes.

This time is to be spent in reading the question paper.

The time given at the head of this Paper is the time allowed for writing the answers.

SECTION *A* is compulsory. Attempt any four questions from SECTION *B*.

The intended marks for questions or parts of questions are given in brackets [ ].

SECTION – A (40 Marks)

(Answer all the questions from this SECTION)

Question 1.

(i) To convert $^{232}_{90}$Th into $^{208}_{82}Pb$ Th. The least number of α and β particles that have to be emitted are

(a) 6,4

(b) 4,6

(c) 8,6

(d) 6,8

Answer. (d)

(ii) Sea water and river water are heated to their boiling points, then

(a) Both boil at the same temperature

(b) River water boils at a lower temperature

(c) Sea water boils at a lower temperature

(d) None of the above

Answer. (b)

(iii) The specific heat capacity is maximum for

(a) Steam

(b) Water

(c) Ice

(d) Alcohol

Answer. (b)

(iv) 100 g of ice is mixed with 100 g of water at 100°C. The final temp. Of the mixture is

(a) 10°C

(b) 20°C

(c) 30°C

(d) 40°C

Answer. (b)

(v) The strength of the magnetic field inside a long-current-carrying solenoid is

(a) Same at all points

(b) Minimum in the middle

(c) More at the ends than at the center

(d) Found to increase from one end to the other

Answer. (a)

(vi) The fuse wire is made of a/an

(a) Tin-lead alloy

(b) Iron-lead alloy

(c) Copper-tin alloy

(d) None of these

Answer. (a)

(vii) In parallel combination of resistances.

(a) The current is the same in each resistor

(b) P.d is the same in each resistor

(c) Both (a) and (b)

(d) None of the above

Answer. (b)

(viii) Which of the following combinations of resistances is different from the others?

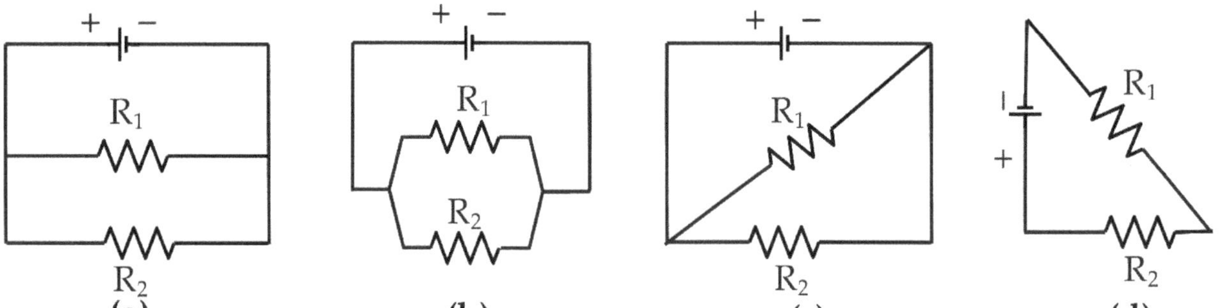

(a) (b) (c) (d)

Answer. (d)

(ix) Total internal reflections occur when:

(a) The light travels from a rarer to denser medium

(b) The light travels from a denser to rarer medium

(c) The light travels from a denser to a rarer medium at an angle greater than the critical angle
(d) None of the above
Answer. (c)

(x) The distance between the principal focus and optical center is called
(a) Displacement
(b) Radius of curvature
(c) Focal length
(d) Light year
Answer. (c)

(xi) The M.A. of an ideal single movable pulley is
(a) 1
(b) Less than 1
(c) Greater than 2
(d) 2
Answer. (d)

(xii) Which of the following quantity remains invariant during a uniform circular motion of a particle
(a) Force
(b) Speed
(c) Acceleration
(d) Velocity
Answer. (b)

(xiii) For a fixed mass, the graph between linear momentum (p) and kinetic energy (k) is best represented by

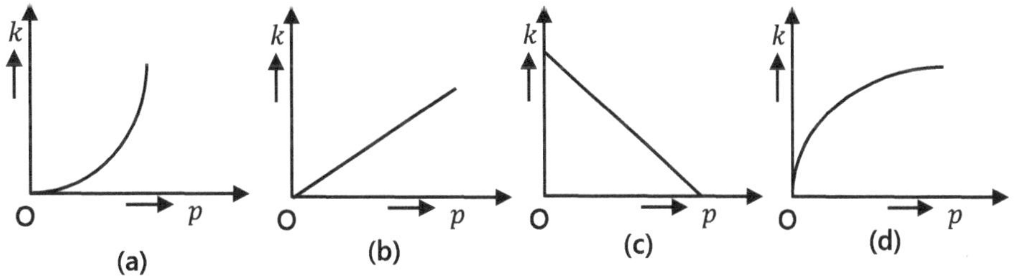

Answer. (b)

(xiv) A man moving towards a vertical cliff at a constant velocity of u, m/s $^{-1}$, fires a gun, and hears the echo after ts If he was at a distance of d m from the cliff when he fired the gun, the velocity of sound in air is......... ms^{-1}.
(a) $\frac{d}{t}$
(b) $\frac{2d}{t}$
(c) $\frac{2d}{t} - u$

(d) $\frac{2d}{t}+u$
Answer. (b)

(xv) A 'SONAR' device fitted in a submarine receives an echo 2 sec. later the signal is transmitted towards another submarine. If the speed of sound in water is 1530 ms^{-1}, the distance between two submarines is

(a) 3060 m
(b) 1530 m
(c) 765 m
(d) 6120 m
Answer. (a)

Question 2.

(i) Explain the refraction. A ray of monochromatic light is incident on a glass slab in the air. Draw a ray diagram and indicate the change in its path till it emerges out of the glass slab. **[3]**

(ii) Shows that a ray of light passes from air to water. In figure four refracted rays A, B, C, and D are shown. Which is the correct refracted ray? **[2]**

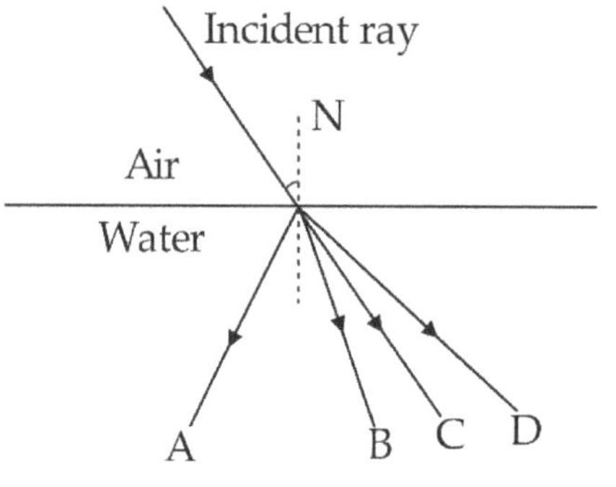

(iii) An electric arc lamp uses 20 A when connected to a 220 V line. Find its resistance **[2]**
Answer. R = 11Ω

(iv) Write CGS and SI units of energy and express the relation between them. **[2]**

(v) What is a magnetic field? And its SI units. **[2]**

(vi) An object is placed in front of a lens between its optical Centre and the focus and forms a virtual, erect, and diminished image. **[2]**

(a) Name the lens which formed this image.
(b) Draw a ray diagram to show the formation of the i = age with the above-stated characteristics.

(vii) What is a fixed pulley? Write one use of a single fixed pulley. **[2]**

Question 3.

(i) How much work is done in moving a charge of 2 coulombs from a point at 20 volts to a point at 40 volts? **[2]**

Answer. $W = 40J$

(ii) Mention two factors on which the internal resistance of a cell depends. **[2]**

(iii) Give one example of each first-order lever where M.A. is **[2]**

(a) Equal to 1, and

(b) More than 1.

(iv) State three uses of an electromagnet. **[2]**

(v) What is an electromagnet? What are its two standard shapes? **[2]**

SECTION – B (40 Marks)

(Attempt any four questions)

Question 4.

(i) Derive the relation $\text{KE} = \frac{1}{2}\text{mv}^2$. **[3]**

(ii) Shows the light (blue + red, green) incident on a prism and on a rectangular glass block. Com plate the ray diagrams by drawing refracted and emergent rays. **[3]**

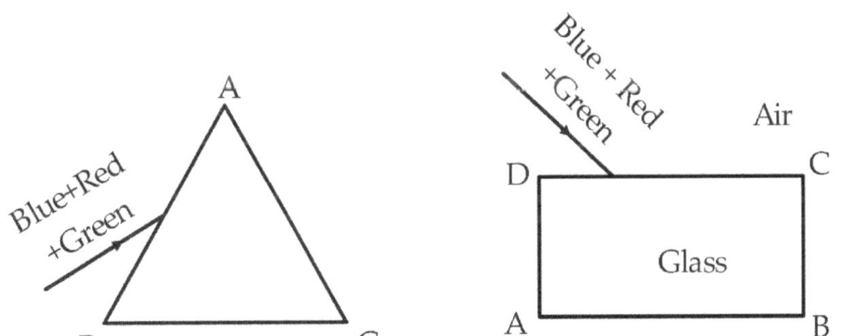

(a) (b)

(iii) The red light of wavelength $6600A^0$ gets refracted into the water from the air. The speed of light in air is 3×10^8 ms^{-1} And refractive index of water is 4/3. Determine: **[3]**

(a) The frequency of light in the air,

(b) The speed of light in water, and

(c) The wavelength of light in water.

Answer.

(a) (a)f = 4.54×10^{14}Hz

(b) V = 2.25×10^{8}m/s

(c) $\lambda = 8800A^0$

Question 5.

(i) A refrigerator is marked 80 W and 220 V. **[3]**

(a) How much energy does it consume in one day if it is used for 20 hours a day ?

(b) What is likely to happen (to the amount of energy consumed) if the voltage drops to 55 V?

Answer. (1.6kWh, 0.1kWh)

(ii) **(a)** What is the principle on which sonar is based?

(b) Calculate the minimum distance at which a person should stand in front of a reflecting surface so that he can hear a distinct echo. (Take the speed of sound in air = 350 m s^{-1}.) **[3]**

Answer. $d = 17m$

(iii) A bulb is connected to a battery of p.d. 4 V and internal resistance of 2.5Ω. A steady current of 0.5 A flows through the circuit. Calculate

(a) The total energy supplied by the battery in 10 minutes,

(b) The resistance of the bulb, and

(c) The energy dissipated in the bulb in 10 minutes. **[4]**

Answer.

(a) $E = 1.2KJ$

(b) $R = 5.5\Omega$

(c) $E = 825J$

Question 6.

(i) The graph represents a cooling curve for a surface being cooled from a higher temperature of a lower temperature.

(a) What is the boiling point of the substance?

(b) What happens in the region DE?

(c) Why is the region DE shorter than the region BC. **[3]**

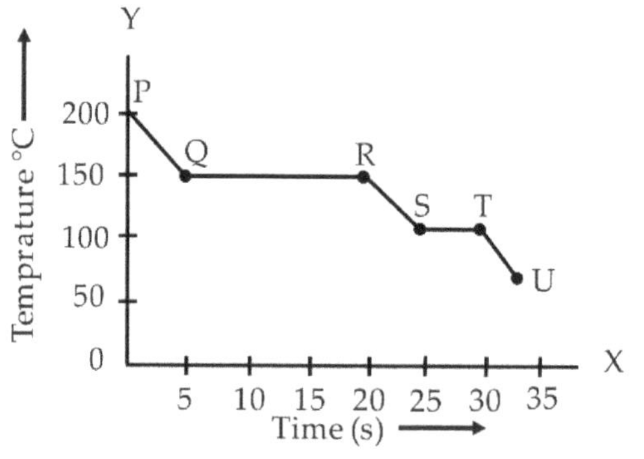

(ii) Why do the surroundings become pleasantly warm when freezing starts in cold countries? **[3]**

(iii) A calorimeter of mass 50 g and specific heat capacity 0.42 $J\ g^{-10}C^{-1}$ contains some mass of water at 20°C. A metal piece of mass 20 gat100°C is dropped into the calorimeter. After stirring, the final temperature of the mixture is found to be 22°C. Find the mass of water used in the calorimeter. Specific heat capacity of the metal piece = 0.3 $J\ g^{-1}C^{-1}$, specific heat capacity of water = 4.2 $J\ g^{-10}C^{-1}$.

Answer.$47^{0}C$

Question 7.

(i) A bullet of mass 0.01 kg moving with a velocity of 500 ms^{-1} strikes a block of mass 2 kg suspended from a 5 m long string. The center of gravity of the block rises vertically upwards through a height of 0.1 m. Find the velocity of the bullet after emerging out of the block. **[3]**

Answer. $V = 220m/s$

(ii) In a meter rod, half of it is made of copper and the rest half of steel. Weights of copper and steel are 9 N and 8 N respectively. Is the center of gravity of the rod at its geometric center? If not, where is it **[3]**

(iii) The diagram given below shows a sky jump. A skier weighing 60kgf stands at A at the top of sky jump. He moves from A to B and takes off for his jump at B.

(a) Calculate the change in the gravitational potential energy of the skier between A and B.

(b) If 75% of the energy in part (a) becomes kinetic energy at B, calculate the speed at which the skier arrives at B. (Take g = 10 m s^{-2})

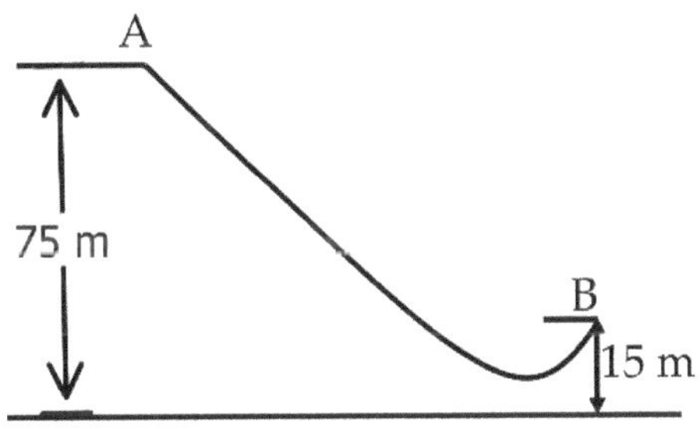

Answer.

(a) $P.E. = 36000J$

(b) $V = 30m/s$

Question 8.

(i) The adjacent diagram shows the displacement-time graph for a vibrating body. **[3]**

(a) Name the type of vibrations produced by the vibrating body.

(b) Give one example of a body producing such Vibrations.

(c) Why is the amplitude of the wave gradually decreasing?

(d) What will happen to the vibrations of the body after some time?

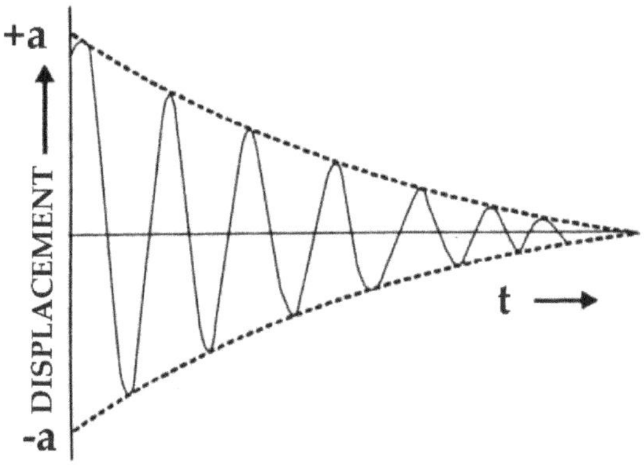

(ii) **(a)** Name two factors on which the magnitude of an induced e.m.f, in the secondary coil depends.

(b) In the adjacent diagram, the arrow shows the motion of the coil towards the bar magnet.

(i) Sate in which direction the current lows: A to B or B to A ?

(ii) Name the law used to come to the conclusion. **[3]**

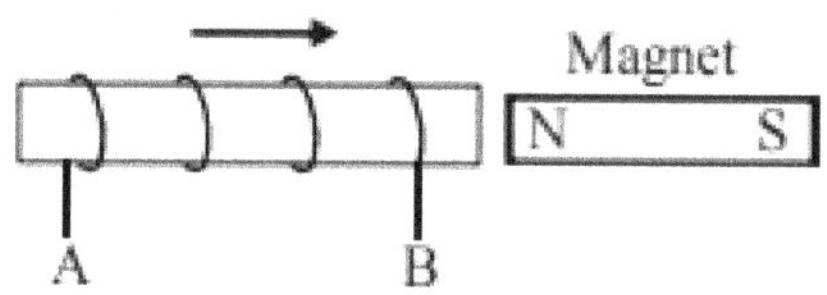

(iii) Prove that: refractive index $= \frac{\text{Real depth}}{\text{Apperent depth}}$ **[4]**

Question 9.

(i) What is Lateral displacement? Write the factors on which the lateral displacement depends. **[3]**

(ii) **(a)** Can the absolute refractive index of a medium be less than one?

(b) A coin placed at the bottom of a beaker appears to be raised by 4.0 cm. If the refractive index of water is 4 . 3. find the depth of water in the beaker. **[3]**

Answer. Depth= 12cm

(iii) A pulley system has a velocity ratio of 5. Draw a labeled diagram of the pulley system to lift a load by applying the effort in a convenient direction. Draw arrows to represent tension in each strand. **[4]**

(a) How many strands do support to lead?

(b) If the efficiency of the system is 80%, find its mechanical advantage.

(c) State two reasons why it is not 100% efficient.

(d) How much force is required to lift a load of 10kgf by this system?

(e) If the load is pulled up by the distance of 2 m in 10s, calculate the power developed by the effort.

ICSE 2023 EXAMINATION
SAMPLE PAPER-5
PHYSICS
(SCIENCE PAPER - 1)

Maximum Marks: 80

Time allowed: Two hours

Answers to this Paper must be written on the paper provided separately.

You will not be allowed to write during first 15 minutes.

This time is to be spent in reading the question paper.

The time given at the head of this Paper is the time allowed for writing the answers.

SECTION *A* is compulsory. Attempt any four questions from SECTION *B*.
The intended marks for questions or parts of questions are given in brackets [ ].

SECTION – A (40 Marks)
(Answer all the questions from this SECTION)

Question 1.

(i) Which one of the following radiations has the least penetrating power?

(a) X-rays
(b) α –particle
(c) β –particle
(d) Both (a) and (b)
Answer. (b)

(ii) The specific heat capacity of water is

(a) $0.42 Jg^{-1} K^{-1}$
(b) $420 Jg^{-1} K^{-1}$
(c) $4200 Jkg^{-1} K^{-1}$
(d) $42000 Jkg^{-1} K^{-1}$
Answer. (c)

(iii) SI Unit of latent heat is

(a) Jkg^{-1}
(b) J
(c) $Jkg^{-1 0}C^{-1}$
(d) $°C^{-1}$
Answer. (a)

(iv) The specific heat of a body depends on the

(a) Mass of the body

(b) Weight of the body
(c) Density of the body
(d) Nature of the material of the body
Answer. (a)

(v) Fleming's left-hand rule is applied when
(a) Electrical energy changes into chemical energy
(b) The direction of force on a current carrying conductor placed in a magnetic field is to be determined
(c) Mechanical energy changes into electrical energy
(d) Electrical energy changes into heat energy
Answer. (b)

(vi) A motor converts__________ energy into________ energy.
(a) Electrical, mechanical
(b) Mechanical, electrical
(c) Thermal, mechanical
(d) None of these
Answer. (a)

(vii) Three resistances R_1, R_2, R_3 are connected in series. The total resistance is
(a) $R_s = R_1 + R_2 + R_3$
(b) $R_s = \frac{1}{R_1} + \frac{1}{R_2} + \frac{1}{R_3}$
(c) $R_s = \frac{R_1+R_2}{R_3}$
(d) $R_s = \frac{R_2}{R_1+R_2}$
Answer. (c)

(viii) Ohm's law is valid when
(a) Temperature increases
(b) Temperature decreases
(c) Temperature remains constant
(d) Graph between I and V is a curve
Answer. (c)

(ix) A magnifying glass forms
(a) A virtual and diminished image
(b) A real and magnified image
(c) A real and diminished image
(d) A virtual and magnified image
Answer. (d)

(x) The process of splitting white light into its seven constituent colours is called

(a) Reflection
(b) Refraction
(c) Scattering
(d) Dispersion
Answer. (d)

(xi) A movable pulley is used
(a) As speed multiplier
(b) Is force multiplied
(c) To change the direction of effort
(d) None of the above
Answer. (b)

(xii) A body is acted upon by two unequal forces in - opposite directions, but not in one line. The effect is that:
(a) The body will have only the rotational motion.
(b) The body will have only the translational motion.
(c) The body will have neither the rotational motion nor the translational.
(d) The body will have rotational as well as translational motion.
Answer. (d)

(xiii) A man has a box of weighs 20 kg. The energy of the box when he keeps the box in his hand for 5 minutes is
(a) $10J$
(b) $200J$
(c) $400J$
(d) Zero
Answer. (d)

(xiv) The energy of the wave that passes through a unit area per unit time is called
(a) Quality
(b) Pitch
(c) Intensity
(d) Amplitude
Answer. (c)

(xv) For an ideal machine, the ratio of mechanical advantage to the velocity ratio
(a) Is greater than one
(b) s less than one
(c) Is equal to one
(d) Depends on the value of the load
Answer. (c)

Question 2.

(i) 45 g of water at 50°C in a beaker is cooled when 50 g of copper at 18°C is added to it. Calculate the final temperature. The specific heat capacity of copper is $0.39 Jg^{-1} K^{-1}$ and that of water is $4.2 Jg^{-1} K^{-1}$. Assume that there is no less heat in the surroundings. **[3]**

Answer. $t = 47^0C$

(ii) What is meant by alpha decay? What is the change: **[2]**

(a) In the mass number and

(b) In the atomic number of the parent nucleus when an alpha decay takes place.

(iii) State the principle of conservation of energy. **[2]**

(iv) A ray of light of wavelength 5400 A° suffers refraction from air to glass. What will be the wavelength of light in air, if $_a\mu_g = 3/2$ **[2]**

Answer. $\lambda = 8100A^0$

(v) An object is placed in front of a converging lens at a distance greater than twice the focal length of the lens. Draw a ray diagram ta show the formation of the image. **[2]**

(vi) What happens to the kinetic energy when the mass of a body is doubled and velocity is reduced to half? **[2]**

(vii) State two characteristics of a primary coil of a step-up transformer when compared to the secondary coil.

Question 3.

(i) Name any four regions of the electromagnetic spectrum (other than visible light) in increasing order of wavelength. **[2]**

(ii) Draw a graph showing the relationship between acceleration and mass when force in constant. **[2]**

(iii) Explain the condition under which resonance occurs. State one example of a phenomenon based on resonance. **[2]**

(iv) Define current, give its mathematical expression, and also give its unit of measurement. **[2]**

(v) Define the efficiency of a machine. Express it mathematically.

$$\left[\eta = \frac{\text{Work output}}{\text{Work input}}\right]$$

SECTION – B (40 Marks)
(Attempt any four questions)

Question 4.

(i) Define the e. m. f. E of a cell and the potential difference V across a resistor R in terms of work done in moving a unit charge. State the relation between these two works and the work done in moving a unit charge through a cell connected across the resistor. Take the internal resistance of the cell as r. Hence obtain an expression for the current l in the circuit. **[3]**

(ii) With the help of a labeled diagram discuss the construction of a U-shaped electromagnet. Give two factors on which the strength of the electromagnet depends. **[3]**

(iii) In the figure shown, calculate: **[4]**

(a) The value of the combined resistances of 40 ohm and R, using the readings of the two meters.

(b) The value of 'R'

(c) The current flowing through 'R'

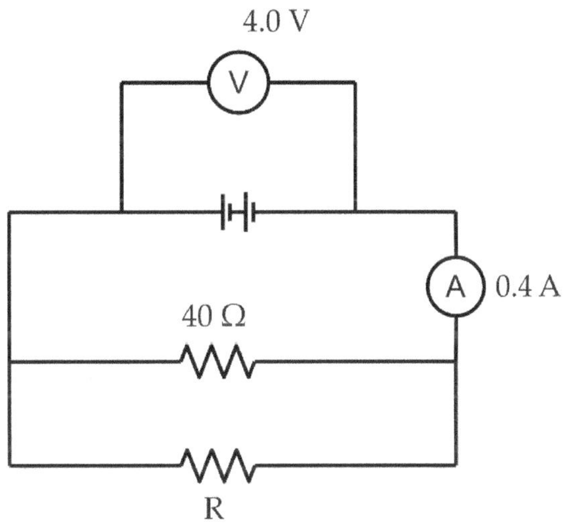

Question 5.

(i) Calculate the amount of ice that is required to cool 150 g of water contained in a vessel of mass 100 g at 30°C such that the temperature of the mixture is 5°C (Take specific heat capacity of material of vessel as $0.4 Jg^{-1}\ °C^{-1}$, specific latent heat of fusion ice = $336 Jg^{-1}$, the specific heat capacity of water = $4.2 Jg^{-1}\ ^3C^{-1}$) **[3]**

Answer. m = 47g ice

(ii) Complete the following nuclear changes: **[3]**

(a) $^{27}_{12}Mg \xrightarrow{\beta} Al \xrightarrow{\gamma}$

(b) $^{24}_{11}Na \xrightarrow{\beta} Mg$

(c) $^{A}_{Z}P \xrightarrow{\beta} Q$

(iii) A piece of iron of mass 2.0 kg has a thermal capacity of $966JK^{-1}$. Calculate: **[4]**

(a) Heat energy needed to warm it by 15°C and

(b) Its specific heat capacity in the S.I unit.

Answer.

(a) $Q = 14{,}490J$

(b) $C = 483J/Kg\ K$

Question 6.

(i) Mention two advantages and two disadvantages of producing hydroelectricity. **[3]**

(ii) A rocket of mass 3×10^6Kg takes off from a launching pad and acquires a vertical velocity of $1\ km \times s^{-1}$At an altitude of 25 km Calculate its K.E and P.E. Given $g = 10\ ms^{-2}$ **[3]**

Answer. $K.E. = 1.5 \times 10^{12}J$

(iii) What do you understand by equilibrium? State necessary conditions for a body to be in equilibrium. **[4]**

Question 7.

(i) A pencil dot appears raised by 7.0 mm when placed under a rectangular glass block of refractive index 1.5. Find the thickness of the glass block. **[3]**

(ii) **(a)** What is meant by 'Dispersion of light'? **[3]**

(b) In the atmosphere which color of light gets scattered the least?

(iii) (a), (b), and (c) in your answer book. Complete the path of the ray's incident normally on the faces of the right-angled isosceles prisms as shown. Draw any normal required, mark important angles, and show clearly where the rays emerge from the prisms, in Each case. Assume critical angle $\theta_{crit} = 42^0$ For the material of the prisms. Also, explain briefly why you chose the particular paths at the boundaries (air-glass and glass-air). **[4]**

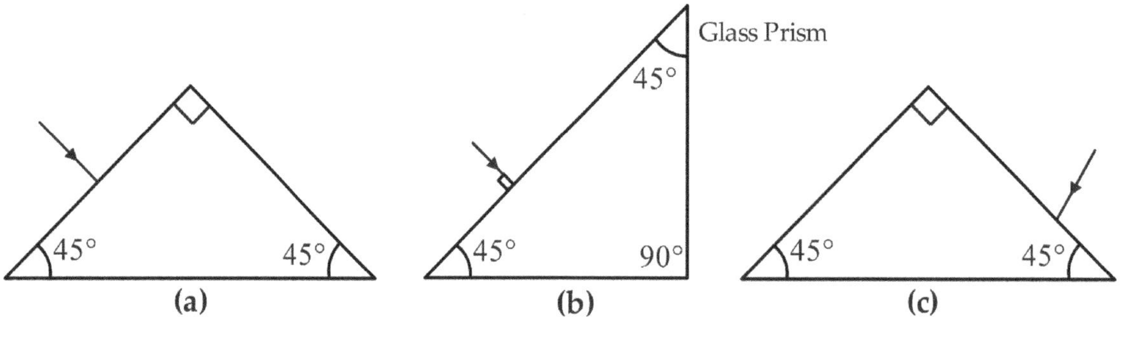

Question 8.

(i) A pulley system has $VR = 4$ and an efficiency 70% When a load of mass 1.4 kg is raised by it, calculate: **[3]**

(a) The M.A. of the system and

(b) The effort (in SI units).

Answer.

(a) $\text{M. A.} = 2.8$

(b) $\text{E} = 49\text{N}$

(ii) State and prove Newton's second law of motion. Under what condition Newton's second law takes the form $\text{F} = ma$, where α is acceleration? **[3]**

(iii) A fixed pulley is driven by a 100 Kg mass falling at a rate of 8.0 m in 4.0 s. It lifts a load of 75.0 Kgf. Calculate: **[4]**

(a) The power input to the pulley taking the force of gravity on 1Kg as 10 N.

(b) The efficiency of the pulley, and

(c) The height to which the road is raised in 4.0 s.

Answer.

(a) 2000W

(b) 0.75

(c) 8.0m

Question 9.

(i) The real view mirror of the motorbike starts vibrating violently at some particular speed of the motorbike. **[3]**

(a) Why does this happen?

(b) What is the name of the phenomenon taking place?

(c) What could be done to stop the violent vibrations?

(ii) A see-saw has a 40kgboy sitting at a distance of 80 cm from one end and his little brother of 30 kg is counterbalanced on the other side. The fulcrum is in the middle of the uniform plank of length 4.0 m How far is the little brother from the other end of the see-saw? **[3]**

Answer. $x = 160cm$

(iii) A person standing between two vertical cliffs and 640m away from the nearest cliff shouted (just once). He heard the after 4sec.and the second echo 3sec. later. Calculate **[4]**

(a) The velocity of sound in air and

(b) The distance between the cliffs

Answer.

(a) $\text{V} = 320\text{m/s}$

(b) $\text{S} = 1760\text{m}$

PREVIOUS YEAR PAPER

ICSE 2023 EXAMINATION

PREVIOUS YEAR PAPER-2019

PHYSICS

(SCIENCE PAPER - 1)

Maximum Marks: 40

Time allowed: Two hours

Answers to this Paper must be written on the paper provided separately.

You will not be allowed to write during first 15 minutes.

This time is to be spent in reading the question paper.

The time given at the head of this Paper is the time allowed for writing the answers.

SECTION A is compulsory. Attempt any four questions from SECTION B.
The intended marks for questions or parts of questions are given in brackets [ ].

SECTION – A (40 Marks)

(Answer all the questions from this SECTION)

Question 1.(a)

The diagram below shows a claw hammer used to remove a nail: **[2]**

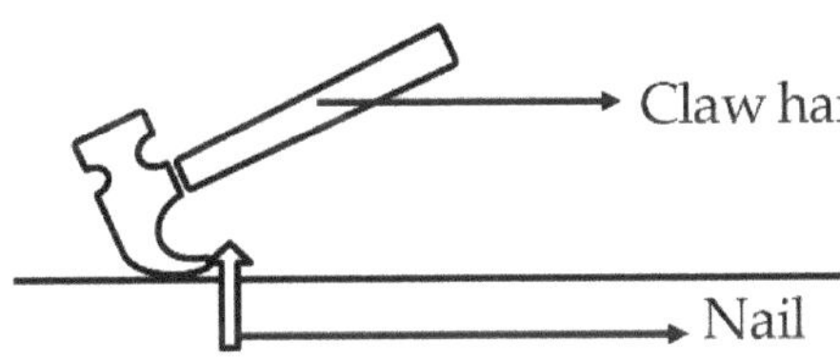

(i) To which class of lever does it belong?

(ii) Give one more example of the same class of lever mentioned by you in (i) for which the mechanical advantage is greater than one.

Answer

(i) A claw hammer belongs to the class I lever.

(ii) Another example of a class I lever is sheared (used to cut metal sheets)

Question 1.(b)

Two bodies A and B have masses in the ratio 5:1 and their kinetic energies are in the ratio 125:9. Find the ratio of their velocities. **[2]**

Answer

Given,

$$\frac{m_A}{m_B} = \frac{5}{1}$$
$$\frac{K_A}{K_B} = \frac{125}{9}$$

$$\frac{K_A}{K_B} = \frac{\frac{1}{2} m_A v_A^2}{\frac{1}{2} m_B v_B^2}$$

$$= \left(\frac{m_A}{m_B}\right) \times \left(\frac{v_A^2}{v_B^2}\right)$$

$$\frac{125}{9} = \frac{5}{1} \times \frac{v_A^2}{v_B^2}$$

$$\Rightarrow \frac{v_3^2}{v_B^2} = \frac{125 \times 1}{9 \times 5}$$

$$\Rightarrow \frac{v_A}{v_B} = \sqrt{\frac{25}{9}} = \frac{5}{3}$$

Hence, the ratio between velocities of *A* and *B* la 5: 3

Question 1.(c)

(i) Name the physical quantity which is measured in calories.

(ii) How is calorie related to the S.I. unit of that quantity? **[2]**

Answer

(i) Heat energy is measured in calories.

(ii) 1cal = 4.2 J where joule is the S.l. unit of heat energy.

Question 1.(d)

(i) Define couple.

(ii) Sate the SI. unit of moment of a couple. **[2]**

Answer

(i) Two equal and opposite parallel forces, not acting along the same line, form a couple.

(ii) The S.I. unit of moment of a couple is Newton meter or Nm.

Question 1.(e)

(i) Define critical angle.

(ii) State one important factor which affects the critical angle of a given medium. **[2]**

Answer

(i) The critical angle is the angle of incidence in the denser medium corresponding to which the angle of refraction in the rares medium is 90°.

(ii) The refractive index of the medium affects the critical angle of a given medium.

Question 2.(a)

Electromagnetic radiation is used for photography in fog.

(i) Identify the radiation.

(ii) Why is this radiation mentioned by you, ideal for this purpose? **[2]**

Answer

(i) Infra-Red radiation.

(ii) Infra-Red radiation has a larger wavelength hence, it is scattered least among visible radiations and thus has deep penetration even in the fog.

Question 2.(b)

(i) What is the relation between the refractive index of water to air $({}_{a}\mu_{W})$ and the refractive index of air to water $({}_{w}\mu_{a})$

(ii) If the refractive index of water to air $({}_{a}\mu_{W})$ is $\frac{5}{3}$. Calculate the refractive index of air to water $({}_{w}\mu_{a})$ **[2]**

Answer

(i) ${}_{a}\mu_{W} = \frac{1}{{}_{w}\mu_{a}}$ i.e., they are inverse of each other.

(ii) Given, $\mu_{W} = \frac{5}{3}$

$${}_{w}\mu_{a} = \frac{3}{5} = 0.6$$

Question 2.(c)

The specific heat capacity of substance A is 3,800 J kg^{-1} K^{-1} and that of a substance B is 400 J kg^{-1} K^{-1}. Which of the two substances is a good conductor of heat? Give a reason for your answer. **[2]**

Answer

Substance *B* is a good conductor of heat energy. For the same heat energy and same mass, the rise in temperature of *B* will be more here, *B* is a good conductor of heat.

Question 2.(d)

A man playing the flute can produce notes of different frequencies. If he does the hales near his mouth, will the pitch of the note produced, increase or decrease? Give a reason. **[2]**

Answer

When the hales near the mouth are closed, the effective length of the air column increases so the pitch of sound decreases as the frequency of note produced is inversely proportional to the length of the air column.

Question 2.(e)

The diagram below shows a light source *P* embedded in a rectangular glass block ABCD of the critical angle 42°. Complete the path of the ray PO till it emerges cut of the block. [Write necessary angles.] **[2]**

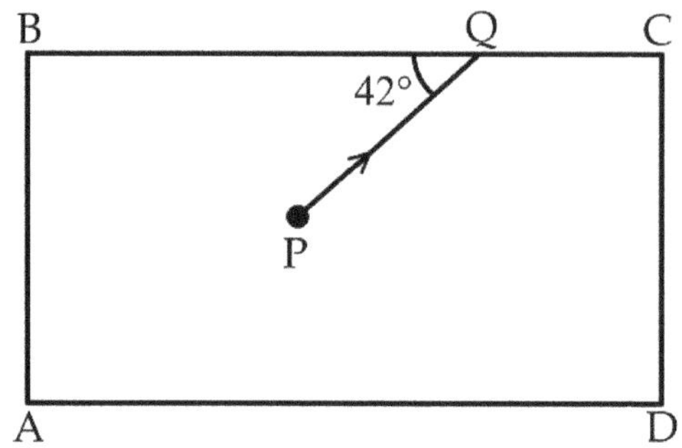

Answer

The path of the ray is as shown.

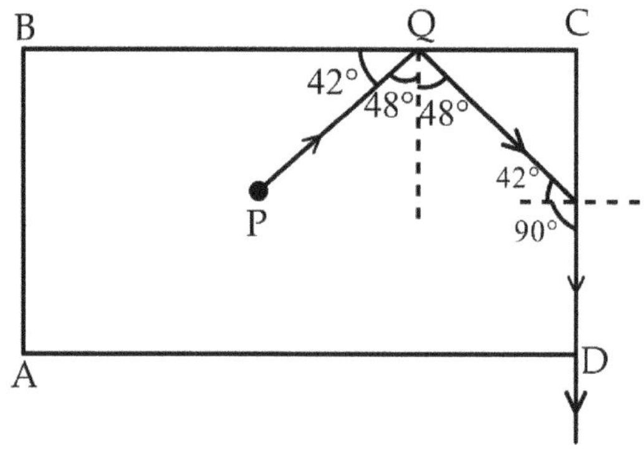

Question 3.(a)

(i) If the lens is placed in water instead of air, how does its focal length charge?

(ii) Which lens, thick or thin has a greater focal length? **[2]**

Answer

(i) The focal length of kens increases.

(ii) A thin lens has a greater focal length as compared to a thick lens.

Question 3.(b)

Two waves of the same pitch have amplitudes in the ratio 1: 3. What will be the ratio of their:

(i) Intensities and

(ii) Frequencies'? **[2]**

Answer

(i) Intensity is the measure of I loudness.

Loudness ∝ (amplitude) ^{2}

$$\therefore \quad \frac{L_1}{L_2} = \left(\frac{a_1}{a_2}\right)^2$$

$$\Rightarrow \quad \frac{L_1}{L_2} = \left(\frac{1}{3}\right)^2$$

$$\Rightarrow \quad \frac{L_1}{L_2} = \frac{1}{9}$$

The Ratio of intensities is 1: 9

(ii) The ratio of frequencies is 1:1 (the same frequency as the pitch is the same for both waves).

Question 3.(c)

How does an increase in the temperature affect the specific resistance of a :

(i) Metal and

(ii) Semiconductor? **[2]**

Answer

(i) On increasing the temperature of metal its Specific resistance increases

(ii) On increasing the temperature of a semiconductor, its specific resistance decreases.

Question 3.(d)

(i) Define resonant variations.

(ii) Which characteristic of sound, makes it possible ta recognize a person by his voice without seeing him? **[2]**

Answer

(i) Resonant vibrations are vibrations of high amplitude which are produced when the natural frequency of vibrations of the vibrating body is equal to the frequency of forced vibration imposed on it.

(ii) Quality (or timbre) is the characteristic of sound that makes it possible ta recognize a person by his voice without seeing him.

Question 3.(e)

Is it possible for a hydrogen (${}_{1}^{1}H$) nucleus to emit an alpha particle? Give a reason for your answer. **[2]**

Answer

No, a hydrogen nucleus is just a proton which obviously cannot give out an alpha particle made of two protons and two neutrons.

Question 4.(a)

Calculate the effective resistance across AB: **[2]**

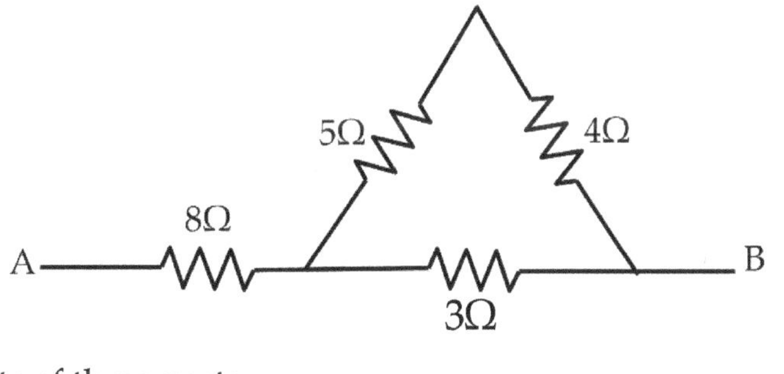

Answer

The given circuit consists of three parts.

In the first part 5Ω and 4Ω are in series and if the equivalent resistance is given by R_p then,

$$R_s = 5 + 4 = 9\Omega$$

Then, in the second part, there is the parallel combination of 3Ω and R_s\{9Ω), if equivalent resistance is R_p

$$\frac{1}{R_p} = \frac{1}{3} + \frac{1}{9}$$

$$\Rightarrow \frac{1}{R_p} = \frac{3+1}{9}$$
$$\Rightarrow \frac{1}{R_p} = \frac{4}{9}$$
$$\Rightarrow R_p = \frac{9}{4}$$
$$\Rightarrow R_p = 2.25\Omega$$

In the third part, B Q and $R_p(2.25Q)$ are in series. Therefore, the equivalent resistance between AB i.e., R_{AB} is

$$8 + 2.25 = 10.25\Omega$$

Hence, the Total rebalance between A and B is 10.25Ω

Question 4.(b)

(i) State whether the specific heat capacity of a substance remains the same what its state changes from solid to liquid.

(ii) Give one example ID to support your answer. **[2]**

Answer

(i) The specific heat capacity of a substance changes when its state changes.

(ii) The specific heat capacity of water is 4.2 J $g^{-1}C^{-1}$ while that of ice (frazer1 water} is 2.1Jg $°C^{-1}$

Question 4.(c)

A magnet kept at the center of two coils A and B is moved to and fro as shown in the diagram. That two galvanometers show deflection. **[2]**

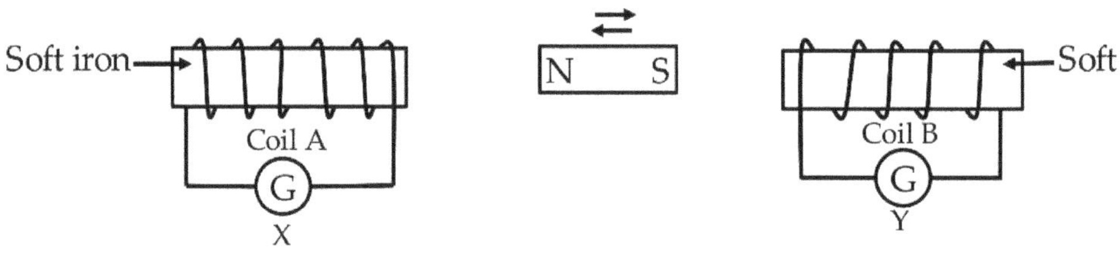

State with a reason whether:

$$x > y$$
or
$$x < y[x \text{ and } y \text{ are magnitudes of deflection }]$$

Answer

$$x < y$$

Since coil A has a smaller number of turns, therefore the e.m.f. generated in this coil will be less, hence the galvanometer x connected to this coil shows less deflection i.e., $x < y$ –

Question 4.(d)

(i) Why is a nuclear fusion reaction calling a thermonuclear reaction? **[2]**

(ii) Complete the reaction:

$$^3He_2 + {}^2H_1 \rightarrow {}^4He_2 + \cdots \ldots + \text{Energy}$$

Answer

(i) A nuclear fusion reaction is called a thermal nuclear reaction because it takes place at a temperature of nearly 10^7 × (10 million)

(ii) $^{3}He_2 + {}^{2}H_1 \rightarrow {}^{4}He_2 + {}^{1}H_1$ + Energy

Question 4.(e)

State two ways to increase the speed of rotation of a D. C. motor. **[2]**

Answer

The two ways of increasing the speed of a D.C. motor are

(i) By increasing the strength of current through the coil.

(ii) By increasing the number of turns in the coil.

SECTION - B (40 Marks)
(Attempt any four questions)

Question 5.(a)

A body of mass of 10 kg is kept at a height of 5 m. It is allowed to fall and reach the ground. **[3]**

(i) What is the total mechanical energy possessed by the body at that height of 2 m assuming it is a frictionless medium?

(ii) What is the kinetic energy possessed by the body just before hitting the ground? Takes $g = 10\ m\ s^{-2}$.

Answer

(i) The speed of the body when at a height of 2 m above the ground i.e., after falling through 3 m is:

$$V^2 = u^2 + 2gh = (0) + (2 \times 10 \times 3)$$
$$= 60$$
$$\therefore V = \sqrt{60} ms^{-1}$$

Mechanical exergy as $2m$ height = P.E. $+ K.E. = mgh + \frac{1}{2} mv^2$

$$= (10 \times 10 \times 2) + \left(\frac{1}{2} \times 10 \times 60\right)$$
$$= 200 + 300$$
$$= 500\ J$$

Hence, total mechanical energy possessed by the body at the height of 2 m = 500 J

(ii) The kinetic energy reaching the grout will be the same as the potential energy at its highest point from which it started falling.

Mechanical energy = Initial potential energy

$$= m \times g \times h = 10 \times 10 \times 5 = 500\ J$$

Hence, kinetic energy possessed by the body just before hitting the ground = 500 J

Question 5.(b)

A uniform meter scale is in equilibrium as shown in the diagram: **[3]**

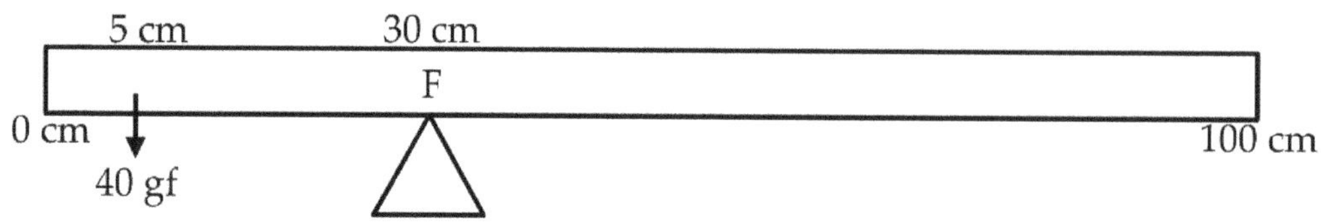

(i) Calculate the weight of the meter scale.

(ii) Which of the following options is correct to keep the ruler in equilibrium when 40gf wt is shifted to the 0 cm mark?

F is shifted towards 0 cm or

F is shifted towards 100 cm.

Answer

(i) Let W gf be the weight of the meter rule which acts as commands from the 50 cm mark.

In equilibrium position, taking moments of a fulcrum.

Anticlockwise moment = $40 \times (30 - 5) = 1000$gf cm

Clockwise moment = $W(50 - 30) = 20$ W gf cm

∴ Using the principle of moments:

$$20 \text{ W} = 1000$$
$$\Rightarrow \text{W} = \frac{1000}{20} = 50 \text{ gf}$$

∴ Weight of the meter scales = 50gf

(ii) In order to keep the ruler in equilibrium, F has shifted towards the 0 cm mark.

Question 5.(c)

The diagram below shows a pulley arrangement: **[4]**

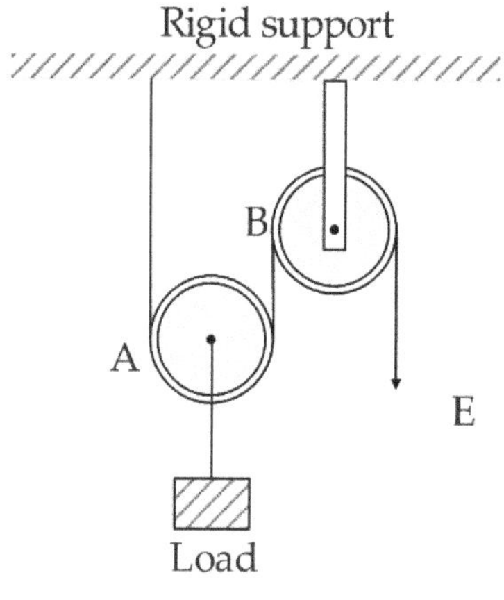

(i) Copy the diagram and mark the direction of tension on each strand of the string.

(ii) What is the velocity ratio of the arrangement?

(iii) If the tension acting and the string is T, then what is the relationship between T and effort E?

(iv) If the free end of the string moves through a distance x_1 find the distance by which the load is raised.

Answer

(i) The direction of tension (T) is marked in the diagram:

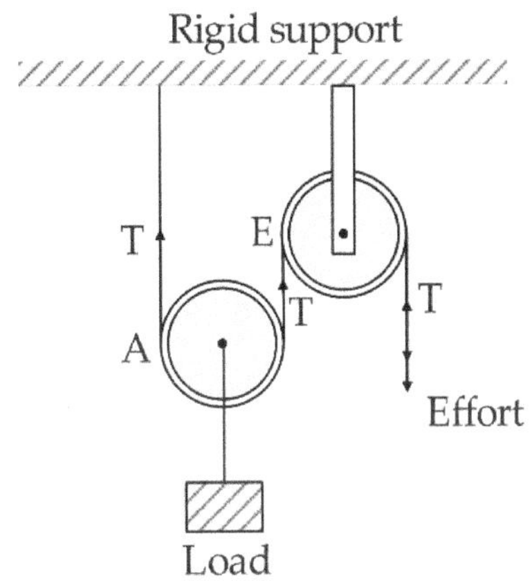

(ii) V.R. = $\frac{\text{Distance moved by the effort}}{\text{Distance moved by the load}} = 2$

(iii) Effort E balances the tensions therefore, $T = E$

(iv) From the relation,

$$\text{V.R.} = \frac{\text{Distance moved by the effort}}{\text{Distance moved by the load}} = 2$$

If the frees end of the string moves through a distance, x then distance moved by load =?
Substituting the values, we get.

$$2 = \frac{x}{\text{Distance moved by load}}$$

$$\Rightarrow \text{Distance moved by load} = \frac{x}{2}$$

Question 6.(a)

How does the angle of deviation formed by a prism change with the increase in the angle of incidence? Draw a graph showing the variation in the angle of deviation with the angle of incidence at a prism surface. **[3]**

Answer

The angle of deviation (δ) produced by a prism first decrease with the increase in the angle of incidence (i) and reaches a minimum value at a certain angle of incidence. With a further increase in the angle of incidence, the angle of deviation also increases.

The graph below shows the variation of the angle of deviation with the angle of incidence:

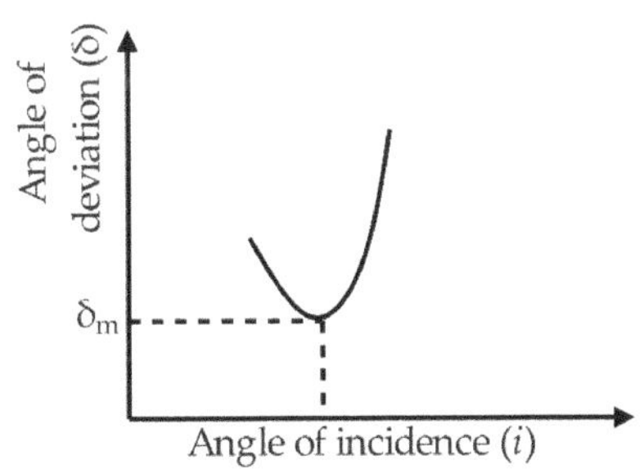

Question 6.(b)

A virtual, diminished image is formed when an object is placed between the optical center and the principal focus of a lens. **[3]**

(i) Name is the type of lens that forms the above image.

(ii) Draw a ray diagram to show the formation of the image with the above-stated characteristics.

Answer

(i) The lens is concave:

(ii) A Ray diagram showing the formation of the image is given below.

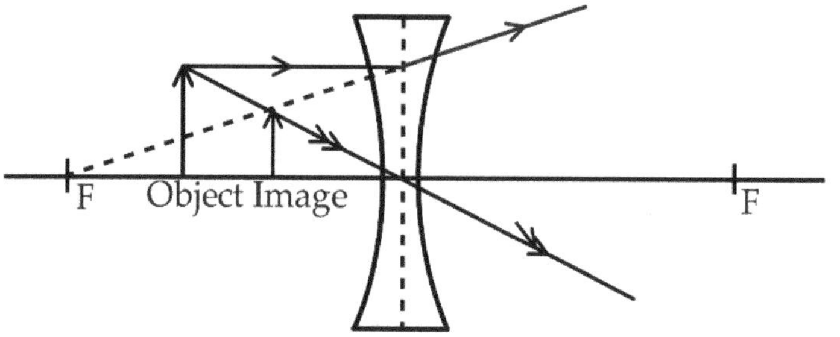

Concave lens

Question 6.(c)

Ars object is placed at a distance of 24 cm in front of a convex lens of focal length of 8 cm. **[4]**

(i) What is the nature of the image so formed?

(ii) Calculate the distance of the image from the lens.

(iii) Calculate the magnification of the image.

Answer

Given $u = 24$ cm (-ve), $f = 8$ cm {+ ve)

(i) The image formed is real, inverted, and diminished.

(ii) Let v is the distance of the image from the optical center. Fram that relation,

$$\frac{1}{v} - \frac{1}{u} = \frac{1}{f}$$

$$\frac{1}{v} + \frac{1}{24} = \frac{1}{8}$$

$$\frac{1}{v} = \frac{1}{8} - \frac{1}{24}$$

$$\frac{1}{v} = \frac{3-1}{24}$$

$$\frac{1}{v} = \frac{2}{24}$$

$$\frac{1}{v} = \frac{1}{12}$$

$$\Rightarrow v = 12 \text{ cm}$$

The distance of the Image from the lens = is 12 cm

(iii) From relation, $m = \frac{v}{u}$

Substituting the values, we get.

$$m = \frac{12}{24}$$

$$\Rightarrow m = 0.5$$

Magnification = 0.5

Question 7.(a)

It is observed that during march-past we hear a base drum distinctly from a distance compared to the side drums. **[3]**

(i) Name the characteristic of the sound associated with the above observation.

(ii) Give a reason for the above reservation.

Answer

(i) Loudness

(ii) The bass drum has a greater surface area compared to the side drums so the amplitude of vibration of the bass drum is greater than the amplitude of vibration of the side drums. Hence Loudness of the bass drum is increased compared to the side drums and it can be d distinctly heard from a distance.

Question 7.(b)

A pendulum has is a frequency of 4 vibrations per second. An observer starts the pendulum and fires a gun. simultaneously. He hears the echo from the cliff after 6 vibrations of the pendulum. If the velocity of sound in air is 340 m s^{-1}, find the distance between the cliff and the observer. **[3]**

Answer

An echo is a heart after 6 vibrations of a pendulum. Since the frequency of the pendulum is 4 vib per sec, so the time taken for the echo to be heard is $t = \frac{6}{4} = 1.5$ s.

If d is the distance between the cliff and the observers, then the velocity of sound $V = \frac{2d}{t}$

Substituting the values in the equation above:

$$340 = \frac{2d}{1.5}$$

$$\Rightarrow d = \frac{340 \times 1.5}{2} = 255\text{cm}$$

Hence, the distance between the cliff and the observer = is 255 cm

Question 7.(c)

Two pendulums C ard D are suspended from a wire as shown in the given figure. The pendulum C is the mate to Dilate by displacing it from its mean position. Hit is seen that D also starts oscillating. **[4]**

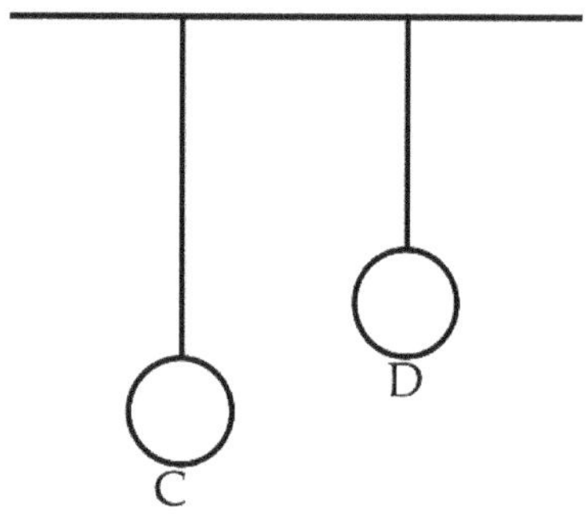

(i) Name the type of oscillation, C will execute.
(ii) Name the type of oscillation, D will execute.
(iii) If the length of D is made equal to C, then what difference will you notice in the oscillation of D?
(iv) What is the name of the phenomenon when the length of D is made equal to C ?

Answer

(i) C executes free vertices (damped if the medium is present).
(ii) D executes forced oscillation.
(iii) If the length of D is made equal ta C, then the amplitude of vibration of pendulum D increases substantially.
(iv) The phenomenon is called resonance.

Question 8.(a)

(i) Write one advantage of connecting electrical appliances in parallel combination.
(ii) What characteristics should a fuse wire have?
(iii) Which wire in a power circuit is connected to the metallic body of the appliance? **[3]**

Answer

(i) The advantage of connecting electrical appliances in a parallel combination is that each appliance works Independently any change In one appliance does not affect the other appliance(s).
(ii) The fuse wire should have high specific resistance and a low melting point.
(iii) The earth wire in is power circuit is connected to the metallic body of the appliance

Question 8.(b)

The diagram below shows a dual control switch circuit connected to a bulb. **[3]**

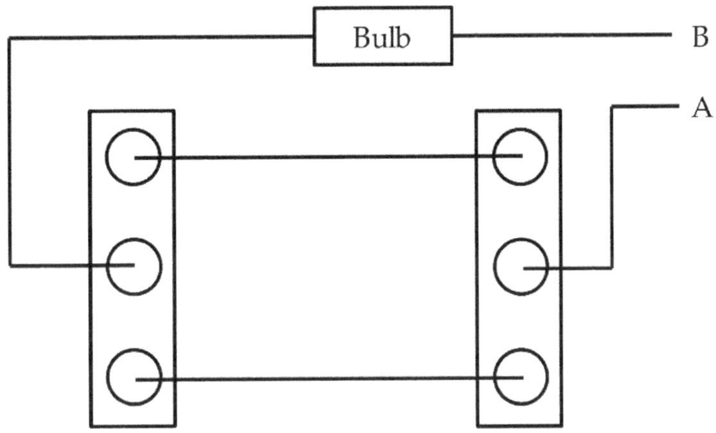

(i) Copy the diagram and complete it so that the bulb is switched ON.

(ii) Out of A& B which one is the live wire, and which one is the neutral wire?

Answer

(i) The following figure shows the completed diagram:

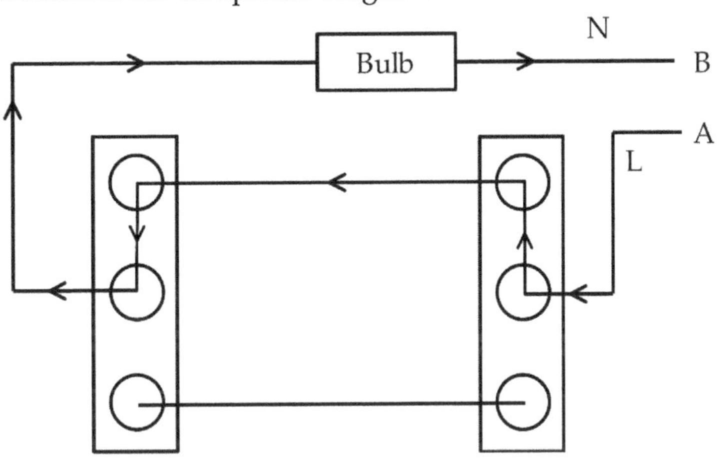

(ii) Wire A is the live wire and wire B is the neutral wire-

Question 8.(c)

The diagram shows a circuit with the key k open. Calculate: **[4]**

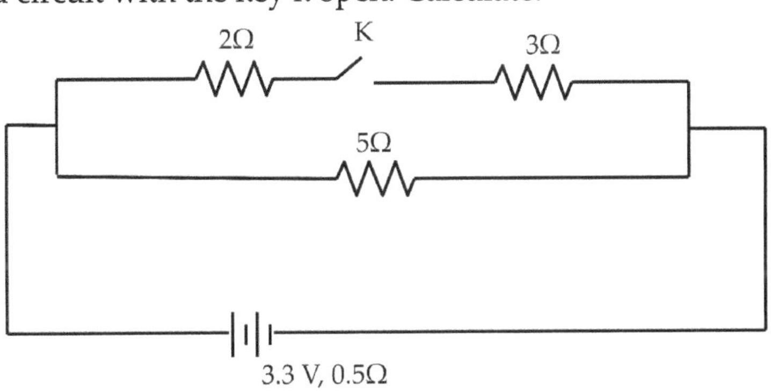

(i) The resistance of the circuit when the key k. Is open.

(ii) The current is drawn from the cell where the key k is open.

(iii) The resistance of the circuit where the key k is closed.

(iv) The current is drawn from the cell when the key k is closed.

Answer

(i) When k is open, resistance is $5 + 0.5 = 5.5\Omega$

(ii) Relation, $V = IR$

$$3.3 = I \times 5.5$$
$$\Rightarrow I = \frac{3.3}{5.5}$$
$$\Rightarrow I = 0.6 \text{ A}$$

The current drawn from the cell when the key k is open = 0.6 A.

(iii) When k is closed, the resistance 2 Ω and 3Ω are in series, therefore their total resistance is 2Ω + 3Ω = 5Ω.

Now since, 5Ω resistance is in parallel to it,

$$\frac{1}{R_p} = \frac{1}{5} + \frac{1}{5}$$
$$\frac{1}{R_p} = \frac{1+1}{5}$$
$$\Rightarrow \frac{1}{R_p} = \frac{2}{5}$$
$$\Rightarrow R_p = 2.50\Omega$$

So now the resistance of circuit is $2.5 + 0.5 = 3\Omega$

(iv) Current drawn $I = \frac{V}{R}$

$$I = \frac{3.3}{3}$$
$$\Rightarrow I = 1.1 \text{ A}$$

Question 9.(a)

(i) Define Calorimetry. **[3]**

(ii) Name is the material used for making a Calorimeter.

(iii) Why is a Calorimeter made up of thin sheets of the above material answered in (ii)?

Answer

(i) The science of measuring the amount of heat exchanged by the system with its surrounding is called calorimetry.

(ii) A copper sheet is used to make a calorimeter.

(iii) It is because Capper is a good conductor of heat, so it soon acquires the temperature of its contents and a thin Copper sheet has low heat capacity, so it takes only a small amount of heat from its contents. Hence, a Calorimeter is made up of thin sheets of copper.

Question 9.(b)

The melting point of naphthalene is 80°C and the room temperature is 30°C. A sample of liquid naphthalene at 100°C is cooled down to room temperature. Draw a temperature-time graph to represent this coaling. In the graph, mark the region which corresponds is the freezing process. **[3]**

Answer

The temperature-time graph representing the coaling of naphthalene is shown below:

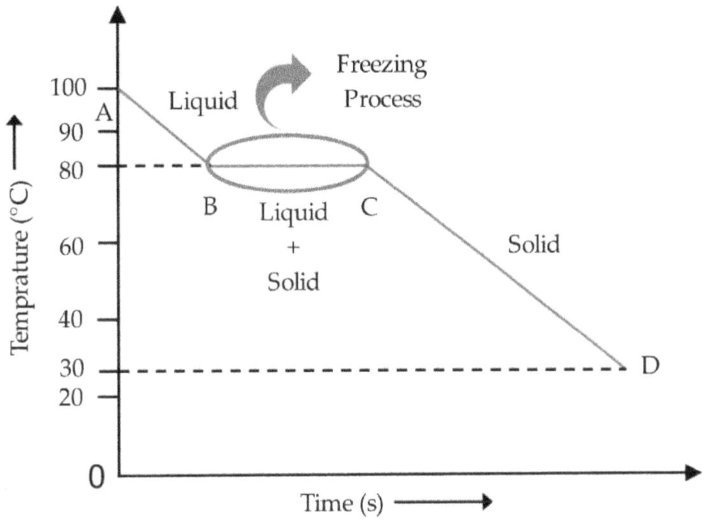

Question 9.(c)

104 g of water at 30°C is taken in a calorimeter made of copper of mass 42 g. When a certain mass of ice at 0°C is added to it, and the final steady temperature of the mixture after the ice has melted was found to be 10^0C. Find the mass of ice added.

[Specific heat capacity of water = $4.2 J g^{-1}\,{}^oC^{-1}$; Specific latent heat of fusion of ice = 336 J g^{-1}. Specific heat capacity of copper = 0.4 J $g^{-1}\,{}^oC^{-1}$] **[4]**

Answer

Given,

Mass of water = 104 g

The temperature of water = 30°C

Final temperature = 10°C

Mass of calorimeter = 42 g

Temperature of ice = 0°C

Heat is given by water $= m \times s \times t$

Heat is given by water $= 104 \times 4.2 \times (30 - 10) = 8736$ J

Heat is given by calorimeter $= m \times s \times t$

Substituting the values we get,

The heat is given by calorimeter $= 42 \times 0.4 \times (30 - 10) = 336.$ J

Let the mass of ice added be gm

Taken took by ice to melt $= mL = 336$ mJ

Heat has been taken by ice-water to reach the mixture temperature $= mst = m \times 4.2 \times (10 - 0) = 42$ mJ

Therefore, from a principle of calorimetry, heat has taken = heat given.

$$336m + 42m = 8736 + 336$$

$$m = \frac{9072}{378} = 24 \text{ g}$$

Hence, mass of Ice added = 24 g

Question 10. (a)

Draw a neat, labeled diagram of an AC generator. **[5]**

Answer

The labeled diagram of an AC general bar is as shown:

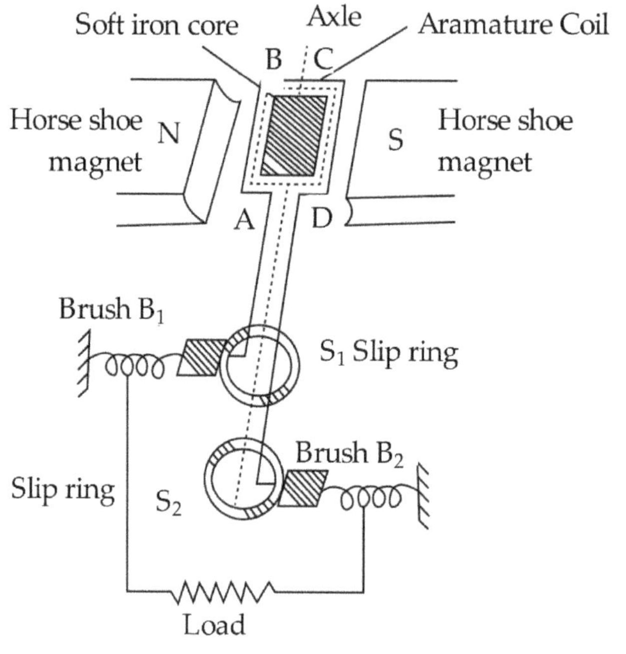

Question 10. (b)

(i) Define nuclear fission. **[3]**

Answer

(i) The process of splitting a heavy nucleus into two lighter nudes of the nearly same mass, when bombarded with slow neutrons, is called nuclear fission.

(ii) $^{235}_{92}U + ^{1}_{0}n \rightarrow ^{144}_{56}Ba + ^{89}_{36}Kr + 3\,^{1}_{0}n + \text{Energy}$

Question 10. (c)

The diagram below shows a magnetic needle kept just below the conductor *AB* which is kept in a North-South direction. **[4]**

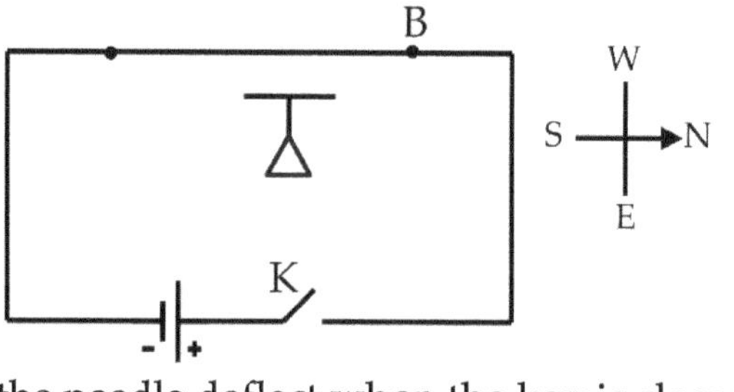

(i) In which direction does the needle deflect when the key is closed?

(ii) Why is the deflection produced?

(iii) What will be the charge in the deflection if the magnetic needle is taken just above the conductor AB?

(iv) Name one device which works in this principle.

Answer

(i) The North pole of the needle deflects towards the east.

(ii) On passing a current through the wire AB, a magnetic field is produced around the wire which aligns the magnetic needle in its direction.

(iii) The direction of deflection gets reversed is now it defects towards west.

(iv) Electric bell works this principle-

ICSE 2023 EXAMINATION
PREVIOUS YEAR PAPER-2020
PHYSICS
(SCIENCE PAPER - 1)

Maximum Marks: 40

Time allowed: Two hours

Answers to this Paper must be written on the paper provided separately.

You will not be allowed to write during first 15 minutes.

This time is to be spent in reading the question paper.

The time given at the head of this Paper is the time allowed for writing the answers.

SECTION A is compulsory. Attempt any four questions from SECTION B.
The intended marks for questions or parts of questions are given in brackets [ ].

SECTION – A (40 Marks)
(Answer all the questions from this SECTION)

Question 1.(a)

(i) Define the moment of force. **[2]**

(ii) Write the relationship between the S.I. and C.G.S. unit of moment of force.

Answer

(i) The moment of force is equal to the product of the magnitude of the force and the perpendicular distance of the line of action of a force from the axis of rotation.

(ii) The S.I. and C.G.S. unit of moment of force are related as follows -
$1 \text{ N m} = 10^5 \text{ dyne} \times 10^2 \text{ cm} = 10^7 \text{ dyne cm}$

Question 1.(b)

Define a kilowatt hour. How is it related to joule? **[2]**

Answer

One kilowatt hour is the electrical energy consumed by an electrical appliance of power 1 kilowatt when it is used for 1 hour.

$$1 \text{ kilowatt hour} = 1 \text{ kilowatt} \times 1 \text{ hour}$$
$$= 1000 \text{ J s}^{-1} \times 3600 \text{ s} = 3.6 \times 10^6 \text{ J}$$

Question 1.(c)

A satellite revolves around a planet in a circular orbit. What is the work done by the satellite at any instant? Give a reason. **[2]**

Answer

The work done is zero because the centripetal force on the body at any instant is directed towards the center of the circular path and the displacement at that instant is along the tangent to the circular path, i.e., normal to the direction of the force on the body. Since $\theta = 90°, \cos 90° = 0$. Therefore, work done is zero

Question 1.(d)

(i) Identify the class of the lever shown in the diagram below: **[2]**

(ii) How is it possible to increase the M.A. of the above lever without increasing its length?

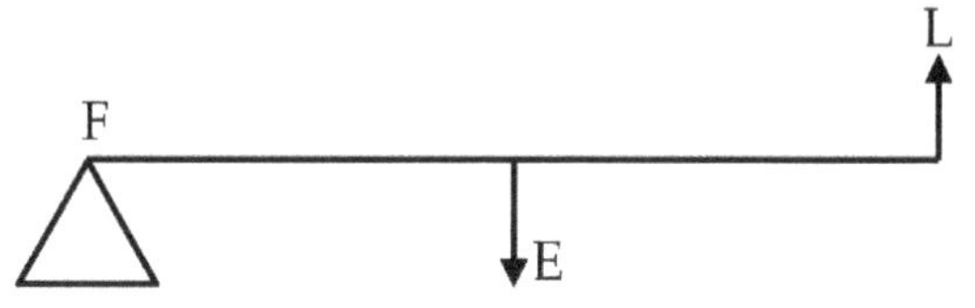

Answer

(i) The class of the lever shown in the diagram is class III.

(ii) By applying effort at a larger distance from the fulcrum i.e., shifting effort *E* towards load *L*, thereby increasing the length of the effort arm.

Question 1.(e)

Give one example of each when: **[2]**

(i) Chemical energy changes into electrical energy.

(ii) Electrical energy changes into sound energy.

Answer

(i) Chemical energy changes into electrical energy - In a battery when current is drawn from it in the external circuit.

(ii) Electrical energy changes into sound energy - In a loudspeaker, electrical signals vibrate the diaphragm of a loudspeaker to produce sound.

Question 2.(a)

A crane 'A' lifts a heavy load in 5 seconds, whereas another crane 'B' does the same work in 2 seconds. Compare the power of crane 'A' to that of crane 'B'. **[2]**

Answer

Let the work done by both cranes be ' W'

Given,

Time is taken by crane A to do work, $t_1 = 5$ s

Time is taken by crane *B* to do work, $t_2 = 2$ s

Power of crane A, $P_A = \frac{W}{t_1}$

Power of crane B, $P_B = \frac{W}{t_2}$

$$\frac{P_A}{P_B} = \frac{Wt_2}{Wt_1}$$

$$\frac{P_A}{P_B} = \frac{t_2}{t_1}$$

$$\frac{P_A}{P_B} = \frac{2}{5}$$

$$P_A : P_B = 2:5$$

Question 2.(b)

A ray of light falls normally on a rectangular glass slab. Draw a ray diagram showing the path of the ray till it emerges out of the slab. **[2]**

Answer

Below is the ray diagram showing the path of the ray till it emerges out of the slab:

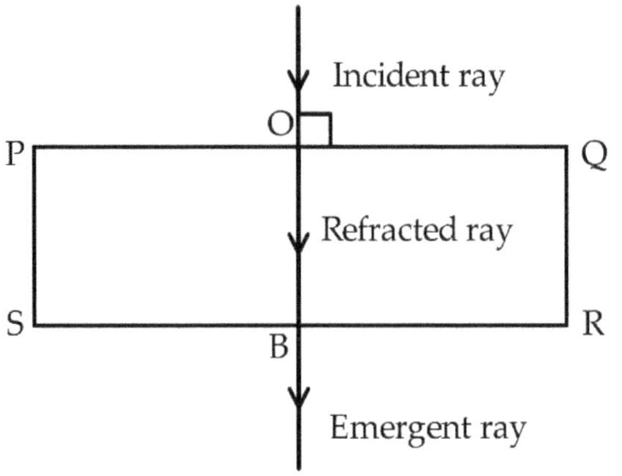

Question 2.(c)

Complete the path of the monochromatic light ray AB incident on the surface PQ of the equilateral glass prism PQR till it emerges out of the prism due to refraction. **[2]**

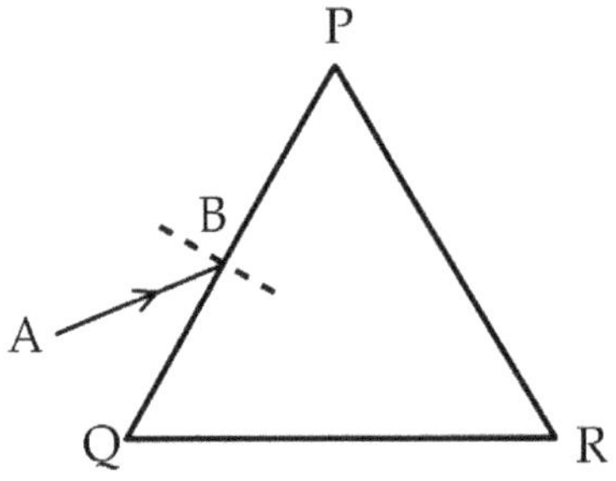

Answer

Below ray diagram shows the path of ray *AB* til it emerges out of the prism:

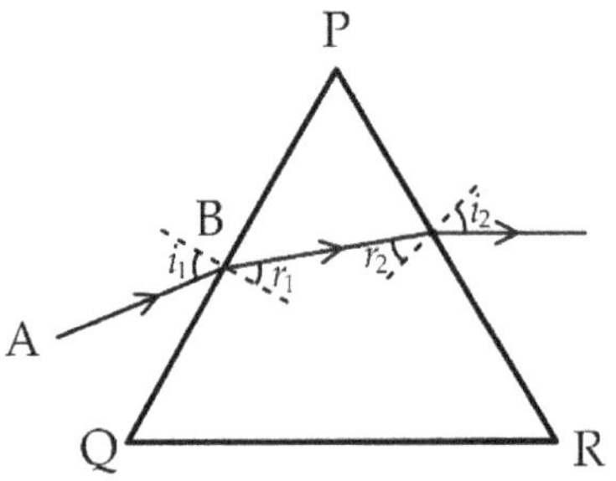

Question 2.(d)

Where should an abject be placed in front of a convex lens in order to get: **[2]**

(i) Enlarged real images.

(ii) Enlarged virtual image?

Answer

(i) In order to get an enlarged real image, the object should be placed between F_1 (ar f) and $2F_1$ (or 2f) distance ie. $2F_1 > u > F_1$

(ii) In order to get an enlarged virtual image, the object should be placed between F_1 and optical center i.t.

Question 2.(e)

A pond appears to be 2.7 m deep. If the refractive index of water is 4/3, find the actual depth of the band. **[2]**

Answer

Given,

apparent depth = 2.7 m

Refractive index of the water $= \frac{4}{3}$

Refractive index of the liquid $= \frac{\text{Actual depth}}{\text{Apparent depth}}$

$$\frac{4}{3} = \frac{\text{Actual depth}}{2.7}$$

$\Rightarrow$ Actual depth $= \frac{4}{3} \times 2.7 = 3.6$ m

Hence, actual depth = 3.6 m

Question 3.(a)

The wave lengths for the light red and blue colors are near 7.8×10^{-7} m and 4.8×10^{-7} m respectively. **[2]**

(i) Which color has the greater speed in a vacuum?

(ii) Which color has a greater speed in glass?

Answer

(i) The speed is the same for both colors in a vacuum because the velocity of light of all colors in a vacuum or air remains the same and it changes only when the medium changes.

(ii) The light of red color has greater speed in glass as it has a larger wavelength.

Question 3.(b)

Draw a graph between displacement from mean position and time for a body executing free vibration in a vacuum. **[2]**

Answer

Below is the graph between displacement from mean position and time for a body executing free vibration in a vacuum:

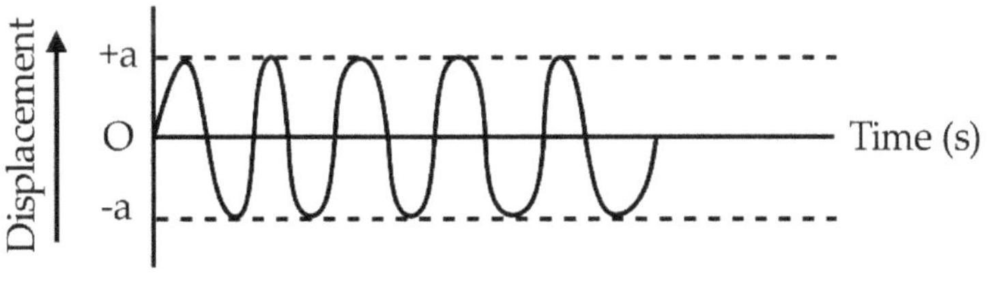

Question 3.(c)

A sound wave traveling in water has a wavelength of 0.4 m. Is this wave audible in the air? (The speed of sound in water = 1400 ms^{-1}) **[2]**

Answer

wavelength = 0.4 m

speed of sound in water = 1400 $m\ s^{-1}$

frequency of wave $= \frac{\text{Speed}}{\text{Wavelength}}$

frequency of wave $= \frac{1400}{0.4}$

frequency of wave = 3500 Hz = 3.5kHz

Hence, we get the frequency of wave = 3500 Hz and this lies in the audible range of frequency (i.e., 20 Hz to 20,000 Hz), hence it is audible.

Question 3.(d)

Why does a stone lying in the sun get heated up much more than water lying for the same duration of time? **[2]**

Answer

The stone lying in the sun gets heated up much more than water lying for the same duration of time because the specific heat capacity of water is much more than that of stone. With the same exposure to the sun, stone acquires higher temperatures due to its low specific heat capacity.

Question 3.(e)

Why is it not advisable to use a piece of copper wire as fuse wire in an electric circuit? **[2]**

Answer

It is not advisable to use a piece of copper wire as fuse wire in an electric circuit because due to its high conductivity, low specific resistance, and high melting point, copper does not melt when heated up and thus does not break the flow of current in the circuit. Thus, the purpose of the fuse wire will not get fulfilled.

Question 4.(a)

Calculate the total resistance across AB: **[2]**

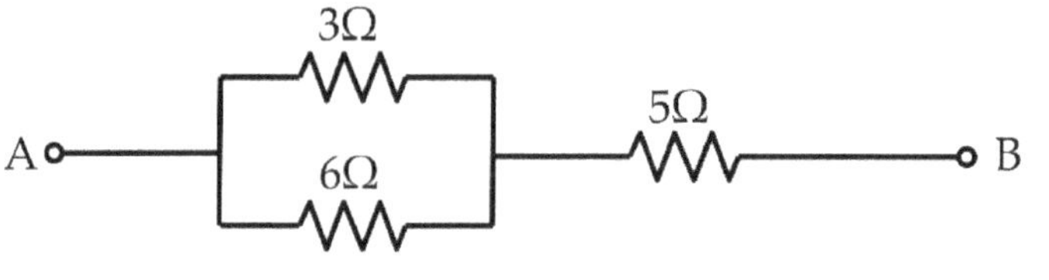

Answer

This circuit consists of two parts. In the first part, the resistances 3ohm and 6ohm are connected in parallel. If R_p is the equivalent resistance, then

$$\frac{1}{R_p} = \frac{1}{3} + \frac{1}{6}$$

$$\frac{1}{R_p} = \frac{2+1}{6}$$

$$\frac{1}{R_p} = \frac{3}{6}$$

$$\frac{1}{R_p} = \frac{1}{2}$$

$$\Rightarrow R_p = 2\Omega$$

In the second part, R_p (2ohm) and 5ohm are in series. If the equivalent resistance = R_5

$$R_5 = 2 + 5 = 7\Omega$$

Hence, equivalent resistance across A and B = 7Ω

Question 4.(b)

Two metallic blocks P and Q having masses in a ratio of 2: 1 are supplied with the same amount of heat. If their temperatures rise by the same degree, compare their specific heat capacities. **[2]**

Answer

The mass of block $P = m_p$ and mass of block $Q = m_Q$

Given,

$$\frac{m_p}{m_Q} = \frac{2}{1}$$

$$Q = m \times s \times \Delta t$$

Heat supplied (ΔQ) and rise in temperature (Δt) is the same for both block P and Q,

$$m_p \times s_p \times \Delta t = m_Q \times s_Q \times \Delta t$$

$$m_p \times s_p = m_Q \times s_Q$$

$$\frac{s_p}{s_Q} = \frac{m_Q}{m_p} = \frac{1}{2}$$

$$s_P : s_Q = 1:2$$

Question 4.(c)

When a current-carrying conductor is placed in a magnetic field, it experiences a mechanical force. What should be the angle between the magnetic field and the length of the conductor so that the force experienced is: **[2]**

(i) Zero

(ii) Maximum?

Answer

(i) In order to experience zero force, the conductor should be parallel to the magnetic field i.e., the angle between the length of the conductor and the magnetic field should be zero.

(ii) In order to experience maximum force, the conductor should be kept perpendicular to the magnetic field i.e., the angle between the length of the conductor and the magnetic field should be 90°.

Question 4.(d)

A nucleus $_{84}X^{202}$ of an element emits an alpha particle followed by a beta particle. The final nucleus is $_{a}Y^{b}$. Find a and b. **[2]**

Answer

The emission of alpha and beta particles is represented below:

$^{202}_{84}X \longrightarrow {}^{198}_{82}Z + {}^{4}_{2}He(\alpha$ particle emission $)$ $^{198}_{82}Z \longrightarrow {}^{198}_{83}Y + {}^{0}_{-1}e(\beta$ particle emission)

$\therefore a = 83$ and $b = 198$

Question 4.(e)

The diagram alongside shows a loop of wire carrying current I: **[2]**

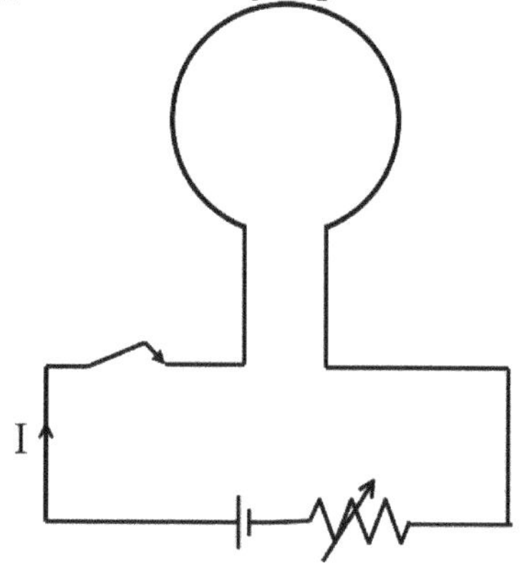

(i) What is the magnetic polarity of the loop that faces us?

(ii) With respect to the diagram, how can we increase the strength of the magnetic field produced by this loop?

Answer

(i) The magnetic polarity of the loop that faces us is the south pole as the current is in a clockwise direction.

(ii) We can increase the strength of the magnetic field produced by this loop by decreasing the value of variable resistance which in turn will increase the current I in the circuit.

SECTION - B (40 Marks)

(Attempt any four question)

Question 5.(a)

The figure alongside shows a simple pendulum of mass of 200 g. It is displaced from the mean position A to the extreme position B. The potential energy at position A is zero. At position B the pendulum bob is raised by 5 m. **[3]**

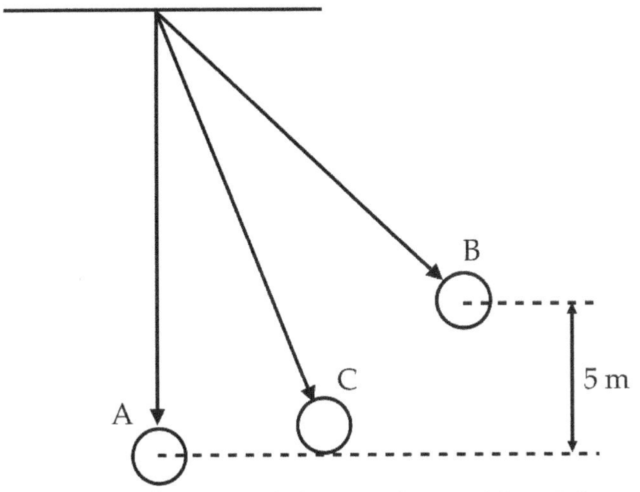

(i) What is the potential energy of the pendulum at the position B ?
(ii) What is the total mechanical energy at point C?
(iii) What is the speed of the bob at position A when released from B ?
(Take $g = 10\ ms^{-2}$ and there is no loss of energy.)

Answer

Given,

$$h = 5\ m,\ m = 200\ g = 0.2\ kg,\ g = 10\ ms^{-2}$$

(i) Potential energy U_B at B is given by

$$U_B = m \times g \times h$$
$$U_B = 0.2 \times 10 \times 5$$
$$\Rightarrow U_B = 10\ J$$

Hence, the potential energy of the pendulum at the position $B = 10$ J

(ii) Total mechanical energy at point C = 10 J

The total mechanical energy is the same at all points of the path due to the conservation of mechanical energy.

(iii) At A, bob has only kinetic energy which is equal to potential energy at B,

$$\frac{1}{2} \times m \times (v_A)^2 = U_B$$
$$0.5 \times 0.2 \times (v_A)^2 = 10$$
$$(v_A)^2 = \frac{10}{0.1}$$
$$\Rightarrow v_A = \sqrt{100}$$
$$\Rightarrow v_A = 10\ m/s$$

Question 5.(b)

(i) With reference to the direction of action, how does a centripetal force differ from a centrifugal force during uniform circular motion? **[3]**
(ii) Is centrifugal force the force of reaction of centripetal force?
(iii) Compare the magnitudes of centripetal and centrifugal force.

Answer

(i) Centripetal force always acts towards the center of the circle along its radius. It is this force that compels the body to move along the circular path. A centrifugal force appears to act away (outward) from the center of a circular path. Thus, the two forces act in opposite directions.

(ii) No, the centrifugal force is not the force of reaction of centripetal force.

(iii) Centripetal force and centrifugal force have equal magnitudes.

Question 5.(c)

A block and tackle system of pulleys has a velocity ratio of 5. **[4]**

(i) Draw a neat, labeled diagram of the system indicating the points of application and direction of load and effort.

(ii) What will be its V.R. if the weight of the movable block is doubled?

Answer

(i) A labeled diagram of the system with direction and points of application of load and effort marked is shown below:

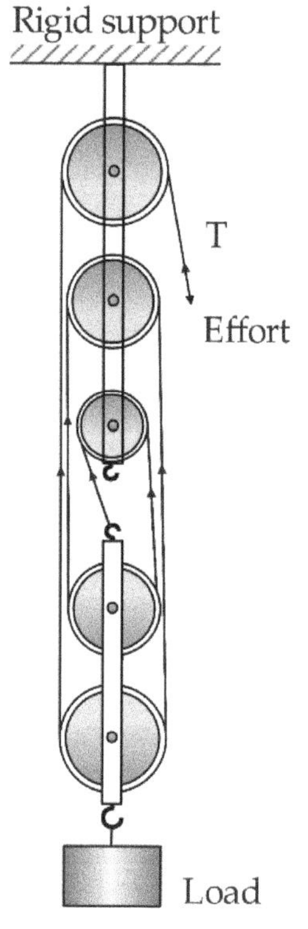

(ii) An increase in the weight of the movable block does not affect the velocity ratio.
Therefore, V.R. = 5

Question 6.(a)

A diver in the water looks obliquely at an object AB in the air. **[3]**

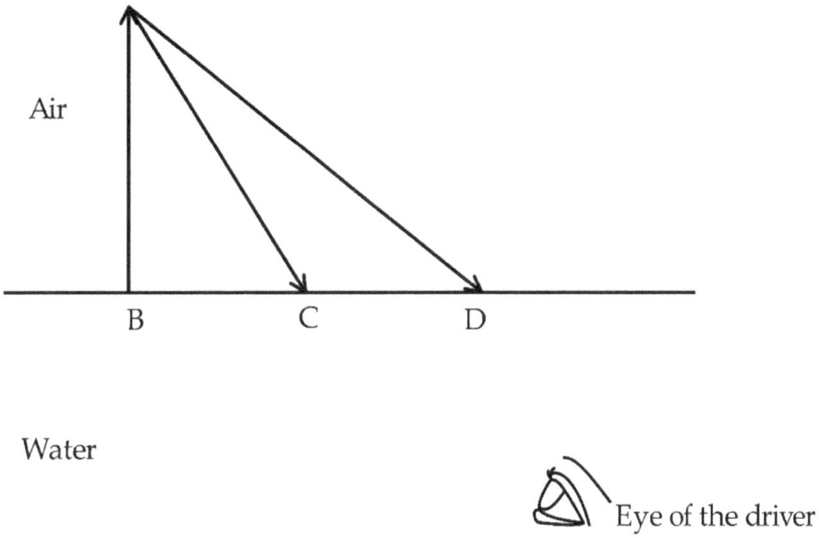

(i) Does the object appear taller, shorter, or of the same size as the diver?

(ii) Show the path of two rays AC & AD starting from the tip of the object as it travels towards the diver in the water and hence obtains the image of the object.

Answer

(i) The object appears taller than the diver.

(ii) Below diagram shows the path of two rays AC&AD :

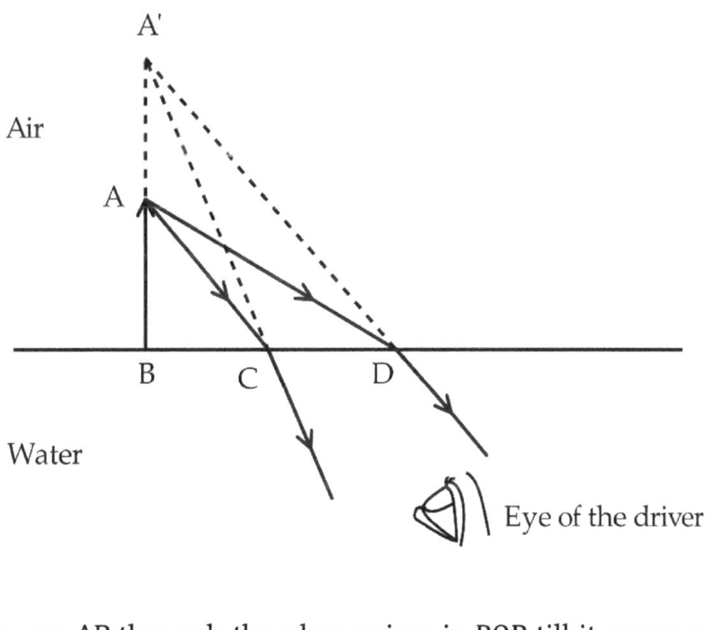

Question 6.(b)

Complete the path of the ray AB through the glass prism in POR till it emerges out of the prism. Given the critical angle of the glass as 42°. **[3]**

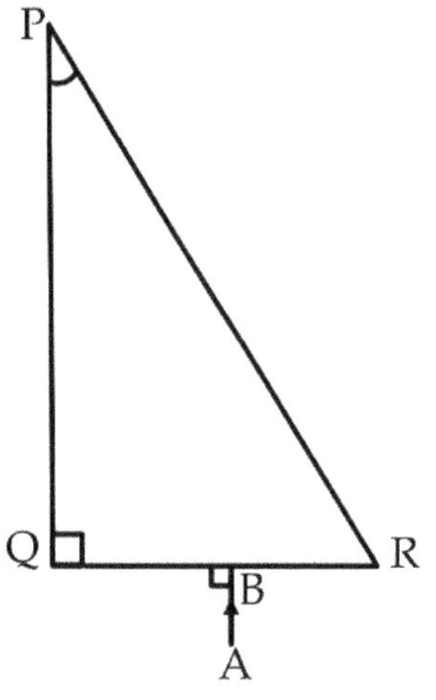

Answer

The path of the ray *AB* through the glass prism in PQR till it emerges out of the prism is shown below:

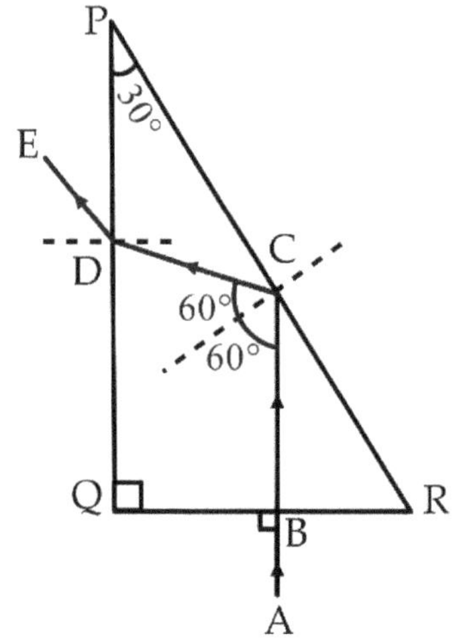

Note that the total internal reflection takes place at C.

Question 6.(c)

A lens of a focal length of 20 cm forms an inverted image at a distance of 60 cm from the lens. **[4]**

(i) Identify the lens.
(ii) How far is the lens present in front of the object?
(iii) Calculate the magnification of the image.

Answer

(i) The lens used is convex.
(ii) Given, $f = +20$ cm, $v = +60$ cm, u =?
From the lens formula,

$$\frac{1}{f} = \frac{1}{v} - \frac{1}{u}$$

Substituting the values in the formula,

$$\frac{1}{20} = \frac{1}{60} - \frac{1}{u}$$
$$\Rightarrow \frac{1}{u} = \frac{1}{60} - \frac{1}{20}$$
$$\Rightarrow \frac{1}{u} = \frac{1-3}{60}$$
$$\Rightarrow \frac{1}{u} = \frac{-2}{60}$$
$$\Rightarrow u = -30 \text{ cm}$$

Hence, the lens If 30 cm In front of the object

(iii) Magnification $m = \frac{v}{u}$

Substituting the values in the formula above we get,

$$m = \frac{60}{-30} = -2$$

Thus, magnification = 2 times

Question 7.(a)

Give reasons for the following: **[3]**

During the day:

(i) Clouds appear white.

(ii) The sky appears blue.

Answer

(i) Clouds are dust particles and water molecules suspended in the atmosphere near the earth of size bigger than the wavelength of visible light. Thus, they scatter all colors of incident white light from the sun to the same extent, and hence where scattered light reaches our eyes, the clouds appear white.

(ii) The air molecules in the atmospheres scatter the blue sand of the spectrum and have shorter wavelengths much more than colors be the red end. In the absence of direct light from the sun, the light reaching our eyes is the scattered light which is rich in blue color. Hence, light from all directions of the sky being rich in blue color makes the sky' appear blue.

Question 7.(b)

(i) Name the system which enables us to locate underwater objects by transmitting ultrasonic waves and detecting the reflecting impulse. **[3]**

(ii) What are acoustically measurable quantities related to pitch and loudness?

Answer

(i) The system which enables us to locate underwater objects by transmitting ultrasonic waves and detecting the reflecting impulse is called sound navigation and rang ling or SONAR. Here, ultrasonic waves from a ship are transmitted in all directions. The reflected waves received in the receiver give the distance and position of the object (e,g, suámarine, etc.) in water.

(ii) The acoustically measurable quantity related to pitch is the frequency and loudness is an Intensity of sound.

Question 7.(c)

(i) When a tuning fork is held close to the ear, one hears a faint hum. The same is held such that its stern is in contact with the table surface, then one hears a loud sound. Explain. **[4]**

(ii) A man standing in front of a vertical cliff fires a gun. He hears the echo after 3.5 seconds. On moving closer to the cliff by 84 m, he hears the echo after 3 seconds. Calculate the distance of the cliff from the initial position of the man.

Answer

(i) When the stern of the tuning fork is placed in contact with a tabletop, it sets the table surface in small vibrators but a large number of air molecules in contact with the table surface also start vibrating, there producing a loud sound.

(ii) Let the man be starting at distance d from the diff and v be the speed of sound in air.

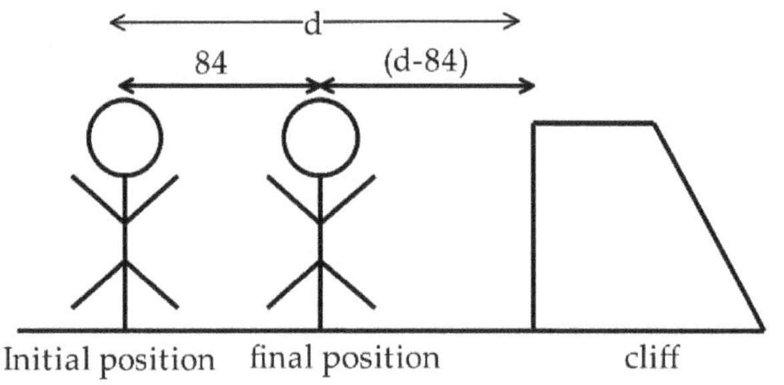

Fur first echo, $t_1 = \frac{2d}{v} = 3.5$ s [Eqn I]

and for the second echo, $t_2 = \frac{2(d-84)}{v} = 3$ s [Eqn II]

Dividing Eqn. (II) by Eqn. (I)

$$\frac{\frac{2(\text{d}-84)}{\text{y}}}{\frac{2\text{ d}}{\text{v}}} = \frac{3}{3.5}$$

$$\Rightarrow \frac{\text{d}-84}{\text{d}} = \frac{3}{3.5}$$

$$= 3.5(\text{ d}-84) = 3\text{ d}$$

$$\Rightarrow (3.5\text{ d}) - (3.5 \times 84) = 3\text{ d}$$

$$\Rightarrow (3.5d) - 3d = 294$$

$$\Rightarrow 0.5\text{ d} = 294$$

$$\Rightarrow \text{d} = \frac{294}{0.5}$$

$$\Rightarrow \text{d} = 588\text{ m}$$

Hence, the distance of the cliff from the initial position of the man = 588 m

Question 8.(a)

The diagram below shows the core of a transformer and its input and output connections **[3]**

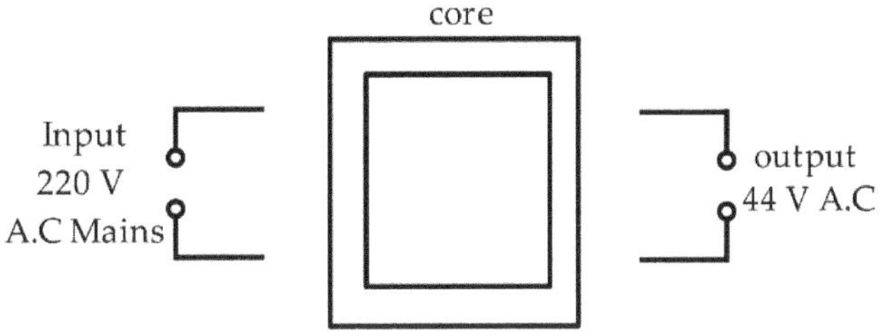

(i) State the material used for the care.

(ii) Copy and complete the diagram of the transformer by drawing input and output coils.

Answer

(i) The core is made up of soft Iron.

(ii) The completed diagram of the transformer is shown below:

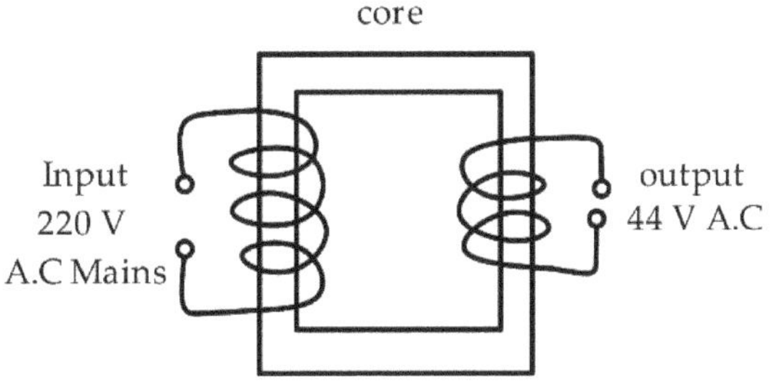

Question 8.(b)

(i) What are superconductors? **[3]**

(ii) Calculate the current drawn by an appliance rated 110 W, 220 V when connected across a 220 V supply.

(iii) Name a substance whose resistance decreases with the increase in temperature.

Answer

(i) A superconductor is a substance of zero resistance (or infinite conductance) at a very low temperature.

(ii) For the given appliance, $P = 110$ W, V = 220 V

$\therefore$ Current $I = \frac{P}{V} = \frac{110}{220} = 0.5$ A

Hence, the current drawn by the appliance = 0.5 A

(iii) The resistance of semiconductors such as carbon, silicon, etc., decreases with an increase in temperature.

Question 8.(c)

The diagram alongside Shaw's three resistors connected across a cell of e.m.f. 1.8 V and internal resistance r. Calculate: **[4]**

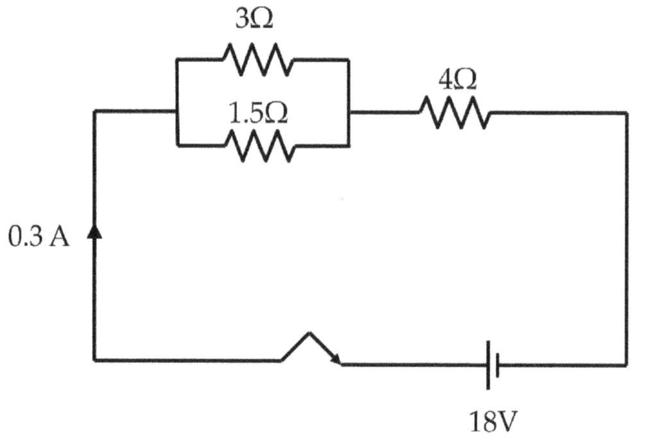

(i) Current through 3Ω resister.
(ii) The internal resistance r.

Answer

(i) The equivalent resistance R_p of resistances, 3Ω and 1.5Ω joined in parallel is given by

$$\frac{1}{R_p} = \frac{1}{3} + \frac{2}{3}\left[\because 1.5\Omega = \frac{3}{2}\Omega\right]$$

$$\Rightarrow \frac{1}{R_p} = \frac{3}{3}$$

$$\Rightarrow R_p = 1\Omega$$

From $\quad V = IR$

the potential drop across this combination $= 0.3 \times 1 = 0.3$ V

$\therefore$Current through 3Ω resistance $= \frac{\text{Voltage}}{\text{Resistance}}$

$$= \frac{0.3}{3} = 0.1 \text{ A}$$

(ii) The total resistance of the circuit $= R_\rho + 4 + r = (5 + r)\Omega$

Current in the circuit,

$$0.3 = \frac{1.8}{5+r}$$

$$0.3 \times (5 + r) = 1.8$$

$$(0.3 \times 5) + (0.3 \times r) = 1.8$$

$$1.5 + (0.3 \times r) = 1.8$$

$$0.3 \times r = 1.8 - 1.5$$

$$r = \frac{0.3}{0.3} = 10$$

Question 9.(a)

(i) Define the heat capacity of a substance. **[3]**

(ii) Write the SI unit of heat capacity.

(iii) What is the relationship between heat capacity and the specific heat capacity of a substance?

Answer

(i) The heat required to raise the temperature of a substance in a body through 1 °C (or 1 K) is called its heat capacity.

(ii) S.I. unit of heat capacity is J^oC^{-1} or JK^{-1}

(iii) Specific heat capacity $= \frac{\text{Heat capacity}}{\text{Mass of body or substance}}$

Question 9.(b)

The diagram below shows the change of phases of a substance on a temperature vs time graph and heating the substance at a constant rate. **[3]**

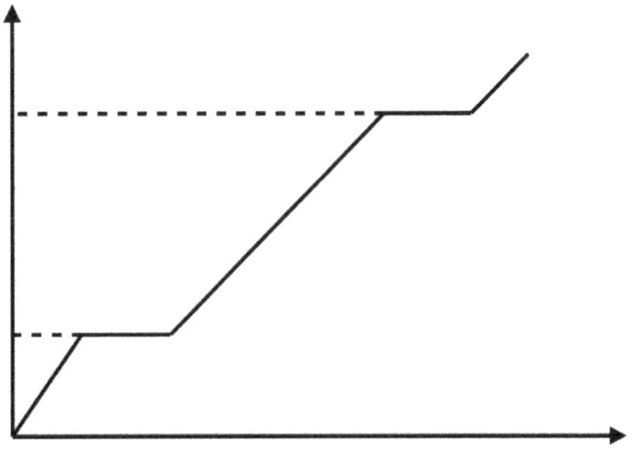

(i) Why is the slope of CD less than the slope of AB?

(ii) What is the boiling and melting point of the substance?

Answer

(i) In part CD, the rate of rising in temperature is slow as the substance in this phase has high specific heat capacity while the temperature rises rapidly in part AB (so higher slope) as the substance has lower specific heat capacity in this phase. The different specific heat capacities are distributed to different phases of state i.e., solid and liquid phases.

(ii) The boiling point of a substance is t_2 and a melting point of a substance is t_1

Question 9.(c)

A piece of ice of mass 60 g is dropped into 140 g of water at 50°C. **[4]**

Calculate the final temperature of the water where all the ice has melted. {Assume no heat is lost to the surrounding}.

Specific heat capacity of water (c) $= 4.2 Jg^{-1}\ km^{-1}$,

Specific latent heat of fusion of ice $(L) = 336 Jg^{-1}$

Answer

Let the final temperature of water be T" "C.

Heat energy is taken by the ice to melt at 0 " C

Q_1 = mass of ice specific latent heat of fusion in ice

$$= 60 \times 336 = 20{,}160 \text{ J}$$

Heat energy taken by the melted ice ta raise its temperature from 0°C in T °C.

Q_2 = mass of ice specific heat capacity of water x rise in temperature

$$= 60 \times 4.2 \times (\text{T} - 0) = 252 \text{ T}J$$

Total heat energy is taken by ice $= Q_1 + O_2$

$$= (20{,}160 + 252T)\text{J}$$

Heat energy is given by water in fall of its temperature from 50°C in T°C

= mass of water *x* specific heat capacity of water *x* fall in temperature

$$= 140 \times 4.2 \times (50 - T)$$
$$= 588(50 - T)\text{J}$$

If there is no heat loss,

heat energy is given by water = total heat energy taken by the ice

Substituting the values we get,

$$588(50 - T) = 20{,}160 + 252T$$
$$(588 \times 50) - 588\text{ T} = 20{,}160 + 252\text{ T}$$
$$29{,}400 - 588\text{ T} = 20.160 + 252\text{ T}$$
$$29.400 - 20.160 = 588\text{ T} + 252\text{ T}$$
$$9240 = 840T$$
$$\Rightarrow \text{T} = \frac{9240}{840}$$
$$\Rightarrow \text{T} = 11°\text{C}$$

Hence: $T = 11°\text{C}$

Question 10. (a)

(i) Draw a neat, labeled diagram of a d.c. motor. **[3]**

(ii) Writer any one use of a d.c. motor.

Answer

(i) Below is the labeled diagram of a d.c. motor.

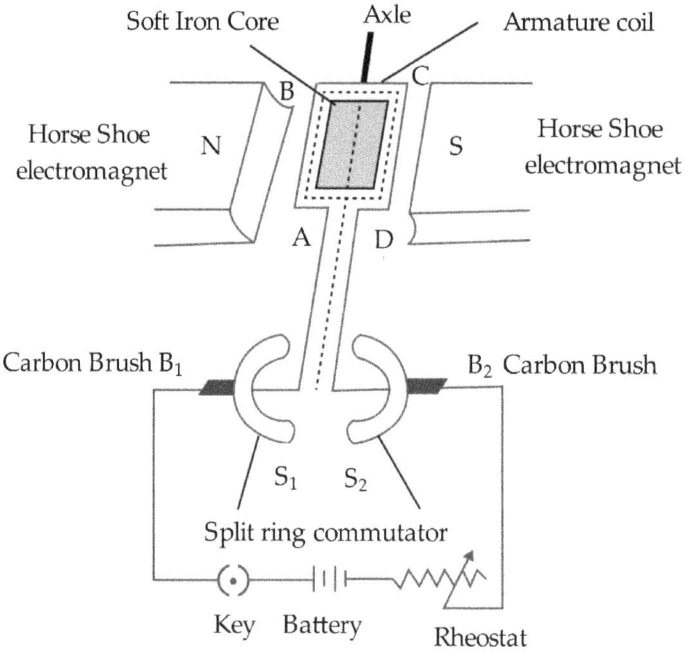

(ii) it is used to produce rotational motion in appliances like fans, mixers, grinders, washing machines, etc.

Question 10. (b)

(i) Differentiate between nuclear fusion and nuclear fission. **[3]**

(ii) State safety precautions in the disposal of nuclear waste.

Answer

(i) The difference between nuclear fusion and nuclear fission is as follows:

Nuclear fusion	Nuclear fission
Nuclear fusion is the process of combining light nuclei to form a larger nucleus at a very high temperature and pressure with the release of energy	Nuclear fission is the process of breaking a heavy nucleus into two nearly equal fragments with the release of energy.
This reaction is possible only at a very high temperature ($\approx 10^7$ K) and very pressure.	This reaction is possible at ordinary temperature and ordinary pressure.

(ii) The nuclear waste should be enclosed in thick casks and buried in deep underground places far from populated areas as they can be horror.

Question 10. (c)

An atomic nucleus A is composed of 84 protons and 128 neutrons. The nucleus A emits an alpha particle and is transformed in a nucleus B. **[4]**

(i) What is the composition of 8?

(ii) The nucleus B emits a β partied and is transformed into a nucleus C. What is the composition of C?

(iii) What is the mass number of nucleus A?

(iv) Does the composition of C change if it emits gammas radiation?

Answer

(i) After the permission of an alpha particle from A the resulting nucleus B has 2 protons and 2 neutrons Less than the part nucleus (i.e., A), therefore, the nucleus B has:
No. of proton = 82
No of neutron = 126

(ii) After the emission of a beta particle from B, the resulting nucleus C 1 proton more and 1 neutron less than the part nucleus (i.e., B) therefore, the nucleus C has:
Na. of portion = 83
Na. of neutron = 125

(iii) The mass number of the nucleus $A = (84 + 128) = 212$.

(iv) No, the composition of a nucleus does not change if it emits gamma radiation.

SEMESTER 1 EXAMINATION
PREVIOUS YEAR PAPER-2022
PHYSICS
(SCIENCE PAPER - 1)

Maximum Marks: 40

Time allowed: Two hours

Answers to this Paper must be written on the paper provided separately.

You will not be allowed to write during first 15 minutes.

This time is to be spent in reading the question paper.

The time given at the head of this Paper is the time allowed for writing the answers.

SECTION A is compulsory. Attempt any four questions from SECTION B.
The intended marks for questions or parts of questions are given in brackets [].

SECTION – A (40 Marks)
(Answer all the questions from this SECTION)

Question 1.

(i) Choose the correct statement with respect to Refraction of light **[1]**

(a) The color always changes when light enters from one optical medium to another.

(b) The absorption of light when it strikes the surface of a medium is refraction.

(c) Speed of light changes when it enters from one optical medium to another of different optical densities.

(d) Speed of light does not change when it enters from one optical medium to another of different optical density.

Answer. (c)

(ii) When a light ray enters from a denser medium to a rarer medium **[1]**

(a) The light ray bends towards the normal.

(b) The angle of incidence is less than the angle of refraction.

(c) Speed of light decreases.

(d) The speed of light remains unchanged.

Answer. (b)

(iii) In the diagram shown below: **[1]**

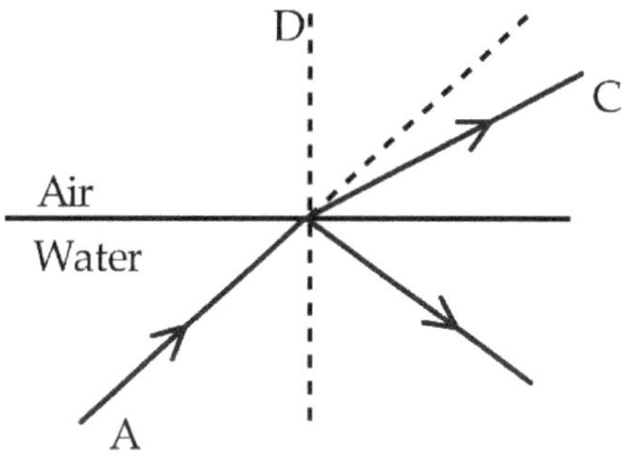

(a) B is an incident ray and C is refracted ray.
(b) A is an incident ray and B is refracted ray.
(c) C is an incident ray and B is refracted ray.
(d) A is an incident ray and C is refracted ray.
Answer. (d)

(iv) From the diagram shown below, identify the characteristics of the image that will be formed. **[1]**

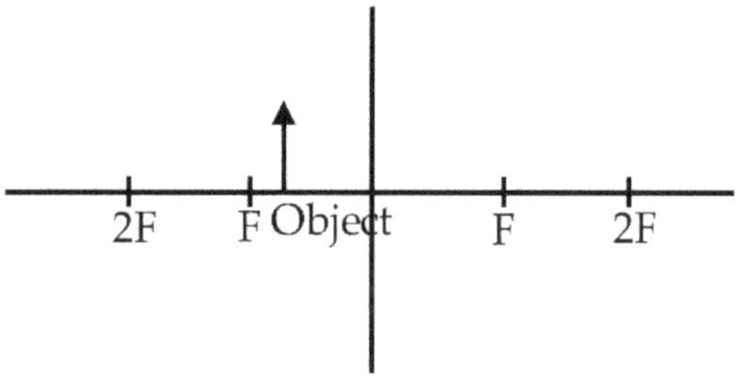

(a) Real.
(b) Diminished.
(c) Formed within the focal length.
(d) Virtual.
Answer. (d)

(v) The wavelength of light in medium A is 600 nm. The wave enters a medium B of the refractive index of 1.5 **[2]**
Steps to find the wavelength of light in medium B is given below. Choose an option that has the correct sequence of steps, to find the wavelength.
I. $\lambda = 1.5 \times 600$
II. $\lambda = \frac{600}{1.5}$
III. $\lambda = 400$ nm
IV. $\lambda = 900$ nm
V. $1.5 = \frac{\lambda}{600}$
(a) I. then III.
(b) II. then III.
(c) I. then IV.

(d) III, I. then IV.

(e) V. then IV.

Answer. (b)

(vi) The diagram below shows an image formed at a distance of 36 cm from the lens LL' ' of focal length 12 cm. With respect to this answer the questions that follow. **[4]**

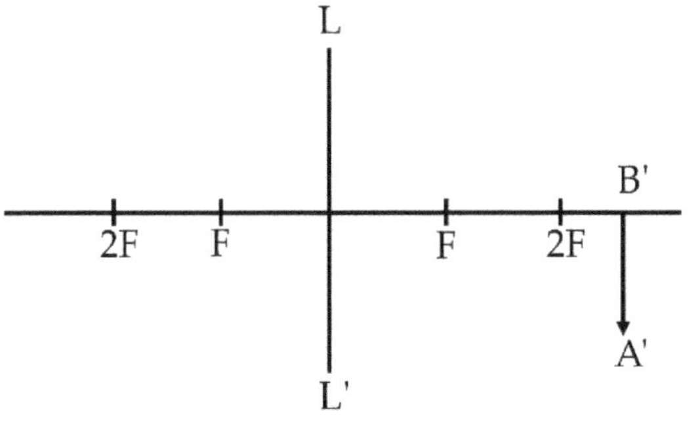

(i) The position of the object on the left-hand side should be

(a) Between 12 cm to 30 cm from the lens.

(b) Beyond 24 cm from the lens.

(c) Between 12 cm to 24 cm from the lens.

(d) Within 12 cm from the lens.

Answer. (b)

(ii) The power of this lens is

(a) -8.33D

(b) $+8.4$D

(c) $+8.33$D

(d) -8.4D

Answer. (c)

(iii) The object distance with sign convention is

(a) -18 cm

(b) -15 cm

(c) -9 cm

(d) $+18$ cm

Answer. (a)

(iv) If the lens L.L' is replaced by another lens of the same type but the focal length of 15 cm then for the same object distance

(a) The size of the image decreases.

(b) The size of the image increases.

(c) The size of the image remains the same.

(d) Information is insufficient to conclude.

Answer. (b)

Question 2.

(i) The usable form of mechanical energy is **[1]**

(a) Elastic potential energy

(b) Kinetic energy

(c) Gravitational potential energy

(d) None of the given options.

Answer. (b)

(ii) One horsepower is equal to **[1]**

(a) 100 W

(b) 735 W

(c) 764 W

(d) 746 W

Answer. (d)

(iii) If A and B of the same mass can climb the third floor of the same building in 3 minutes and 5 minutes respectively, then the ratio of their powers of A is to B in an ideal situation is **[1]**

(a) 1:1

(b) 3: 5

(c) The information is insufficient to form a conclusion.

(d) 5: 3

Answer. (d)

(iv) If the center of gravity of a meter scale of mass 80 g lies at the 45 cm mark, then which one of the following diagrams will show the balanced position of the scale?

(a) 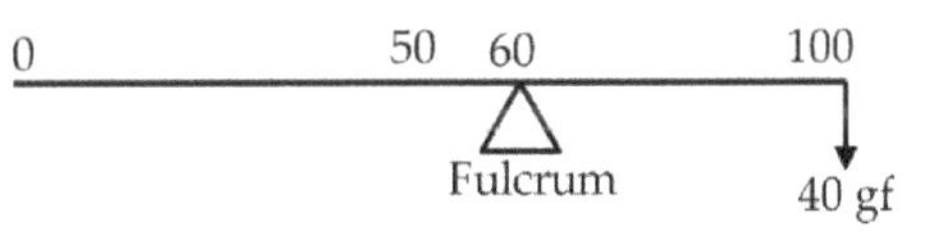

(b) 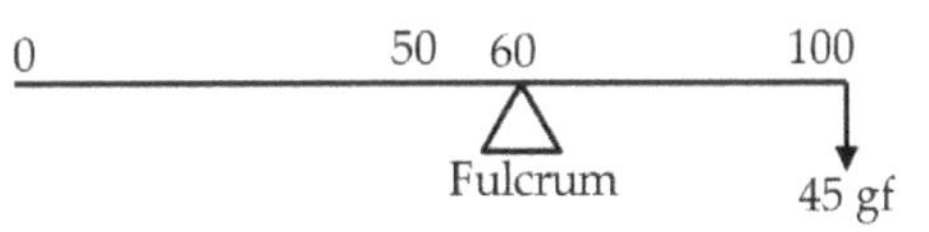

(c) 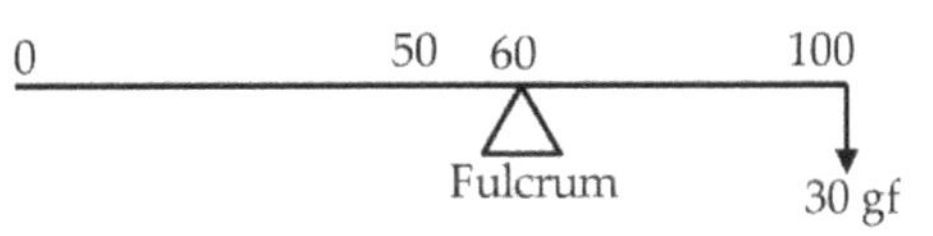

(d) 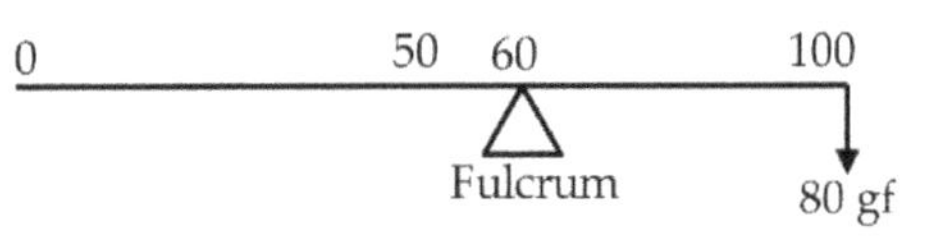

Answer. (c)

(v) A body has a kinetic energy of 250 J. If the mass of the body is 5 kg, then choose its velocity and momentum from the following options. **[2]**

(a) 50 m/s
(b) 50 kg. m/s
(c) 20 kg. m/s
(d) 15 m/s
(e) 10 m/s
(f) 100 kg. m/s
Answer. (b)

(vi) A girl at rest at the gate of her society which is 3.2 m above the road comes down the slope AB on a cycle without paddling. [g = 10 N/kg] **[4]**

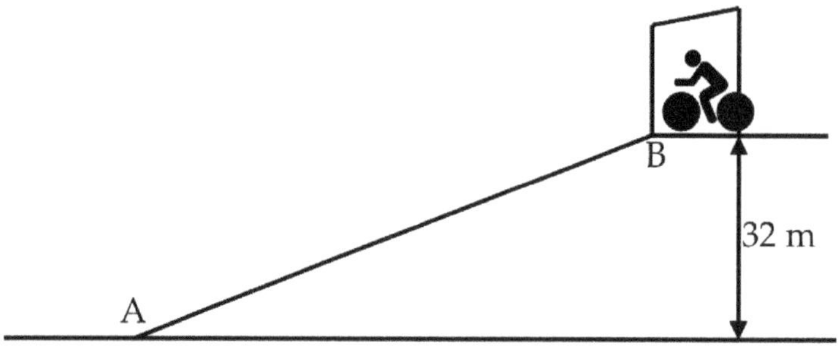

(i) The mechanical energy possessed by the girl at B is
(a) Vibrational kinetic energy.
(b) Translational kinetic energy
(c) Elastic potential energy.
(d) Gravitational potential energy.
Answer. (d)

(ii) The velocity with which the girl reaches point A is
(a) 32 m/s
(b) 10 m/s
(c) 8 m/s
(d) Insufficient information to calculate velocity.
Answer. (c)

(iii) If the mass of the girl is 40 kg then the kinetic energy of the girl at A is [Assuming no loss of energy.]
(a) 1280 J
(b) 1600 J
(c) 400 J
(d) 3200 J
Answer. (a)

(iv) The potential energy of the girl (of mass 40 kg) when she reaches the midpoint of the slope of AB

(a) 800 J

(b) 200 J

(c) 1600 J

(d) 640 J

Answer. (d)

Question 3.

(i) Mechanical advantage (M.A.), load(L), and effort(E) are related as **[1]**

(a) M.A. = LXE

(b) M.A. = E/L

(c) M.A. XE = L

(d) M.A. XL = E

Answer. (c)

(ii) Which one of the following statements is correct? **[1]**

(a) A machine is used to have more output energy as compared to input energy.

(b) The mechanical advantage of a machine can never be greater than 1.

(c) If a machine gives the convenience of direction, then its mechanical advantage should be greater than 1.

(d) For a given design of a machine, even if the mechanical advantage increases, the velocity ratio remains the same.

Answer. (d)

(iii) If a block and tackle system with a convenient direction has 3 movable pulleys, then its velocity ratio

(a) Is either 6 or 7

(b) Should be 6

(c) Should be 7

(d) Is 3

(e) None of these

Answer. (e)

(iv) Work done by a body moving on a circular track is zero at every instant because **[1]**

(a) Displacement is zero.

(b) Displacement is perpendicular to the centripetal force.

(c) There is no force acting.

(d) The reason is not mentioned in the other options.

Answer. (b)

(v) Identify the conditions required to hear a clear and distinct echo by humans, in the air **[2]**

(a) The reflecting surface should be rough.
(b) The size of the reflecting surface should be smaller than the wavelength of sound.
(c) Sound should not be reflected back within 0.1 s.
(d) The incident sound should have a frequency of more than 25000 Hz.
(e) The size of the reflecting surface should be larger than the wavelength of sound.
Answer. (e)

(vi) A person standing in front of a vertical cliff fires a gun and hears its echo in 3 s. The speed of sound in air is 340 m/s **[4]**

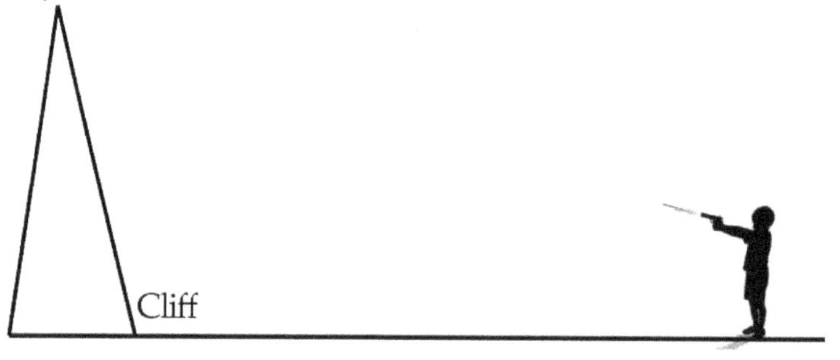

(i) Calculate the distance at which the person is standing in front of the cliff. Steps are given to calculate the distance. Select the correct sequence of the steps from the given options:

I. $340 = \frac{2d}{3}$
II. $340 = \frac{d}{3}$
III. $d = 170 \times 2 = 510$ m
IV. $d = 340 \times 3 = 1020$ m
(a) (ii) then (iv)
(b) (iii) then (ii)
(c) (i) then (iii)
(d) (iii) then (i)
(e) then (iv)
Answer. (c)

(ii) If the speed of sound changes to 350 m/s then how much distance should the person move towards or away from the cliff in order to hear the echo at the same time? Steps are given to calculate the distance. Select the correct sequence of the steps from the given option.

I. $\frac{340+350}{2} = \frac{2d}{3}$
II. $350 - 340 = \frac{2d}{3}$
III. $d = \frac{345 \times 3}{2} = 517.5$ m
IV. $d = \frac{30}{2} = 15$ m
V. 7.5 m
(a) II. , III. Then V.
(b) IV. then II.

(c) IV. then V.
(d) II. then IV.
(e) I. , IV. , and V.
Answer. (d)

Question 4.

(i) Assuming all lenses shown below are of the same material, state which lens has the maximum power. **[1]**

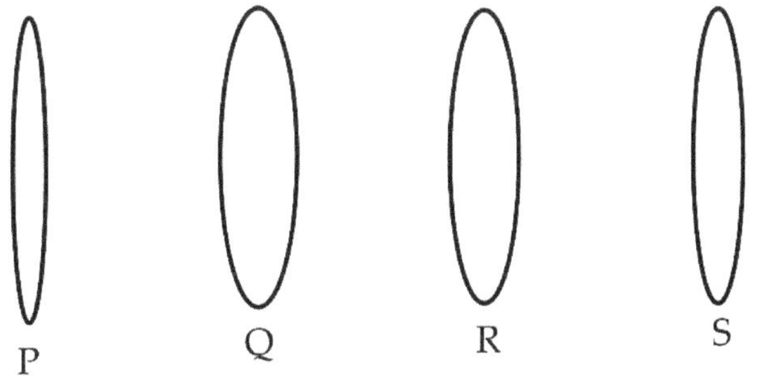

(a) R
(b) P
(c) Q
(d) S
Answer. (c)

(ii) In an electric cell while in use, the change in energy is from: **[1]**
(a) Chemical to mechanical
(b) Chemical to electrical
(c) Electrical to mechanical
(d) Electrical to chemical
Answer. (b)

(iii) The diagram below shows a pendulum having a bob of mass of 80 g. A and C are extreme positions and B is the mean position. The bob has a velocity 5 m/s at position B. Assuming there is no loss of energy, select the correct statements from the options given below: **[2]**

[g = 10 N/kg]

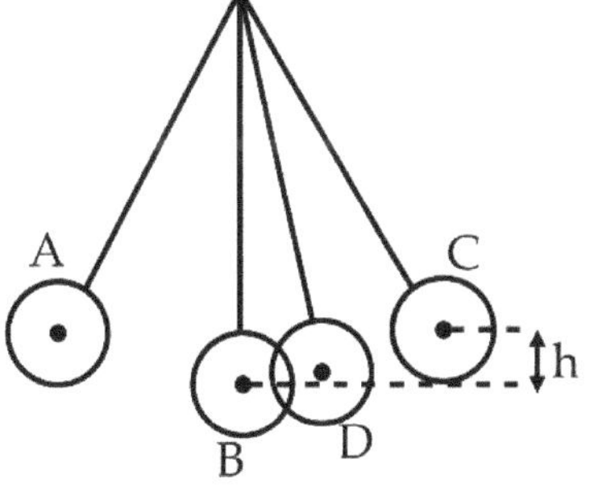

(a) At point A the bob will have only kinetic energy.

(b) The maximum potential energy gained by the bob will be $1000J$.
(c) The maximum height ' h ' reached by the bob will be 125 cm.
(d) At point D the bob will have maximum kinetic energy.
(e) The maximum potential energy gained by the bob will be 1 J
(f) At point B the energy possessed by the bob is 1000 J.
Answer. (c)

(iv) Select correct options for Total internal reflection in a medium. **[2]**
(a) Can take place in an optically denser medium as compared to an optically rarer medium.
(b) Takes place for any angle of incidence greater than 42 degrees.
(c) This reflection does not obey the laws of reflection.
(d) Can take place if the angle of incidence in a denser medium is more than the critical angle.
Answer. (a)

(v) The diagram shows the path of light through a right-angled prism of a critical angle 42°. Observe the diagram and answer the questions that follow. **[4]**

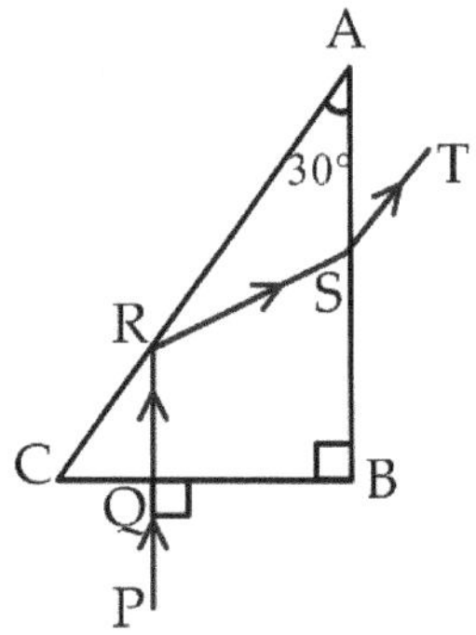

(i) The phenomenon at the surface AC is
(a) Refraction
(b) Partial reflection
(c) Total internal reflection
(d) Scattering
Answer. (c)

(ii) The angle of incidence at the surface AC is
(a) 30°
(b) 45°
(c) 0°
(d) 60°
Answer. (a)

(iii) The angle of incidence at the surface AB is
(a) 30°
(b) 0°
(c) 45°

(d) 60°

Answer. (d)

(iv) Which of the following statement is wrong?

(a) Speed of light ray PQ is equal to the speed of light ray ST.

(b) Speed of light ray QR is equal to the speed of light ray RS.

(c) Speed of light ray *PQ* is greater than the speed of light ray RS.

(d) Speed of light ray RQ is greater than the speed of light ray ST.

Answer. (d)

SEMESTER 2 EXAMINATION

Previous Year Paper 2022

(SCIENCE PAPER - 1)

Maximum Marks: 40

Time allowed: One and a half hour

Answers to this Paper must be written on the paper provided separately.

You will not be allowed to write during first 15 minutes.

This time is to be spent in reading the question paper.

The time given at the head of this Paper is the time allowed for writing the answers.

SECTION A is compulsory. Attempt any four questions from SECTION B.

The intended marks for questions or parts of questions are given in brackets [ ].

SECTION – A (40 Marks)

(Answer all the questions from this SECTION)

Question 1.

Choose the correct answers to the questions from the given options. (Do not copy the question. Write the correct answer only.)

(i) Free vibrations are:

(a) The vibrations under the influence of a periodic force

(b) The vibrations with larger amplitude

(c) The vibrations when the frequency continuously decreases

(d) The vibrations with a constant frequency and constant amplitude

Answer: (d)

(ii) The diagram below shows four sound waves. Which sound has the highest pitch?

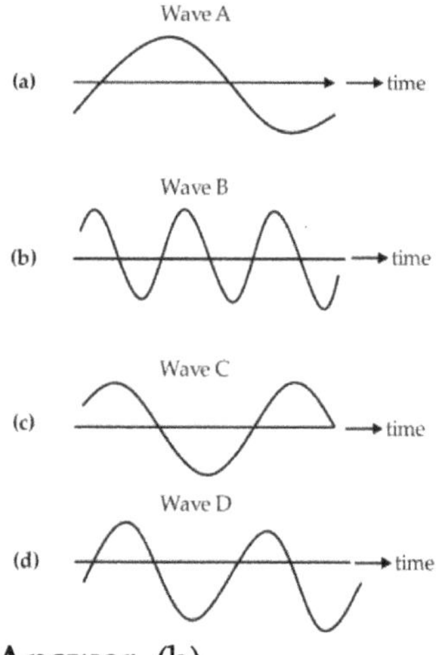

Answer. (b)

(iii) The graph plotted for potential difference (V) against the current (I) for ohmic resistors is:

(a) A curve passing through the origin

(b) A straight line not passing through origin

(c) A straight line passing through origin

(d) A circle centered at the origin

Answer. (c)

(iv) A main switch in the main distribution board is present in:

(a) A live wire

(b) A neutral wire

(c) A live as well as a neutral wire

(d) An earth wires

Answer. (c)

(v) A conductor AB is kept along north-south direction of the earth above a magnetic needle as Shown below. When the key K is closed then:

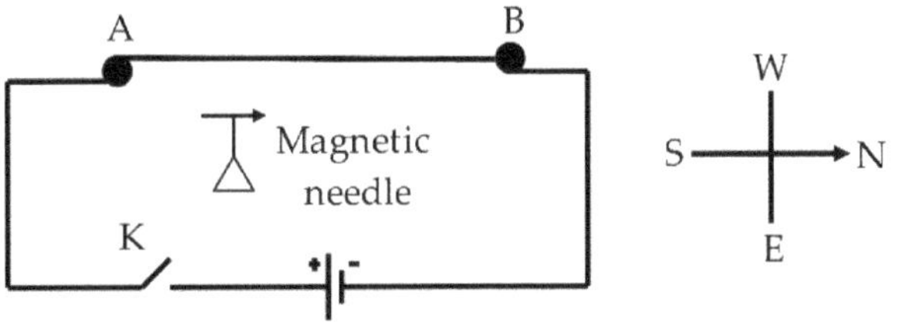

(a) The needle will not show any deflection

(b) The needle will deflect toward east

(c) The needle will turn in the opposite direction i.e. Toward the south

(d) The needle will deflect towards west.

Answer. (d)

(vi) A coil wound around a piece of soft iron can become an electromagnet only when:

(a) The circuit is open

(b) A magnetic compass is present in the vicinity

(c) A galvanometer is connected to the circuit

(d) A current flow in the circuit.

Answer. (d)

(vii) If water absorbs 4000 joule heat to increase the temperature of 1 kg water through, 1°C then The specific heat capacity of water is:

(a) $4 Jkg^{-1}\,°C^{-1}$

(b) $400 Jg^{-1}\,°C^{-1}$

(c) $4 Jg^{-1}\,°C^{-1}$

(d) $4.2 Jg^{-10}C^{-1}$

Answer. (c)

(viii) Water is used in car radiators because:

(a) It is a good conductor of heat.

(b) It conducts heat faster as compared to the other substances and cools the engine quickly.

(c) Its specific heat capacity is very low.

(d) Its specific heat capacity is very high so it can cool the engine without a greater increase in its own temperature,

Answer. (d)

(ix) The heaviest nuclear radiation is:

(a) X-radiation

(b) α-radiation

(c) γ-radiation

(d) β-radiation

Answer. (b)

(x) To study the age of excavated material of archaeological significance we study the rate of Decay of an isotope of:

(a) Uranium

(b) Cobalt

(c) Carbon

(d) Chlorine

Answer. (c)

SECTION – B (40 Marks)

(Attempt any three questions from this SECTION.)

Question 2.

(i) The diagram below shows a magnetic compass kept closer to a coil AB wound around hollow cylindrical cardboard:

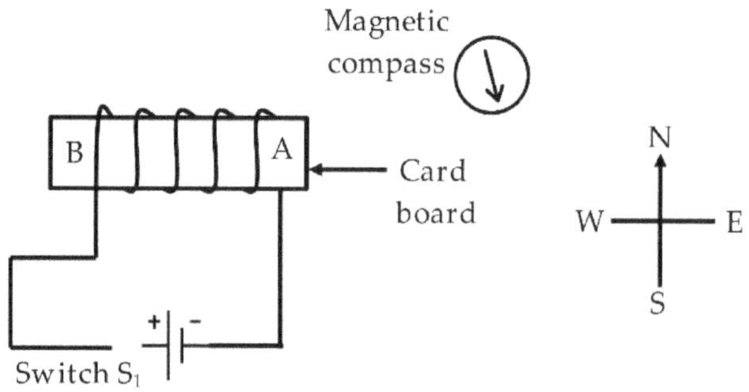

(a) After studying the circuit and the magnetic compass carefully, state whether the switch S_1 Is open or closed?

(b) How did you arrive at the conclusion in?

(c) What is the purpose of placing the magnetic compass in the above setup?

Answer.

(a) Switch S_1 Is closed.

(b) Magnetic compass shows no deflection due to which we can say that no current **Is** flowing through the solenoid.

(c) To check whether the magnetic field produces or not.

(ii) **(a)** Give an important reason for copper to be used as a material for a calorimeter. **[3]**

(b) Calculate the thermal capacity of 40 g of water.

[Specific heat capacity of water = $4200 \text{Jkg}^{-1 0}\text{C}^{-1}$].

Answer.

(a) Copper has a low-specific heat capacity

The good conduct of heat

(b)

$$\begin{aligned} m &= 40 \text{ g} \\ C &= 4200 \text{ J/kg °C} \\ C &= mC \\ &= \frac{40}{1000} \times 4200 \\ &= 168 \text{ J °C}^{-1} \end{aligned}$$

(iii) In the above circuit diagram, calculate:

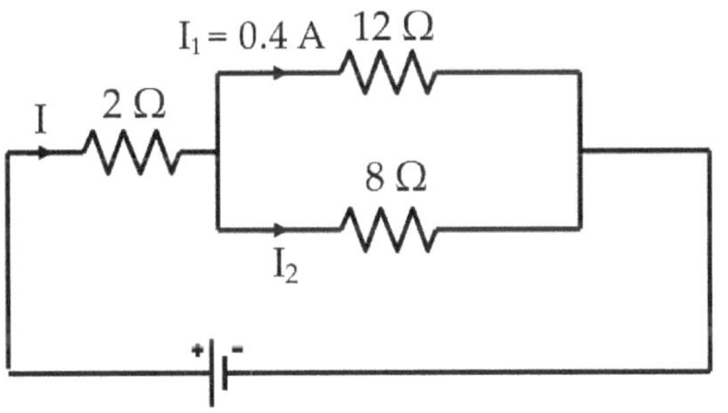

(a) The external resistance of the circuit

(b) The current I_2

(c) The current I.

Answer.

(a)

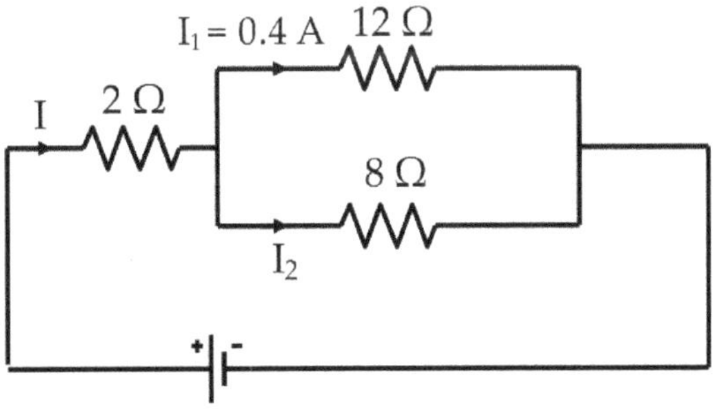

External Resistance.

R_2& R_3 Are in parallel

$$R' = \frac{R_2R_3}{R_2+R_3} = \frac{12\times 8}{12+8} = \frac{24}{5} \Rightarrow 4.8\Omega$$

R_1&R' Are in series

$$R_{eq} = R_1 + R' = 4.8 + 2 \Rightarrow 6.8\Omega$$

(b) Current (I_2) =?

$$V_2 = I_1R_2 = 0.4 \times 12$$
$$V_2 = 4.8\text{ V}$$
$$I_2 = \frac{V_2}{R_3} = \frac{4.8}{8} = 0.6\text{ A}$$

(c)

$$I = I_1 + I_2 = 0.4 + 0.6 = 1A$$

Question 3.

(i) Three wires with proper color coding are connected to the three terminals of a three pin Socket. Match the color of the wire with the proper terminals A, B, and C of the socket.

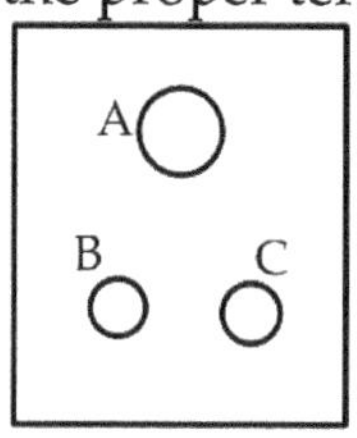

(a) Brown
(b) Green
(c) Light blue **[3]**

Answer.

(a) Brown → C
(b) Green→ A
(c) Light blue→ B

(ii) **(a)** Why does it become colder after a hailstorm than during or before the hailstorm?

(b) 'If two bodies have the same specific heat capacities, then they will always absorb the same Amount of heat if their temperature increases by the same amount.' State whether the given Statement is true or false.

Answer.

(a) After the hailstorm, the ice balls begin to melt and take latent heat from the surrounding atmosphere. The temperature of the surrounding atmosphere thus decreases to a large extent.

(b) False

(iii) A metal piece of mass 420 g present at 80°C is dropped in 80 g of water present at 20°C in a Calorimeter of mass 84 g. If the final temperature of the mixture is 30°C then calculate the spe Cufic heat capacity of the metal piece. **[4]**

[Specific heat capacity of water = $4.2 Jg^{-1} °C^{-1}$,

Specific heat capacity of the calorimeter = $200 Jkg^{-1} °C^{-1}$]

Answer.

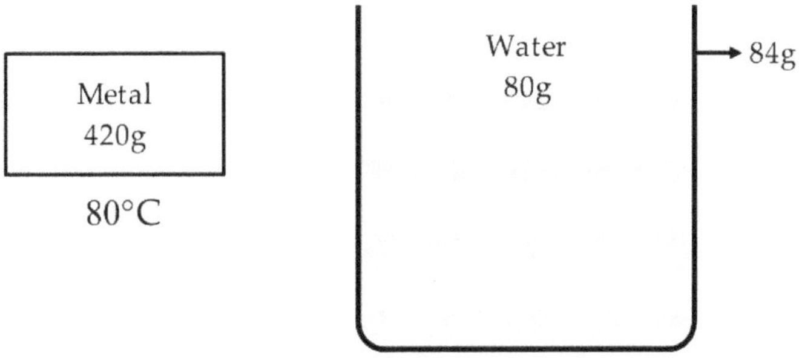

Metal	Water	Calorimeter
$m_1 = 420g$	$m_2 = 80g$	$m_3 = 84g$
$t_1 = 80°C$	$c_2 = 4.2 J/g°C$	$c_3 = 200 J/kg°C$
	$t_2 = 20°C$	$t_2 = 20°C$

Final Temperature (t) = 30°C

Acc. To the principle of calorimetry

Heat loss by hot body = Heat gain by cald

$$m_1c_1\Delta t = m_2c_2\Delta t + m_3c_3\Delta t$$

$$420 \times c_1(80 - 30) = 80 \times 4.2 \times (30 - 20) + 84 \times 0.2 \times (30 - 20)$$

$$420 \times c_1(50) = (30 - 20)[80 \times 4.2 + 84 \times 0.2]$$

$$21000C_1 = 10[336 + 16.8]$$

$$21000C_1 = 10[352.8]$$

$$C_1 = 0.168 J/g°C$$

Question 4.

(i) Rohit playing a flute and Anita playing the piano emit sounds of the same pitch and loudness.

(a) Name one characteristic that is different for waves from the two different instruments.

(b) If now the loudness of the sound from the flute becomes four times that of the sound from the piano, then write the value of the ratio $A_F : A_P$. (A_F – The amplitude of sound waves from flute, Ap_P - amplitude of sound wave from the piano)

(c) Define 'Pitch' of a sound.

Answer.

(a) Quality/Timber

(b) $\frac{\text{Amplitude }(F)}{\text{Amplitude }(P)} = ?$

$$L \propto A^2$$

L = Loudness

A = Amplitude.

$$\frac{A_F^2}{A_P^2} = \frac{L_F}{L_p}$$

$$\frac{A_F}{A_P} = \sqrt{\frac{L_F}{L_P}}$$

$$= \sqrt{\frac{4x}{x}}$$

$$= \sqrt{\frac{4}{1}}$$

$$\frac{A_F}{A_p} = \frac{2}{1} = 2:1 \text{ Ans.}$$

(c) Pitch is the shrillness of a note which enables us to differentiate between two Sound with equal loudness coming from different sources and having different frequencies.

(ii) **(a)** Name two factors on which the force experienced by a conductor carrying current, placed In a magnetic field, depends. Also state how these factors affect the force.

(b) With the help of which rule you can determine the direction of force acting on a current Carrying conductor placed in a magnetic field?

Answer.

(a) Force $\propto$ length of conductor

Force $\propto$ current

(b) Flaming's left, Rule.

(iii) **(a)** What is nuclear energy? **[3]**

(b) After the emission of nuclear radiation, the atomic number of the daughter nucleus in Creases by 1. Identify the nuclear radiation.

(c) Write a nuclear reaction indicating the nuclear change mentioned in (b).

(d) What is the special name given to the parent and daughter nucleus when this radiation is emitted?

Answer.

(a) The energy released when unstable nuclear split or when two small weights nuclear Combined.

(b) β

(c) $zX^A \longrightarrow {}_{Z+1}Y^A + {}_{-1}\beta^0$

(d) Isobars

Question 5.

(i) An appliance rated 440 W, 220 V is connected across 220 V supply.

(a) Calculate the maximum current that the appliance can draw.

(b) Calculate the resistance of the appliance.

Answer. $P = 440W$

$V = 220V$

(a)

$$P = V \times I$$

$$440 = 220 \times I$$

$$I = \frac{440}{220}$$

$$I = 2A$$

(b)

$$P = \frac{V^2}{R}$$

$$440 = \frac{(220)^2}{R}$$

$$R = \frac{220 \times 220}{\frac{440}{2}}$$

$$R = 110\Omega$$

(ii) The diagram below shows a vibrating tuning fork E mounted on a sound box X. When the vibrating tuning forks A, B, C and D are placed on the sound box Y one by one, it is observed that a louder sound is produced when the tuning fork B is placed on Y.

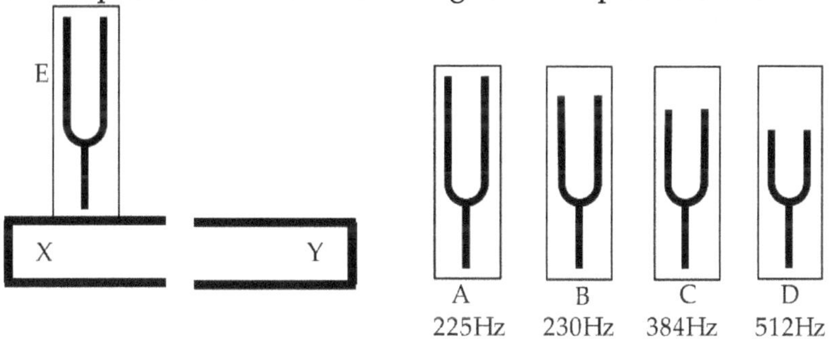

(a) What is the frequency of tuning fork E?

(b) Why does B produce a louder sound?

Answer.

(a) Frequency of Tuning fork = $320hz$

(b) Due to resonance

(iii) **(a)** From the graph of heating curve given below state the melting point and boiling point of The substance.

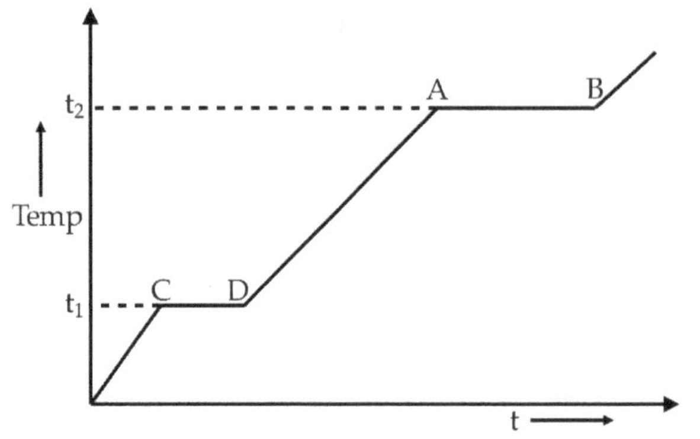

(b) Complete and rewrite the following nuclear reaction by filling the blanks.

$$^{235}U \rightarrow {}_{90}Th + {}^{4}_{2}He$$

Answer.

(a) Melting point=40°C

Boiling point=160°C

(b)

$$^{235}_{92}u \longrightarrow\longrightarrow {}^{231}_{90}Th + {}^{4}_{2}He$$

Question 6.

(i) Study the above figure and answer the following:

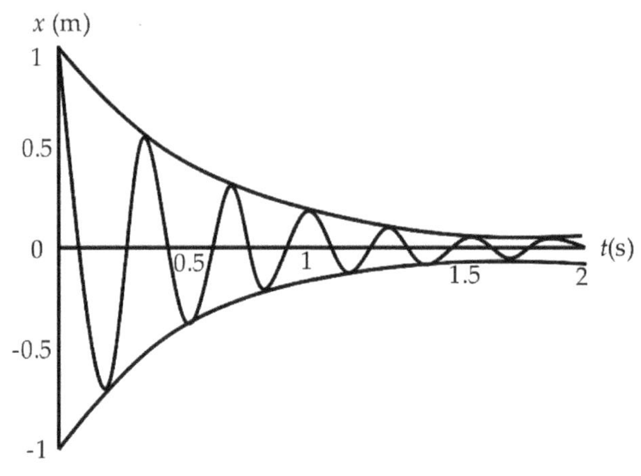

(a) What type of vibration does the above figure represent?

(b) State one reason for which the amplitude of the vibration decreases with time.

(c) Write an example of natural vibrations.

Answer.

(a) Damped vibration

(b) Due to energy loss.

(c) When we strike the keys of a piano various strings are set in vibration each at its Own natural frequency because they are of different thickness and under different tension.

(ii) A certain beam of α particles, β particles and γ radiations travel through a region of electric field produced between two oppositely charged parallel plates A(+) and B(−). **[3]**

(a) Which of the above three has the maximum speed?

(b) Which one deviates the most from its original path?

(c) Which one does not deviate at all when passing through a region of electric or magnetic field?

Answer.

(a) Y-radiation

(b) β - radiation

(c) Y – radiation

(iii) If a wire of resistance 2Ω gets stretched to thrice its original length: **[4]**

(a) Calculate the new resistance of the wire.

(b) What happens to the specific resistance of the wire?

Answer.

(a)

$$R_1 = 2\Omega \; R_2 = ? \; f_1 = f_2$$
$$l_1 = l \; l_2 = 3l$$
$$A_1 = A \; A_2 = A/3$$
$$R_1 = P_1 \frac{l_1}{A_1}$$
$$R_2 = P_2 \frac{l_2}{A_2}$$
$$\frac{R_1}{R_2} = \frac{l1}{A_1} \times \frac{A_2}{l_2}$$
$$\frac{2}{R_2} = \frac{l}{A} \times \frac{A/3}{3/l}$$
$$\frac{2}{R_2} = \frac{1}{A} \times \frac{A}{9}$$
$$R_2 = 18\Omega$$

(b) Remains the same

MOST EXPECTED QUESTIONS PAPER

ICSE 2023 EXAMINATION

SAMPLE PAPER - 1

PHYSICS

(SCIENCE PAPER - 1)

Maximum Marks: 80

Time allowed: Two hours

Answers to this Paper must be written on the paper provided separately.

You will not be allowed to write during first 15 minutes.

This time is to be spent in reading the question paper.

The time given at the head of this Paper is the time allowed for writing the answers.

SECTION A is compulsory. Attempt any four questions from SECTION B.
The intended marks for questions or parts of questions are given in brackets [ ].

SECTION – A (40 Marks)

(Answer all the questions from this SECTION)

Question 1.

(i) The change of a substance directly from solid to vapor state at constant temperature is called

(a) Sublimation
(b) Evaporation
(c) Condensation
(d) Regelation

Answer. (a)

(ii) Which one of the following is most harmful to the human body

(a) X-rays
(b) γ- rays
(c) β-rays
(d) α-rays

Answer. (b)

(iii) The force of attraction between the molecules of a substance is maximum. The substance exists in

(a) Solid state
(b) Liquid state
(c) Gaseous state
(d) None of these

Answer. (a)

(iv) The amount of heat (ΔQ) required to change the state of a body of mass (m) from solid to liquid at the melting point of solid or from liquid to gas at the boiling point of the liquid (in terms of latent heat of the substance) is given by

(a) $\triangle Q = mL$

(b) $\Delta \mathrm{Q} = \frac{m}{\mathrm{L}}$

(c) $\Delta \mathrm{Q} = \mathrm{m}^2 \mathrm{~L}$

(d) $\Delta \mathrm{Q} = \mathrm{mL}^2$

Answer. (a)

(v) An electric current that converts electric energy into mechanical energy is called:

(a) Electric motor

(b) Transformer

(c) Dynamo

(d) Electric generator

Answer. (a)

(vi) In fig., Fleming's right-hand rule is applied. The center finger points along

(a) Induced current

(b) Electric field

(c) Gravitational field

(d) None of these

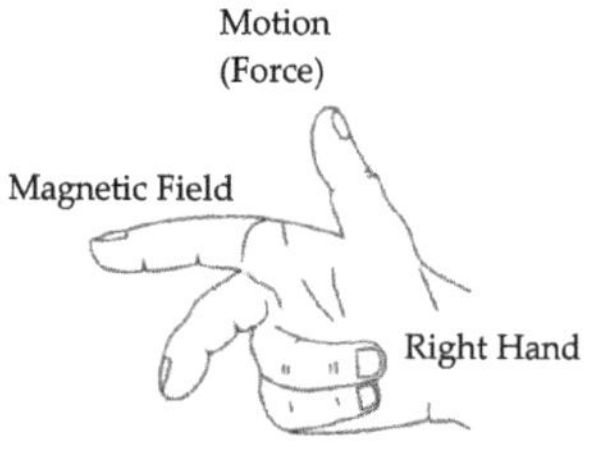

Answer. (a)

(vii) Which one of the following is correct?

(a) $\frac{1 \text{ volt}}{1 \text{ ampere}} = 1\Omega$

(b) $\frac{1 \text{ volt}}{1 \text{ ampere}} = 1 \mathrm{~J}$

(c) $\frac{1 \text{ volt}}{1 \text{ ampere}} = \text{Siemen}$

(d) $\frac{1 \text{ volt}}{1 \text{ ampere}} = 1\Omega - m$

Answer. (a)

(viii) What is the resistance between P and Q ?

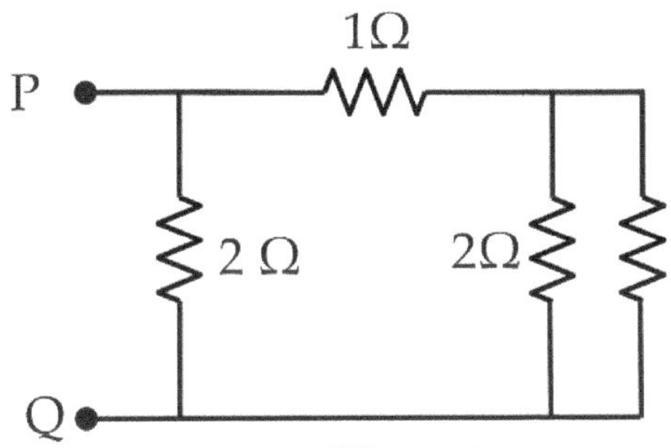

Fig. 31

(a) 1Ω
(b) 2Ω
(c) 3Ω
(d) 2.5Ω
Answer. (a)

(ix) Which of the following diagrams shows the refraction of a ray of light through a concave lens?

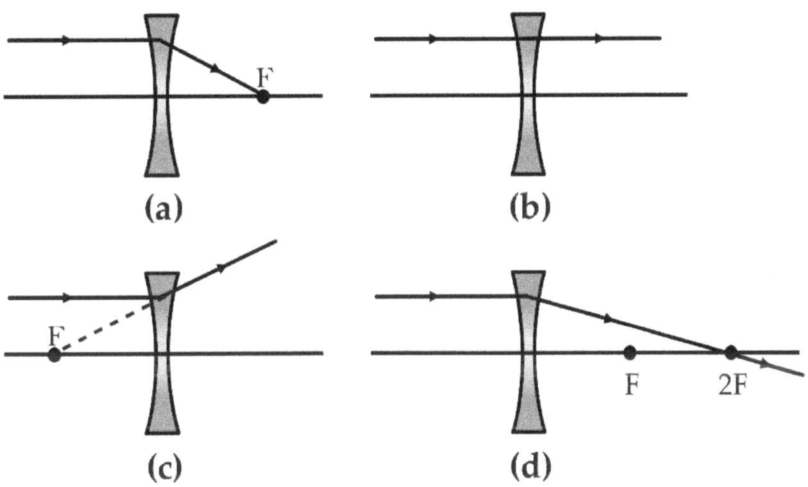

Answer. (c)

(x) The term 'bending of light when it passes from one medium into another medium of different refractive index is called
(a) Dispersion
(b) Reflection
(c) Refraction
(d) Scattering
Answer. (c)

(xi) A block and tackle system of 4 pulleys in each block have an efficiency of 90%. If a load of 320 N is lifted by the system, its velocity ratio is

(a) 2
(b) 4
(c) 6
(d) 8
Answer. (b)

(xii) The unit of moment of force is:
(a) N
(b) $\frac{N}{m}$
(c) kg m^2 s^{-1}
(d) Nm
Answer. (d)

(xiii) The relationship between kgf and N is:
(a) 1kgf = 1 N
(b) 1kgf = 9.8 N
(c) 9.8kgf = 1 N
(d) 1kgf = 100 N
Answer. (b)

(xiv) If a force $\vec{F}$ applied on a body moves it with a velocity $\vec{v}$, then power will be
(a) $\frac{\vec{v}}{\frac{\vec{v}}{v}}$
(b) $\vec{F}, \vec{v}$
(c) $\frac{F}{\vec{v}}$
(d) $F\vec{v}$
Answer. (d)

(xv) A normal human being can hear sound having an intensity level of maximum
(a) 80db
(b) 40db
(c) 20db
(d) 100db
Answer. (a)

Question 2.

(i) What will be the work done in the following cases? **[3]**
(a) A boy carrying a suitcase on his head
(b) A coolie standing with a load of 25 kgf on his head.
(c) A man pushing a wall
Answer.
(a) Zero
(b) Zero

(c) Zero

(ii) State the condition for total internal reflection. **[2]**

(iii) Write the wavelength range of **[2]**
  (a) Visible spectrum
  (b) Ultraviolet spectrum and
  (c) Infrared spectrum.

(iv) What is meant by a parallel combination of resistors? Deduce an expression for the equivalent resistance when two resistors are connected in parallel. **[2]**

(v) If 2×10^{-3}J of work is done in moving a particle carrying a charge of 10×10^{-6} coulomb from infinity to a point P. What will be the potential at this point? **[2]**
Answer. V = 200v

(vi) What do you understand about electromagnetic induction? **[2]**

(vii) Name the material of which the calorimeter is made. Give two reasons in support of your answer. **[2]**

Question 3.

(i) Calculate the amount of heat energy required to raise the temperature of 100g of copper from 20°C to 70°C Specific heat capacity of copper = 390J kg^{-1} K^{-1}. **[2]**
Answer. Q = 1950J

(ii) Draw a graph showing difference between ac and dc. **[2]**

(iii) On what factors refractive index depends? **[2]**

(iv) Explain free and forced vibration and resonance. Give one example of each. **[2]**

(v) Distinguish between a real and a virtual image. **[2]**

SECTION – B (40 Marks)
(Attempt any four questions)

Question 4.

(i) Given below gives an arrangement of single-moving pulleys. Copy the diagram. If the effort applied at the free end of the string is E, **[3]**
  (a) Show the direction and the magnitude of the forces exerted by the four strings marked (1) to (4).

(b) What is the load that can be lifted by the effort?

Calculate the mechanical advantage of the system of pulleys

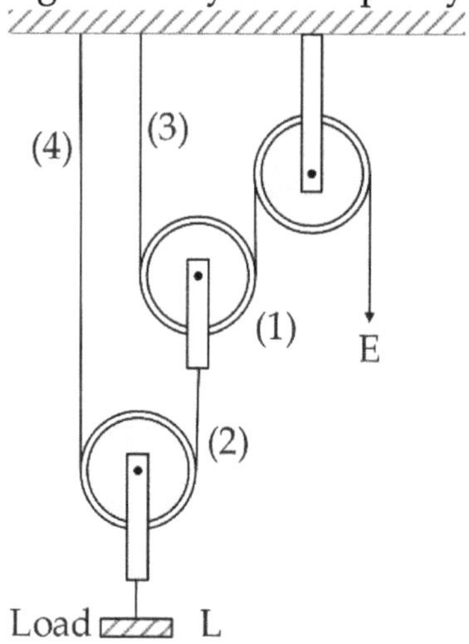

(ii) Fig. shows two forces each of magnitude 10 N acting at points A and B at a separation of 50cm, in opposite directions. Calculate the resultant moment of the two forces about the point

(a) A,

(b) B and

(c) O situated exactly at the middle of the two forces. **[3]**

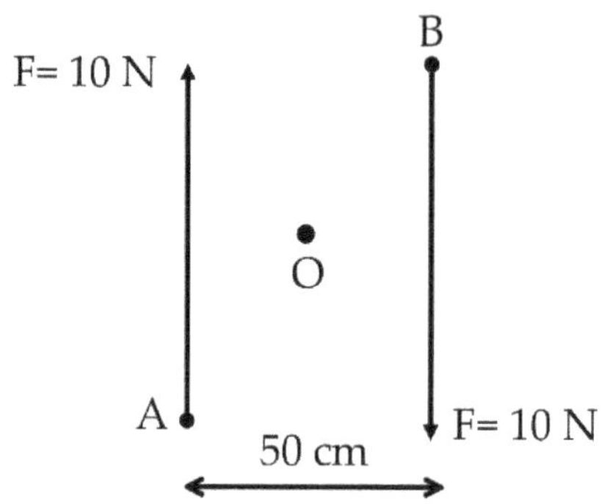

Answer.

(a) 5 N m clockwise

(b) 5 N m clockwise

(c) 5 N m clockwise

(iii) How are kinetic energy and momentum related? Derive the relation. **[4]**

Question 5.

(i) A beam of light consisting of red, blue, and yellow colors is incident normally on the face AB of an isosceles right-angled prism ABC as shown in Fig. Complete the ray diagram showing the refracted and the emergent rays the critical angle of glass-air interface for yellow color is 45°. **[3]**

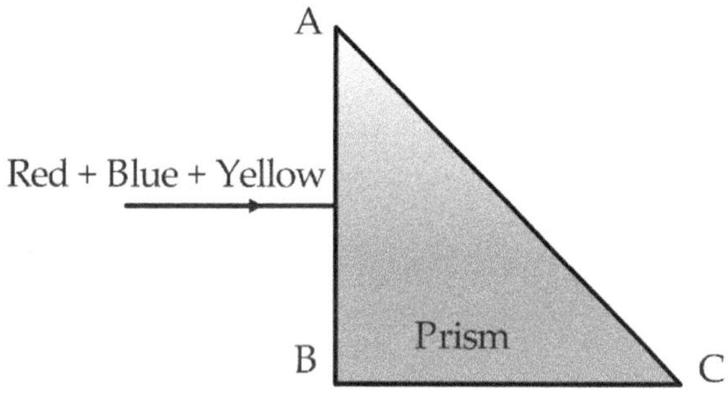

(ii) The refractive index of water is $\frac{4}{3}$ and of glass is $\frac{3}{2}$. What is the refractive index of glass with respect to water? **[3]**

Answer. 1.125

(iii) An object placed 4 cm in front of a converging lens produces a real image 12 cm from the lens. **[4]**

(a) What is the magnification of the image?

(b) What is the focal length of the lens?

(c) Draw a ray diagram to show the formation of the image. Mark F and 2 F in the diagram?

Answer.

(a) $m = -3$

(b) $f = +3cm$

Question 6.

(i) $1300J$ of heat energy is supplied to raise the temperature of 0.5 kg of lead from 20°C to 40°C Calculate the specific heat capacity of lead. **[3]**

Answer. $C = 130J/Kg^0C$

(ii) Calculate the current flowing in a nichrome wire immersed in 500 g of turpentine oil at 20°C Such that the temperature of the oil rises to 70°C in5 minutes when the wire is connected to a battery of emf 24 V. The specific heat capacity of the oil is $750Jkg^{-1}{}^{o}C^{-1}$ **[3]**

Answer. $I = 2.6A$

(iii) 1 kg of ice at 0°C is being continuously heated through an electric heater of 1 kW. Assuming that all the heat is transmitted to ice, calculate the time intervals in seconds for **[4]**

(a) Ice to completely melt into the water at 0°C.

(b) Water to get heated from to. [Given: Specific latent heat of ice, the specific heat capacity of water.]

Answer.

(a) $t = 336sec$

(b) $4{,}20{,}000J,\ 3{,}36000J/Kg, 4200J/Kg$

Question 7.

(i) Convert 1kWh into joule. **[3]**

(ii) Two bulbs a and b are rated 100 W – 120 V and 10 W – 120 V respectively. These are connected in parallel across a 120 V source. Find the current in each bulb. Which bulb will consume more energy? **[3]**

Answer. [0.83A, 0.083A, BulbA]

(iii) Find the equivalent resistance for the combination of resistance shown in fig. **[4]**

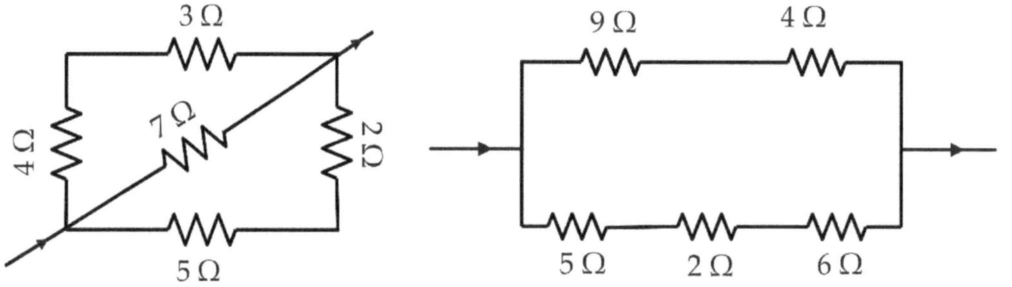

Answer. 2.33Ω, 6.5Ω

Question 8.

(i) See fig. **[3]**

(a) Copy and complete the diagram given alongside by showing and labeling the paths of alpha, beta, and gamma radiations in an electric field.

(b) Name the radiations which have the least penetrating power.

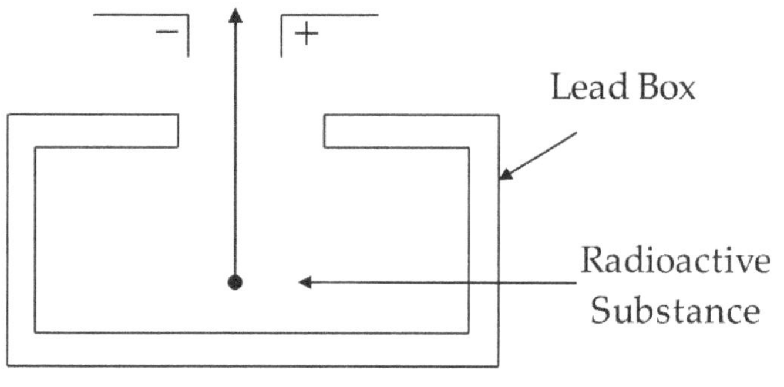

(ii) Show with the aid of a diagram how a wire is wound on a U-shaped piece of soft iron in order to make it an electromagnet. Complete the circuit diagram and mark the poles of the electromagnet. **[3]**

(iii) Describe briefly the properties of **[4]**

(a) α-particles,

(b) β-particles and

(c) γ-rays.

Question 9.

(i) A uniform meter rule rests horizontally on a knife edge at the 60 cm mark when a mass of 10 g is suspended from one end. Draw a diagram of the arrangement. **[3]**

(a) At which end must this mass be suspended?

(b) What is the mass of the rule?

(c) The 10 g mass is now shifted to the 9cm mark. In which direction must the knife edge be shifted to male the rule horizontal again?

ICSE 2023 EXAMINATION

SAMPLE PAPER - 2

PHYSICS

(SCIENCE PAPER - 1)

Maximum Marks: 80

Time allowed: Two hours

Answers to this Paper must be written on the paper provided separately.

You will not be allowed to write during first 15 minutes.

This time is to be spent in reading the question paper.

The time given at the head of this Paper is the time allowed for writing the answers.

SECTION A is compulsory. Attempt any four questions from SECTION B.
The intended marks for questions or parts of questions are given in brackets [ ].

SECTION – A (40 Marks)

(Answer all the questions from this SECTION)

Question 1.

(i) In a β-decay, a nucleus emits

(a) Electrons and neutrino

(b) Positron only

(c) Electrons only

(d) None of the above

Answer. (c)

(ii) The specific latent heat of fusion of water is:

(a) 80 J kg^{-1}

(b) 80Jg^{-1}

(c) 80calg^{-1}

(d) 800calg^{-1}

Answer. (c)

(iii) The quantity of heat required to change the temperature of a unit amount of a substance by 1°C is called its

(a) Specific heat

(b) Heat of friction

(c) Heat of vaporization

(d) Total energy

Answer. (a)

(iv) One kilocalorie is the amount of heat that increases the temperature of

(a) 1 kg of water through 1°F
(b) 1 kg of water through 1°C
(c) 1 g of water through 1°C
(d) 1 g of water through 1°F
Answer. (b)

(v) The material of the core of a strong electromagnet is
(a) Copper
(b) Steel
(c) Soft iron
(d) Brass
Answer. (c)

(vi) The rating of a fuse connected to the lighting circuit is
(a) 5 A
(b) 10 A
(c) 15 A
(d) 20 A
Answer. (a)

(vii) Lenz's law gives the direction of
(a) Magnetic field.
(b) The motion of the conductor.
(c) Induced current.
(d) Current in any electrical circuit.
Answer. (c)

(viii) When a current of 1 ampere flows through a conductor of resistance R for time t seconds, the electrical energy? Spent is
(a) IR^2t
(b) IRt
(c) I^2Rt
(d) I^2R^2/t
Answer. (c)

(ix) The direction of current in a conductor is the direction of flow of
(a) Protons
(b) Electrons
(c) Atoms
(d) Positive charge
Answer. (d)

(x) The focal length of a lens is 50 cm Its power would be

(a) 50 diopters

(b) 2 diopters

(c) 20 diopters

(d) None of these

Answer. (b)

(xi) The angle of incidence for which the angle of refraction is X is called the critical angle. Then equals

(a) 90°

(b) 60°

(c) 45^0

(d) 30°

Answer. (a)

(xii) Which of the following has a minimum refractive index?

(a) Air

(b) Water

(c) Diamond

(d) Alcohol

Answer. (a)

(xiii) The ratio of the output by a machine to the input on the machine is called the

(a) Mechanical advantage

(b) Velocity ratio

(c) Efficiency

(d) None of these

Answer. (c)

(xiv) S.I. unit of a couple is:

(a) N

(b) Nm

(c) Nm^{-1}

(d) Nm^{-2}

Answer. (b)

(xv) The K.E. of a body of mass of 0.1 kg and momentum $20kgms^{-1}$ is

(a) 10^3 J

(b) 2×10^3 J

(c) 4×10^3 J

(d) 0.5×10^3 J

Answer. (b)

Question 2.

(i) A body of mass of 40 kg runs up a flight of 15 steps, each 0.15 cm high in 10 seconds. Find the work done and power developed by the boy. (g = 10 ms^{-2}) **[3]**

Answer. $900J, 90W$

(ii) Write two limitations of using hydro energy for producing electricity. **[2]**

(iii) Distinguish between the thermal capacity and specific heat capacity of a body. **[2]**

(iv) Complete the following sentences

(a) The current at the face of loop is clockwise, so it behaves as______pole. **[2]**

(b) According to Fleming's right-hand rule, the thumb represents________.

(v) A ray of light enters a glass slab ABCD as shown in fig. and strikes at the centre O of the circular part AC of the slab. The critical angle of the glass is 42^0 complete the path of the ray till it emerges out from the slab. Mark the angles in the diagram wherever necessary. **[2]**

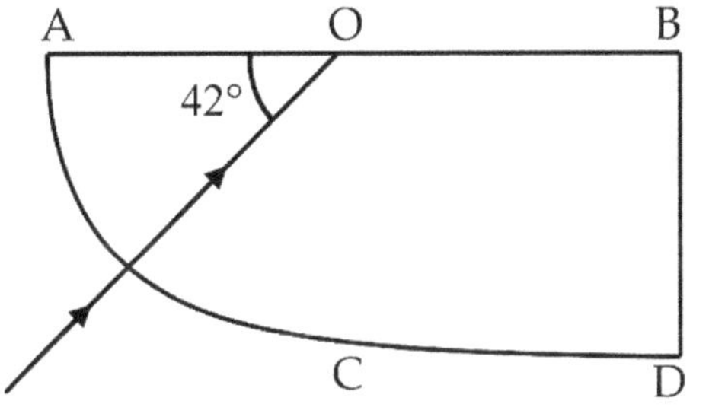

(vi) **(a)** The speed of light in glass is 2×10^5 km/s. What is the refractive index of glass?

(b) Name two factor that affects the lateral displacement of light as it passes through a rectangular glass slab. **[2]**

Answer. (a) 1.5

(vii) **(a)** State the safe limit of sound level in terms of decibel for human bearing. **[2]**

(b) Name the characteristic of sound in relation to its waveform.

Question 3.

(i) An electrical heater is rated 4 kW, 220 V. Find the cost of using this heater for 12 hours. If one kWh of electrical energy costs ₹ 3.25. **[2]**

Answer. ₹117

(ii) An element ${}_Z S^A$ decays to ${}_{85}R^{222}$ after emitting 2α-particle and 1β-particle. Find the atomic number and atomic mass of the element S. **[2]**

Answer. $A = 230, Z = 90$

(iii) A certain radioactive nucleus emits a particle that leaves it unchanged but increases its atomic number by one. Identify the particle and write its symbol. **[2]**

(iv) State the characteristics required in a material to be used as an effective fuse wire. **[2]**

(v) State one point of similarity and one point of difference between an AC generator and a DC motor. **[2]**

SECTION – B (40 Marks)
(Attempt any Four questions)

Question 4.

(i) 250 g of water at 30°C is contained in a copper vessel of mass 50 g. Calculate the mass of ice required to bring down the temperature of the vessel and its contents to 5°C. Given: specific latent heat of fusion of ice $= 336 \times 10^3 \text{ J kg}^{-1}$, the specific heat capacity of copper $=$ $400 \text{ J kg}^{-1} \text{ K}^{-1}$, the specific heat capacity of water $= 4200 \text{ J kg}^{-1} \text{ K}^{-1}$. **[3]**

Answer. $\text{m} = 0.74\text{Kg}$

(ii) Two wires of the same material and same length have radii r_1 and r_2 respectively. compare:

(a) Their resistance, and **[3]**

(b) Their resistivities.

(iii) A pulley system has a velocity ratio of 5. Draw a neat, labeled diagram of the pulley system to lift a load by applying the effort in a convenient direction. Marks the tension in your diagram.

(a) If the efficiency of the system is 80% find its mechanical advantage. **[4]**

(b) If a load of 10 kg$f$ is pulley up by a distance of 2 m in 10 s, calculate the power developed by the effort. (Given $\text{g} = 10 \text{ ms}^{-2}$)

Answer.

(a) $\text{M. A.} = 4$

(b) $\text{P}_\text{I} = 25\text{W}$

Question 5.

(i) **(a)** Write an expression for the heat energy liberated by a hot body. **[3]**

(b) Some heat is provided to a body to raise its temperature by 25°C. What will be the corre spending rises in temperature of the body as shown on the kelvin scale.

(c) What happens to the average kinetic energy of the molecules as the ice melts at 0°C?

(ii) Some ice is heated at a constant rate, and its temperature is recorded after every few seconds, till steam is formed at 100°C. Draw a temperature-time graph to represent the change. Label the two-phase changes in your graph. **[3]**

(iii) Find the result of mixing 10g of ice at -10^0C with 10g of the water at 10^0C. Specific heat capacity of ice = 2.1 J $g^{-1}K^{-1}$, specific latent heat of ice = 336J g^{-1} and specific heat capacity of water = 4.2J$g^{-1}K^{-1}$ **[4]**

Answer. 0.625 g ice will melt, and temperature will remain 0^0C

Question 6.

(i) **(a)** Write a relationship between the angle of incidence and the angle of refraction for a given pair of media. **[3]**

(b) When a ray of light enters from one medium to another having different optical densities it bends. Why does this phenomenon occur?

(c) Write one condition where it does not bend when entering a medium of different optical density?

(ii) A lens produces a virtual image between the object and the lens. **[3]**

(a) Name the lens.

(b) Draw a ray diagram to show the formation of this image. **[3]**

(iii) What do you understand by the term 'Scattering of light'? Which color of white light is scattered the least and why? **[4]**

Question 7.

(i) **(a)** What is an echo?

(b) What is the audible range of frequencies? **[3]**

(c) Write a relation between the velocity of sound, distance of the source of sound from the reflecting body, and time for bearing an echo.

(ii) **(a)** Draw a displacement-distance graph for two waves A and B such that the amplitude of wave A is three times that. **[3]**

(b) Give two examples of forced vibration.

(iii) An electric bulb marked 220 V, 100 W is connected to a 220 V supply. **[4]**

(a) Calculate the resistance of the filament and the current flowing through the filament.

(b) Is the filament resistance of the glowing bulb greater, smaller, or the same compared to its resistance when it is not glowing

Answer. 484Ω

Question 8.

(i) An engine can pump 30000 liters of water to a vertical height of 45m in 10 sec ($g = 9.8$ ms^{-2} Calculate the work done by the machine and its power (density of water 1000kgm^{-3} And 1000 liter = $1m^3$). **[3]**

Answer. p = 22050w, W = 1.3×10^7J

(ii) Derive the expression for the kinetic energy of a body.

(iii) **(a)** Define Radioactivity. **[3]**

(b) A radioactive substance is oxidized. What change would you expect to take place in the nature of its radioactivity? Give a suitable reason. **[4]**

Question 9.

(i) **(a)** Which particles are responsible for current in conductors? **[3]**

(b) To which wire should the fuse be connected?

(ii) **(a)** Name the transformer used in the power transmitting station of a power plant. **[3]**

(b) What type of current is transmitted from the power station?

(c) At what voltage is this currently available to our household?

(iii) A battery of emf 12 V and internal resistance 2Ω relates to two resistors A and B of resistance 4Ω and 6Ω respectively joined in series. **[4]**

Find:

(a) Current in the circuit.

(b) The terminal voltage of the cell

(c) The potential difference across 6Ω Resistor.

(d) Electrical energy spent per minute in 4Ω

Answer.

(a) $I = 1A$

(b) $V = 10v$

(c) $V_6\Omega = 6v$

(d) $E = 240J$